Contents

Family break-up

Twenty-first-century families come in all sorts of shapes and sizes. Gone are the days when 'family' automatically meant a pair of married parents and their children.

A hundred years ago, family break-up was much less common than it is now. When people got married, they expected to stay married to the same person until one or other of them died. They had children who lived with them until the children found husbands and wives of their own.

People still get married, have children and live together happily ever after, but the fact is that a lot of them do not. Nearly half of all US and Australian marriages end in **divorce**, and so do many British marriages. Today's children are much more likely than their grandparents to experience the break-up of their family – around one in four of them will spend at least part of their childhood with only one parent.

The family you live with right now might be your mother and father plus you and some brothers and sisters. Another typical modern family could be a mother and father and just a single child. One friend might live with her mother and her mother's new **partner** and their children – another might live with his father and brothers and sisters.

You may also know people living with a grandparent or an aunt or an older cousin who looks after them.

Confusing? You bet

Things can get still more confusing. Even families that seem happy and settled can fall apart. A family member may die or leave, or parents separate because they can no longer live together. Whatever the reasons behind family break-up, its impact on everyone involved can be enormous.

For some people, it is only slightly less painful than dealing with death. They can experience the same kind of feelings when their family breaks up as they do when someone close to them dies – disbelief, anger, sadness. For others, it may be easier.

This book looks at the reasons why families break up and what happens when they do.

Need to Know

Family Break-up

Keeley Bishop
Penny Tripp

Heinemann
LIBRARY

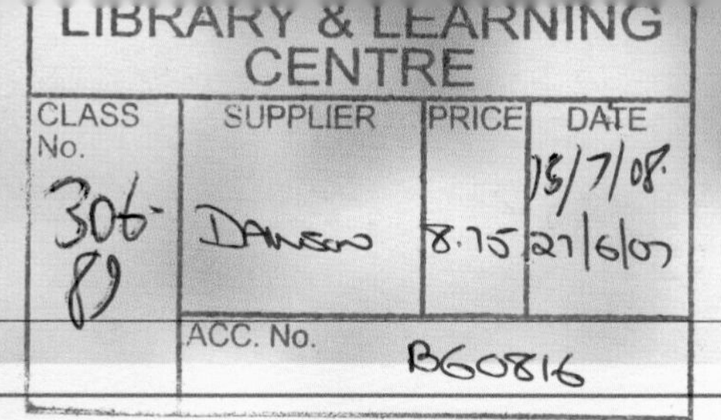

www.heinemann.co.uk/library
Visit our website to find out more information about **Heinemann Library** books.

To order:
 Phone 44 (0) 1865 888066
 Send a fax to 44 (0) 1865 314091
 Visit the Heinemann Bookshop at www.heinemann.co.uk/library to browse our catalogue and order online.

Produced by Roger Coote Publishing
Gissing's Farm, Fressingfield, Suffolk IP21 5SH, UK

First published in Great Britain by Heinemann Library, Halley Court, Jordan Hill, Oxford OX2 8EJ, part of Harcourt Education.
Heinemann is a registered trademark of Harcourt Education Ltd.

Editorial: Penny Tripp
Design: Jamie Asher
Picture Research: Sally Smith
Production: Viv Hichens

Originated by Ambassador Litho Ltd
Printed and bound in China by South China Printing Company

ISBN 0 431 09810 7 (hardback)
07 06 05 04 03
10 9 8 7 6 5 4 3 2 1

ISBN 0 431 09815 8 (paperback)
08 07 06 05 04
10 9 8 7 6 5 4 3 2 1

British Library Cataloguing in Publication Data
Bishop, Keeley
Family break-up. - (Need to know)
1.Divorce - Juvenile literature 2. Children of divorced parents - Juvenile literature 3. Teenagers - Family relationships - Juvenile literature
I.Title II.Tripp, Penny
306.8'9

Acknowledgements
The Publishers would like to thank the following for permission to reproduce photographs: AKG London p. 10-11 (Erich Lessing); Collections pp. 1 top (Kim Naylor), 7 top (Kim Naylor), 33 (Graeme Peacock), 38 (Nigel Hawkins), 42 (Liz Stares); Corbis pp. 5 (Ariel Skelley), 19 (SIE Productions), 48 (Julian Hirshowitz); Format pp. 23 (Paula Solloway), 34 (Michael Ann Mullen), 39 (Ulrike Press), 50-51 (Paula Solloway); ImageState *front cover (foreground);* John Birdsall Photography pp. 7 bottom, 8, 9, 31; Mary Evans Picture Library p. 6; Network Photographers pp. 25 (Jenny Matthews), 35 (Jenny Matthews); Photofusion pp. 1 bottom (Ute Klaphake), 17 (Ute Klaphake), 21 (Christa Stadtler), 27 (Christa Stadtler), 28 (Ute Klaphake), 29 (Ute Klaphake), 37 (Ute Klaphake), 41 (Paul Baldesare); Popperfoto p. 13; Rex Features pp. 14-15 (Bill Ray/Timepix), 45, *front cover (background)* (Amanda Knapp); Sally and Richard Greenhill pp. 20, 43; Science Photo Library p. 46-47 (Will and Deni McIntyre); Skjold Photographs p. 36.

Every effort has been made to contact copyright holders of any material reproduced in this book. Any omissions will be rectified in subsequent printings if notice is given to the publishers.

Any words appearing in the text in bold, **like this**, are explained in the Glossary.

What is a family?

There have been families as long as there have been people. They are different all over the world, but until as recently as a hundred years ago, most children in **Westernized societies** – in the UK, USA, Europe and Australia for example – lived with their father and mother. They might well have had many brothers and sisters – in 1900 the average number of children in a British family was seven. This kind of **nuclear family** is much less common now – and not just because adult couples tend to have fewer children.

A twenty-first-century family can be said to exist when a child lives with at least one parental figure. Children today might live with two or more adults, or just one. A pair of adults in a family group might be married to each other, or they might not. They might belong to the same sex, or be one male and one female. One of the adults might be the child's **biological parent** – their mother or father – or both of them might be. Some children live in families parented by adults who are not related to them in any way, because they are **adopted** or **fostered**. Others live with members of their **extended family** – someone like their grandparents, or an aunt or older cousin. In some countries – Russia, China and in southern Asia, for example – most family units are still large. Grandparents, aunts, uncles and older children continue to live together.

Large, close-knit families bound together by marriage – like this American family a hundred years ago – are less common today.

An alternative lifestyle

In other places, all over the world, families join together to live and work in **communes**. Different communes have different reasons for existing. Some people live in them because they think they offer a better way of sharing responsibilities – including caring for children – than more traditional family units. Others do so because they want to live and work with people who have the same goals in life. Many communes are based on shared religious ideas, while some focus more on what it means to live together and support other people as members of a group.

Children brought up in such groups may think of themselves as having many parents, rather than just two biological parents. They have close family-type relationships with many people who are not related to them.

"A family is somewhere you live and are loved and cared for."

(Rupinder, aged 14)

Today's parents are less likely to be married for life than their grandparents were.

What is family break-up?

Some family break-ups happen after a long period of unhappiness. Others are sudden. All are difficult to handle, and everyone experiences them in different ways.

Separation and divorce

Parents who decide to part may do so for one reason or for many. They may no longer share the same interests, or feel the same way about each other, as they once did. Disagreements may have turned into constant arguments. One might find the other's behaviour impossible, or have met someone else they want to live with.

When an adult leaves after a long period of unhappiness and anger, those remaining may feel relieved that they have gone. If the break-up is sudden, they are more likely to be angry, confused and bewildered.

Children often feel that their parents' break-up is somehow their fault. They may understand very little about what has happened, and the remaining adult may be so upset or angry that they cannot easily talk about it with them.

Death or disappearance of a family member

Some families are broken up by death. Some deaths happen suddenly, while others are expected. Someone dying after a long illness may leave the rest of the family feeling sad, but relieved they are now out of pain. The sudden death of a family member can lead to feelings of grief, anger or sadness that can be very difficult to express.

Sometimes, people simply go missing. There may have been an argument, or the person who left may have felt that they just could not continue living as part of the family any more. They may have felt unloved, or as if they were to blame for everything bad that happened.

Some families stay together forever, but others may not.

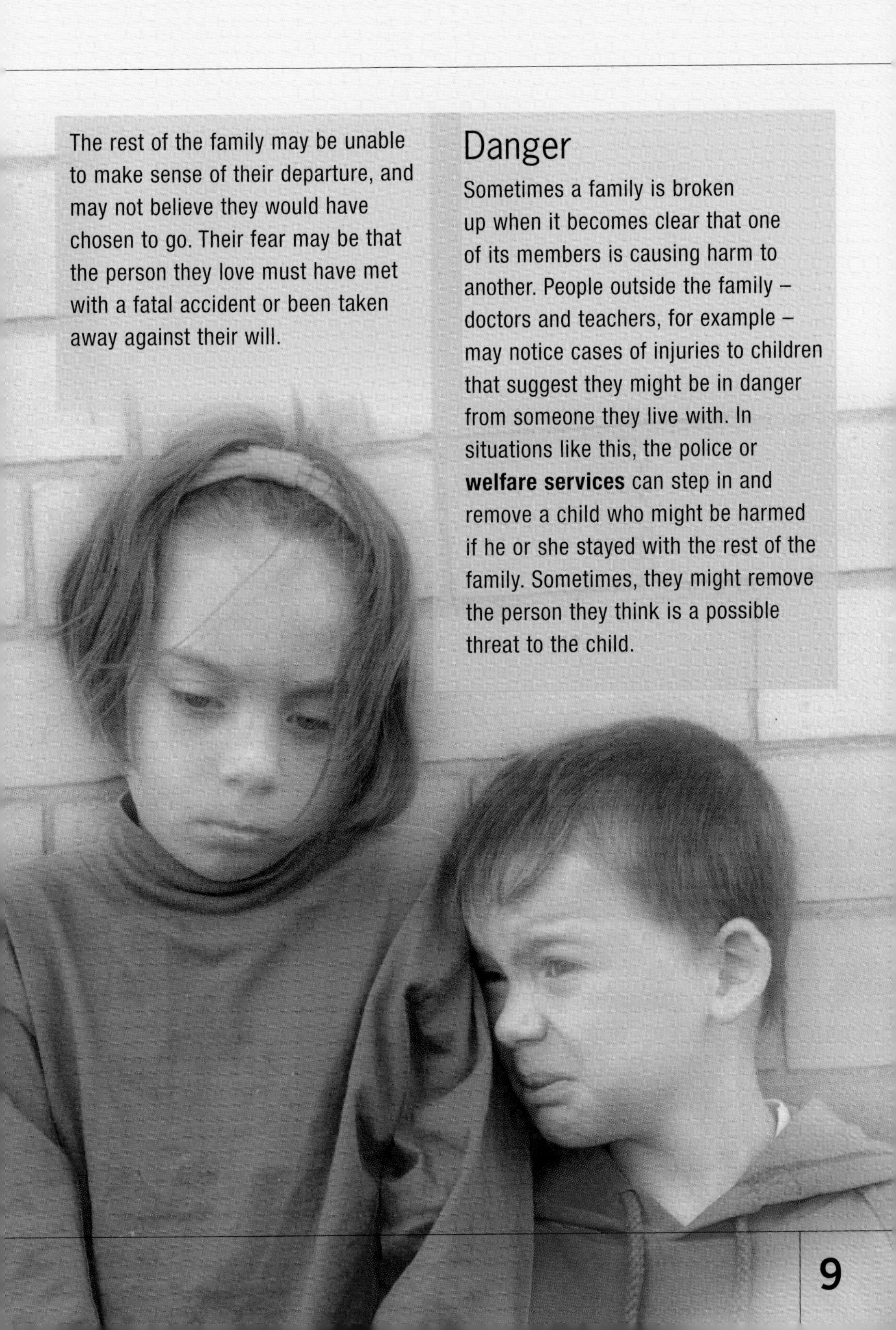

The rest of the family may be unable to make sense of their departure, and may not believe they would have chosen to go. Their fear may be that the person they love must have met with a fatal accident or been taken away against their will.

Danger

Sometimes a family is broken up when it becomes clear that one of its members is causing harm to another. People outside the family – doctors and teachers, for example – may notice cases of injuries to children that suggest they might be in danger from someone they live with. In situations like this, the police or **welfare services** can step in and remove a child who might be harmed if he or she stayed with the rest of the family. Sometimes, they might remove the person they think is a possible threat to the child.

The first families

Why did family groups first appear?

There have been people on Earth for almost two million years. Our species has survived where others have not, despite the fact that in some ways it seems badly equipped. Many animals fend for themselves almost from the moment of birth, but our young need care for many years if they are to make it into healthy adulthood. They rely heavily on their parents' **nurturing** instinct – a strong in-built desire to look after their offspring – and survival skills. Without these they die, and so does the species.

Early humans lived wherever they could find shelter, food and water. Their world was full of powerful predators. Even a relatively strong grown-up could be killed by a mammoth or savaged by a sabre-toothed cat. Our ancestors had no food unless they caught it, killed it, picked it off a plant or dug it up.

Males, females and their young probably banded together with other small family groups because that way they were more powerful – and therefore more likely to survive – than they were by themselves. A single **nuclear family** would have had no chance if one of its adults became sick, was injured or died.

Families through time

Slowly, over tens of thousands of years, living conditions changed. Even so, family groups formed the basis of societies all over the world. Deep-rooted instinctive, emotional and social ties kept them together.

In some cultures, it was the parents of a nuclear family who had primary responsibility for

Ancient Egyptian paintings and sculptures often show husbands and wives with their arms around each other.

the welfare of their own children. Others organized themselves into societies based on **communes**, where children were looked after by the group as a whole rather than by their **biological parents**. If a parent left the group for any reason, children still had others they could depend on until they could look after themselves.

By 5000 years ago, the Ancient Egyptians had written laws about what a family was – and penalties for those who broke them. People who ignored or did not conform to the rules laid down by their religions – or who just acted differently from those around them – had a price to pay.

Families in Ancient Egypt

- A girl was usually married by the time she was 14. Her husband was probably aged around 20.
- There was no official marriage ceremony. People were 'married' when they started living together, and '**divorced**' when they split up.
- Some couples' marriages were arranged for them by their parents – especially if both families were rich and powerful, and wanted to become even more so – but others married because they loved each other.
- Important men often had many wives, and some kings had hundreds.
- The chief wife was her husband's equal. She ran the house, owned all the household goods, and had her own servants.

Family break-up in history

A hundred years ago a typical family in the USA, Europe or Australia was usually made up of a married couple and their children. Men were generally the people responsible for making decisions in public life – in business and politics, for example. They usually only got married when they had enough money to support a wife and children. They might inherit this money when their parents died or, more often, have to work for it. Women rarely worked outside the home. Their job was to run the household – using the money their husband supplied – and bring up the children.

Marriage was considered to be the foundation for a proper family life, and anybody who had a sexual relationship outside marriage was frowned upon. Women who became pregnant without a husband were often sent away from home until their babies were born, and were thought to have brought shame on their families. Their **illegitimate** children had no father's name on their birth certificate, and few legal rights.

Marriage may have been the only way anybody could have a 'proper' sexual relationship and **legitimate** children a hundred years ago, but that did not mean all marriages were happy. An unhappy marriages could be brought to a legal end by **divorce**. This process was difficult and involved having to prove that one partner – usually the wife – had been guilty of unacceptable behaviour.

A woman's adultery – having a sexual relationship outside her marriage – was sufficient reason for a husband to divorce her, but she could not divorce him if he did the same thing! A divorced woman's children became her ex-husband's property, and he could stop her from ever seeing them. Adulterers and **divorcees**, especially women, were thought to be a bad influence on children and incapable of caring for them properly. Getting married for a second time, unless a previous husband or wife had died, was almost unheard of.

During the 20th century, huge numbers of men left home – sometimes for years on end – to fight for their countries during two world wars. Families broke up while they were away, sometimes forever. Many women filled the jobs the men left empty and, instead of depending on their husbands for financial

support, earned their own money for the first time. Those whose husbands were killed brought up their children as best they could.

Even in the 1950s, society and its laws still decreed that marriage was for ever, and that there was no place for sex – or children – outside it. Childcare experts said that parents who separated or divorced would damage their children, and people believed them.

During World War II, women who had never worked outside their homes took on jobs previously done only by men.

Family break-up since 1960

Families in the middle of the 20th century had fewer children than before, partly because they no longer had to have lots to make sure that one or two survived until adulthood. Some of the childhood illnesses that used to kill children in their thousands could now be cured, and others prevented altogether. People were generally eating better food, had access to better medical care and were living longer lives. More and more women were working outside the home, and some were even earning enough to be financially independent. They no longer had to rely on finding a suitable husband to look after them, because they could look after themselves.

Marriage and children, though, still went hand-in-hand. Many young people were pressurized into marriage because their relationship had led to an unplanned pregnancy.

The 1960s

Boys and girls in their late teens in the 1960s had more options than to stay at home and wait to get married in order to be independent of their parents. They could find jobs and earn a living, or go away to college and continue their education. It became more common for young people to move away from home before they were married. They no longer had to rely on their parents for money.

By the late 1960s, people could have sexual relationships without having children, because the **contraceptive** pill was widely available – even to unmarried women. It was gradually becoming more acceptable for men and women to live together without being married, and getting married was something that people could now choose to do rather than have to. They also wanted the same freedom to get **divorced** if a marriage did not work out.

The 1970s onwards

Since the 1970s, fewer people have chosen to marry. There are twice as many single-parent families today as there were then. Some are that way because parents have divorced, others because people have chosen to bring up their children without being married. By 1998, around one in four US-based children lived with a single parent – 84% of them with their mothers – and in the UK, 8% of families with children were headed by an unmarried couple living together.

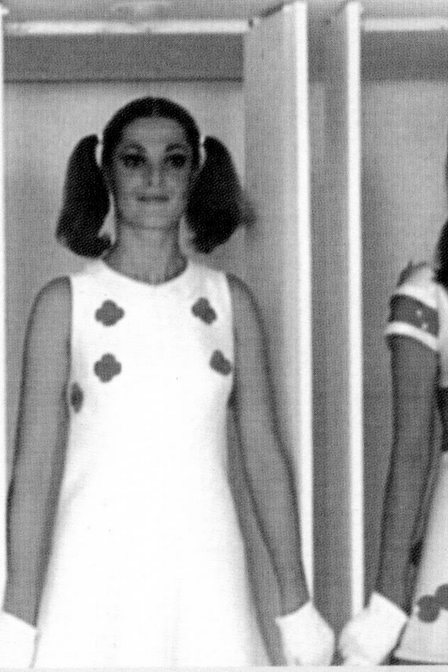

Young people in the 1960s not only started to dress differently from their parents, but to think differently too. Many of the old rules were changing.

Family change in the USA

	1970	**2000**
Family groups with children	30 million	37 million
Single-mother families	3 million (12% of all families)	10 million (26% of all families)
Single-father families	393,000 (1% of all families)	2 million (5% of all families)

(Source: US Census Bureau, 2001. www.census.gov)

Current trends

So many families have experienced break-up of some kind that it is no longer considered unusual. Statistics show that all the industrialized nations are experiencing similar trends – family units are breaking up and becoming smaller, and fewer children are being born.

Marriage is becoming less popular, and almost half end in **divorce**. Every day in the UK, 650 children see their parents separate or divorce. In Australia, around a quarter of the country's 4.6 million under-18s live with only one of their **biological parents**.

Families today

Single-parent families are twice as common as they were in the 1970s. At one time, the children of divorcing parents were automatically thought to be better off living with their mothers, with their fathers giving financial support and having **contact** or visiting rights. More fathers are now successfully arguing that they are just as capable of bringing children up on their own as mothers are. Divorced mothers and fathers are increasingly being encouraged to share responsibility for the children they brought into the world.

Being divorced does not now make it impossible to marry again, or to set up home with someone else. Families formed when this happens – **step-families** – are becoming more common: two-and-a-half million children in the UK live with people to whom they are not related by birth. **Blended families** are formed when a parent goes on to have children with a new **partner**, who may also have children from a previous relationship.

Some children are born to parents who cannot take responsibility for them. Young mothers and fathers who are still at school, for example, may want a better life for their child than they feel they can give. Other parents may suffer from a physical or mental illness that makes it very hard for them to look after a child. In this kind of situation, a child can be **adopted** or **fostered** by another family. The law is changing in some countries to allow adoption by unmarried couples who can show that they can offer a child a stable home and meet its needs.

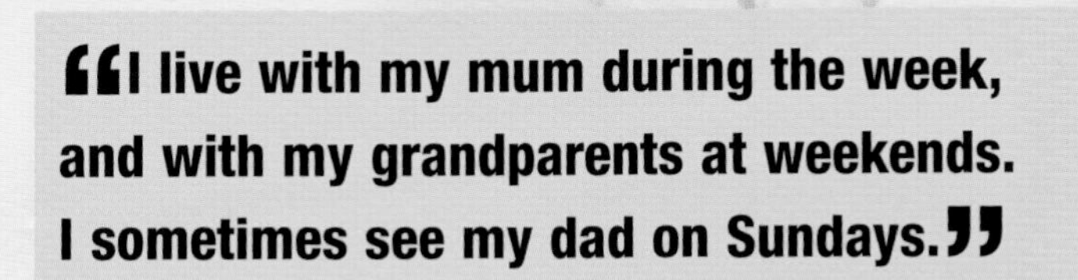

“I live with my mum during the week, and with my grandparents at weekends. I sometimes see my dad on Sundays.”

(Michael, aged 14)

Many children today live with their mother for part of the week, and their father for the rest of the week.

Reasons why families break up

Family break-up can happen after a long period of unhappiness, or very suddenly. A family may split apart after years of arguments and violent disagreements, in spite of many attempts to keep it whole. Parents may look for outside help either separately or together – from **counsellors** or members of their church, for example – before making a final decision to part. Another family might experience the sudden – and permanent – departure of one of its members. A parent or child could die, for instance, or might suddenly leave because they feel they can no longer stay.

Drifting apart

Shared interests, ideas and values are the basis for many relationships but interests and ideas can change, or differences of opinion become more important than they once were. A couple might gradually realize that they no longer have anything in common, and that there does not seem to be any point in staying together.

Wanting to be with someone else

Even people who think they are happy together can – slowly or in an instant – fall in love with someone else. They cannot imagine living without them, even though they know that leaving their present **partner** will be difficult and painful. Falling in love is not something that people choose to do – many say that 'it just happened' – but it is a powerful feeling and hard to ignore.

Wanting to go in different directions

When a couple get together, they tend to agree on the direction their lives will take. They know what kind of work they want to do, how they will spend their free time, what their long-term ambitions are. Their plans cannot take into account something they haven't even thought of – like one partner's realization that they cannot get what they really want if they stay with their partner.

Failure to agree

Many couples argue about money, but it is not the only thing they disagree about. When they find little common ground on anything, and arguments arise all the time without being settled, life becomes so difficult that parting may be the only option. Other families may accept that their arguments are a normal part of family life, and remain strong and settled in spite of them.

Some parents argue all the time and still have a strong relationship, but others become frustrated and angry if they feel they cannot agree on anything.

Abuse

Most people today agree that it is never acceptable to use physical violence against a child, or for one adult to use violence against another. Violence within a family is often hidden, and can sometimes go on for a long time without anyone outside knowing about it. So can sexual **abuse** of one family member by another. People who misuse alcohol or other drugs can become aggressive and violent towards other family members, or neglect their parental responsibilities. Sometimes breaking up a family is the only way to keep non-abusing family members safe and well.

The normal family

'Normal' families in 21st-century industrialized societies reflect the fact that family break-up is far more common than it was 50 years ago. In the USA alone, 20 million children live with just one parent. Families arrange themselves in so many different ways after break-up that it is hard to know now what 'normal' is.

When couples separate, they sometimes feel a lot of bitterness and anger towards their ex-**partner** and find it hard to agree on who their children should live with. In some situations it is obvious where they will be better off, in others less so. Children's own views are more often listened to than they used to be.

Parents who no longer live with their children are usually encouraged to see them regularly – they do not stop being a parent when they **divorce** – unless they are thought to be a danger to the child.

Living with mother

Around 84% of children live with their mother after their parents split, sometimes in the same family home as before, sometimes in a new one. Some – over four million of them in the USA – live with their mother in their grandparents' house. Many see their fathers regularly, but some do not.

Living with father

It is becoming more common for children to live with their father after a separation. For many years it was thought that fathers could not look after their children properly, but this is changing as men become more involved in parenting and more women take on demanding full-time jobs.

Step-families

When a child's mother or father divorce to form a relationship with someone new, their new partner may have children of their own. If they then marry, the two families join together and the children find themselves living with step-brothers and sisters.

Joint custody

Some children live with their mothers for some of the time, and with their fathers for the rest. Their parents share responsibility for their welfare just as they did before they broke up.

Flexible arrangements

When parents divorce, they have to decide where their children will live and who will look after them. These arrangements do not have to stay the same forever, and can be changed later as long as everyone involved agrees.

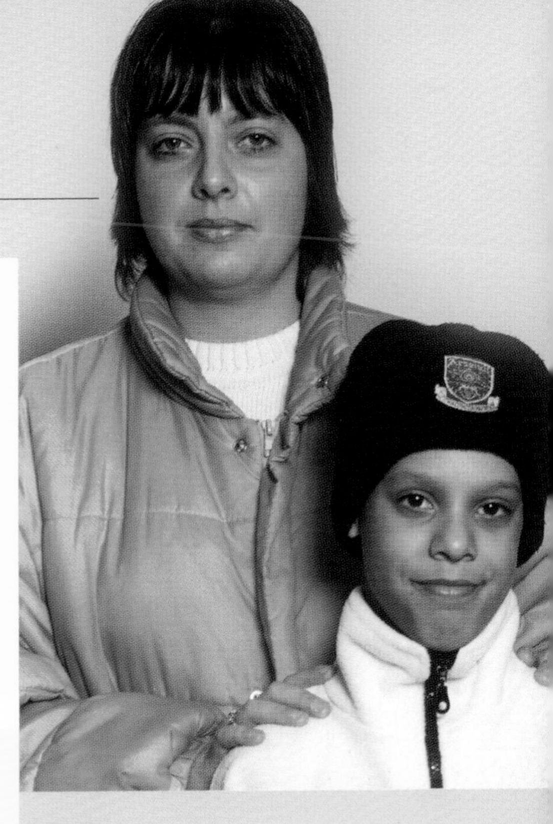

Leonie

Leonie's mum formed another relationship with a man who was also divorced. He had two children of his own who lived with their mother, but who stayed with their dad every other weekend. In the beginning, this was on the same weekends that Leonie was away seeing her dad.

'I used to get really cross at first,' says Leonie. 'Ian and Lucy came and stayed in my room, and got to do fun things with their dad and my mum. My room was always a mess, and I know they went through my things. I hated it. I couldn't believe my mum would let them do this.'

Leonie's mum and dad changed their weekends around, and relationships improved. Leonie now joins in the family's activities, and no longer feels she is missing out.

Changes

Family is the most important and powerful thing in the lives of most children. If one of their parents dies, or their mother and father split up, or someone they care about leaves their family, children may think that the love and stability they knew have gone forever. Although it can feel like that at first, most children eventually get used to the kind of changes a family break-up brings. If family life has meant a lot of arguments and unhappiness, a break-up can be a relief and things may seem a lot better afterwards.

Frequently-asked questions

Faced with huge changes, children and young people ask questions. Some are very difficult to answer, and parents have to deal with them while they cope with their own fears about what the future holds.

Who will be responsible for me?

Children sometimes fear that a parent leaving means that they are going to end up completely on their own. They may even be afraid that the other parent will disappear, too.

Where will I live? Do I have any choice?

If the parent leaving is the one they feel closest to, children may be deeply troubled at the thought of not going with them. They may fear having to choose between two people they love. When they associate a parent with violence or **abuse**, they may be afraid that they will be forced to stay with them or have to see them even if they don't want to.

What will I say to my friends?

Children often think that their own family is the only one that has ever been through a break-up. They may not realize that they know lots of other people it has happened to. They may worry that their friends will see them and their family as odd, or embarrassing. If the break-up means a move out of the area, they may be afraid that they will never see their friends again.

Young people whose lives are changing can find it helpful to talk to friends. Girls often find this easier than boys.

Is it my fault?

Although parents say their children are never to blame for family break-up, children do not always see it that way. They remember times when they made a parent angry, or when they seemed to be the reason for a disagreement. They think that if only they had been good, this would not be happening. But families do not break up because children have been naughty.

What will happen to my pets?

Worrying that one change will automatically lead to others, children may feel that they are going to lose everything that is important to them.

Will we be poor?

Children may worry about whether they can still have treats, outings and birthday presents, especially if the parent they will be living with does not work outside the home.

Can I make contact with Mum or Dad when I want?

Children who are close to a parent who is leaving want to know if they can stay in touch. Telephone calls, emails, letters, visits and outings can all help, and they need to know whether they can make the first move rather than just wait. On the other hand, a child who has had bad experiences with the parent who is leaving needs reassurance that they will not be forced to see them if they do not want to.

Will we live as a family again?

A child who loves both their parents and cannot really understand why they are breaking up may hope for a long time that they will get back together again.

Email can be a good way of sharing news with family members who live somewhere else.

Making changes

Making changes can be hard when people do not agree on what should happen next. Most families who break up work things out by themselves, maybe with the help of friends and relations and other advisors. Others find it more difficult. Professional **mediators** – people who are trained to help others reach agreement – can work with quarrelling parents to sort out arrangements about who lives where, how the bills are going to be paid, and ways of keeping in contact with each other.

If families cannot agree, a **judge** or **magistrate** may have to decide for them, and make a **court order** that tells them what they can and cannot do. Before they do this, they find out what both parents and children want.

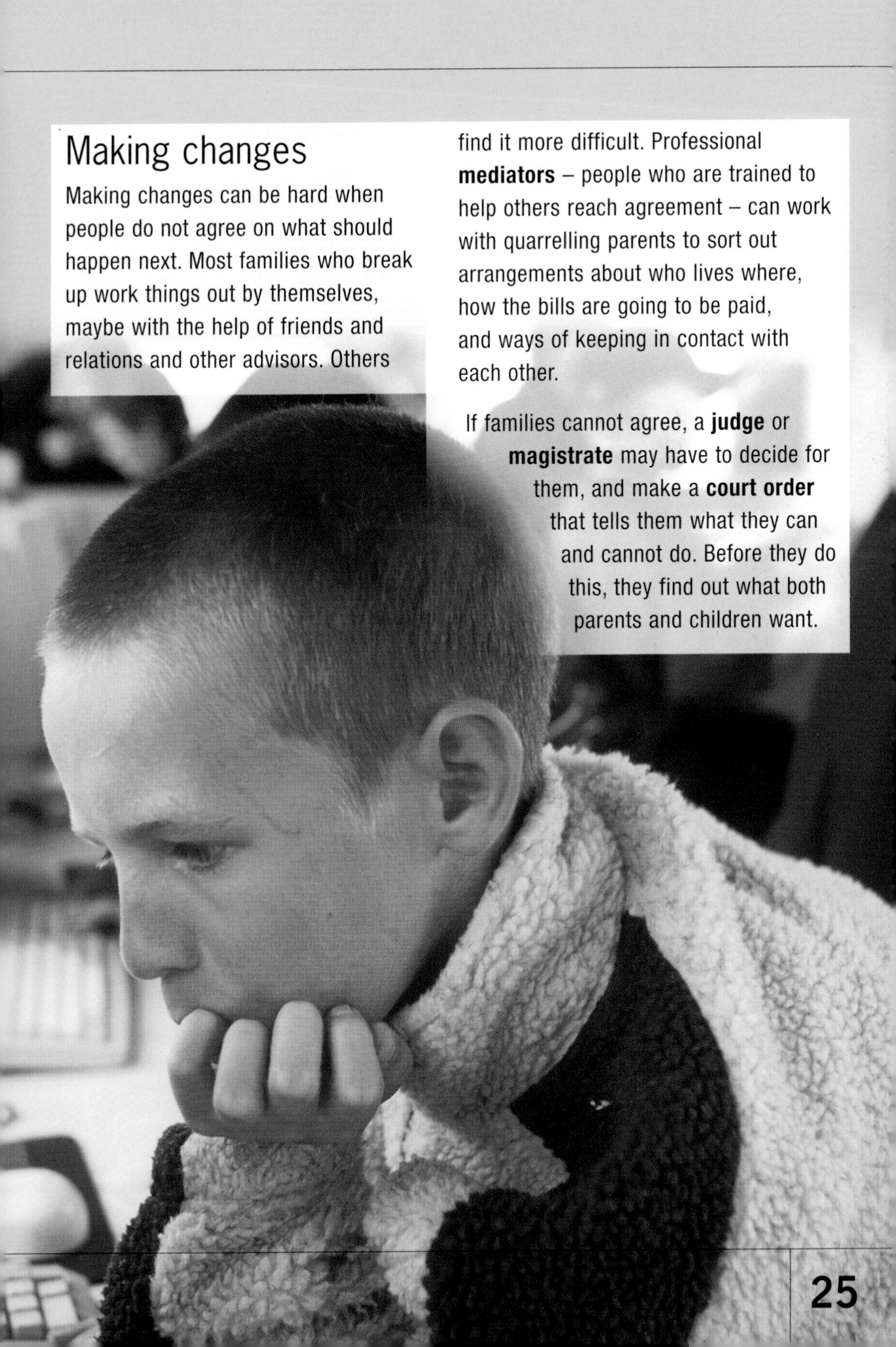

Common reactions

Most young people who have experienced a separation from one or both of their parents clearly remember the moment they realized what was happening. How they react depends on the reasons for the separation, the kind of atmosphere surrounding it – fear, sadness, relief or hostility – and how old they are. Although a family break-up may feel frightening and difficult at first, most people find that things get easier over time.

Birth to two years old

Children under two years old are highly dependent on their parents. They are especially close to the person who they are with the most. These children do not understand what is happening to their family, but they are acutely aware of the stress and anxiety of those around them. If a person who usually looks after them is away for any length of time, they miss them and fret for them.

Two to five years old

Separation can be a major shock to children in this age group. Anger, sadness and anxiety are common reactions, and children as young as this can even show signs of **depression**. They may show their distress by behaving as they did when they were younger, doing things they seemed to have grown out of – like bedwetting, having nightmares and thumb-sucking. Some start using 'baby-talk' again. Pre-school children make sense of their world in very different ways from older children, and may make up stories to explain things they do not understand.

Six to eight years old

It is the children in this age group who seem to have the hardest time coping with family break-up. They commonly experience great sadness, and feelings of being unlovable. They often feel that the departing parent is rejecting them. They may find it hard to concentrate at school, and start behaving in ways that alert friends, teachers and parents to the fact that they are feeling bad. They cannot explain how they feel in words. They want their family back how it was, and often do and say things to try and make this happen.

Nine to twelve years old

At this age, most children have friends and interests outside their family. Although their family is still very important to them, it is no longer their only world. They feel shock and sadness when their family breaks up, and these feelings often turn to anger against the parent who leaves. Although they understand more about what is happening than younger children do, they can still feel powerless, helpless and rejected. They worry about the future and what will happen to them. Their school work often suffers. Unlike younger children, however, they can put their feelings into words and accept help and reassurance from those around them.

Adolescents

Young people over the age of 12 are usually more independent of their families, and more influenced than younger children by reactions from their friends. They tend to distance themselves from both parents while they try to understand their feelings. They worry about what the break-up will mean for their future – will they be able to stay at the same school? Go to college? Keep their current friends? If they have been aware for a long time that relationships within the family were difficult, they may feel relief that the stress is over.

Feeling lonely and sad is a very common reaction to family break-up.

Long-term reactions

Ten years on from family break-up, young people report many mixed feelings about what happened. How they manage to cope with it seems in all cases to be directly related to the way their behave. An atmosphere of parental co-operation rather than conflict means that children can adjust to the changes in their own way and their own time. Constant parental fighting leaves children with long-term feelings of sadness and insecurity, and they find it hard to feel good about themselves.

"After the divorce my mum started acting like she was my best friend. She even wanted to talk about this guy she fancied, and was always pinching my make-up and clothes. I got really fed up about this. My mates were all talking about her and I told her to back off. In the end though I just had to realize it was just a phase she was going through."

(Mia, aged 16, from *Torn in Two* by Matthew Whyman, 1997)

Social and welfare services

Sometimes family break-ups involve more people than those who are directly concerned. Neighbours, teachers or health workers who deal regularly with family members may become worried about their health, or their safety, or how they are behaving. In some cases they may report their concerns to the police – or others who are legally responsible for the welfare of people in the community – who may then step in.

Some of these people work for government-funded social and **welfare services**. Others are employed by locally based public authorities to make sure that individuals and families – especially children – get help when they need it.

Why do welfare services get involved?

Parents who are physically or mentally ill may not be able to look after their children properly. Others may have drug-use or alcohol habits that affect how they behave. Some may have violent tempers that they cannot control. When they are angry, they may lash out at people close to them and hurt them. Some adults – called **paedophiles** – are sexually attracted to children rather than people their own age, and try to involve children in illegal sexual relationships.

In situations like these, where children are neglected or hurt, the welfare services can call on the power of the law to remove them from the family to protect them and keep them safe.

How do welfare services get involved?

Those who come into contact with children – teachers and health workers, for example – are trained to recognize the signs of neglect or **abuse**. If they suspect that a child is not being properly looked after, they may report their concerns to the welfare services or police, and explain why they are worried. Sometimes neighbours or friends raise the alarm.

Outsiders sometimes step in to help sort out family difficulties. This kind of help is not always easy to accept.

There are special police units whose job it is to help families in difficulties. They protect children and other people at risk, often working closely with welfare services. They may suggest classes or **counselling** sessions for parents who find it hard to support their children, but who want to stay together as a family. They have the power to remove a family member who is in danger, or who is a threat to others. In situations where children are thought to be in immediate or serious danger, they can be removed from their family. This can only happen after a proper investigation, and may involve presenting a **judge** with evidence in **court**.

Removing children from their families is a last resort. It is done when they are thought to be in real danger – from neglect or harm – if they remain. If their own family environment is not safe, children then need to be found a new home. There may be family friends or relations who can offer them one. If not, they may be found one with people who will **foster** them for a while, or **adopt** them permanently.

Fostering

Foster families are people willing to care for children who are not their own, until the children can go back to their own homes or be found a permanent one elsewhere. Anyone wanting to be a foster parent is checked carefully by the welfare services to make sure that they can offer children a safe and secure place to live. In return, they get financial support from the welfare services who place children with them.

Some foster parents have children of their own, but others do not. Children are often placed with foster parents who live close by, so that they can see other members of their own family and their friends, and keep going to the same school. Some foster children may stay only until they can go back to their own families, or until they move to a family that wants to adopt them.

Adoption

Children who cannot live with their own family for some reason may be adopted, and become a permanent and legal part of a new family. They may be adopted because their own parents have died, perhaps by someone belonging to their **extended family**. Children becoming part of a **step-family** are sometimes adopted by their step-father or step-mother. Other children may be adopted by individuals or couples completely unrelated to them – people who have said they want to bring them up as their own, and shown that they can offer the right kind of home.

After family break-up

Once a family has broken up, it is unlikely to come back together again in the same shape. The difficulties and differences that cause parents to part do not vanish just because they have separated or have a piece of paper that tells them they are **divorced**. The children of separated parents may at least see their **absent parent** sometimes, but it can take a long time for a family to get used to living without a parent who has died.

The year after break-up in particular sees everyone making practical and emotional adjustments to a new way of life. It can be a confusing and unsettling time, but it does not last forever.

Living with one parent and visiting the other

Children used to living with two parents can find it hard to adjust to seeing one of them all the time, and the other only occasionally. Sometimes formal arrangements are laid down – in a divorce agreement, for example – about who can see each other. There may be rules about how often this can happen, where visiting takes place, and how long each visit can last. Children can feel torn between their parents, especially if there has been disagreement over who they are to live with.

It takes time to get used to moving to a new school, and to spending more time with one parent than another.

Everybody reacts to family break-up in their own way.

Having two homes

Children may have two homes – one they live in most of the time, and another where they visit the parent who has left. Some find this exciting and different, others find it confusing. All may find leaving one of their homes to go to the other hard to cope with.

Changing schools

Older children may find a move and a change of school especially difficult, as their lives outside the family are important to them. School means stability and friendships, and moving to a new one may leave them feeling unsettled and lost.

Not seeing one parent

Children may be prevented from seeing a parent because they are thought by the **welfare services** to be at risk if they do. Their feelings in this situation may be complex – even if a parent has been neglectful, or has harmed someone in the family, they may still be loved by their children. On the other hand, everybody may be glad the parent is no longer involved with the family, but still find it hard to adjust to their absence.

New families

Step-families

Single parents may re-marry or form new long-term relationships that bring children into **step-families**. The new partner becomes a step-parent to the children, and their children become step-brothers and step-sisters.

Life in a step-family can be very difficult to begin with. Children tend to compare their new step-parent with their 'real' parent. They may have to share a home with people they do not know well. They also have to share their parent – with the parent's new partner, and with other children. There may be new family rules to get used to. As the initial strangeness wears off and relationships form, things usually get better.

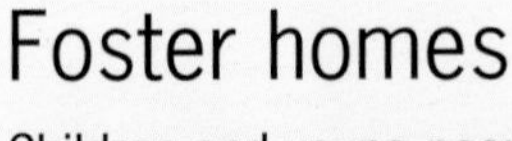

Foster homes

Children and young people removed from their families by outside agencies – like the **welfare services** – often do not understand why they have to leave. They may find themselves separated from their brothers and sisters as well as their parents, and living with a **foster** family they do not know. It might be just for a few weeks – while the parent who normally cares for them is in hospital, for example – or for a longer time. They are often angry and confused. They think that people are not listening to them, and are not interested in what they want. Their parents may be angry and resentful that the family has been broken up, but unable or unwilling to make the changes that would mean it could come together again.

Adoptive homes

Children may be **adopted** by their step-parents, or by people previously unknown to them who can offer the kind of stable, settled home their own parents cannot provide. Fitting into any new family can be hard at first, especially if a child has already experienced a lot of changes in his or her family life. Sometimes social or welfare workers may visit to help sort out any difficulties.

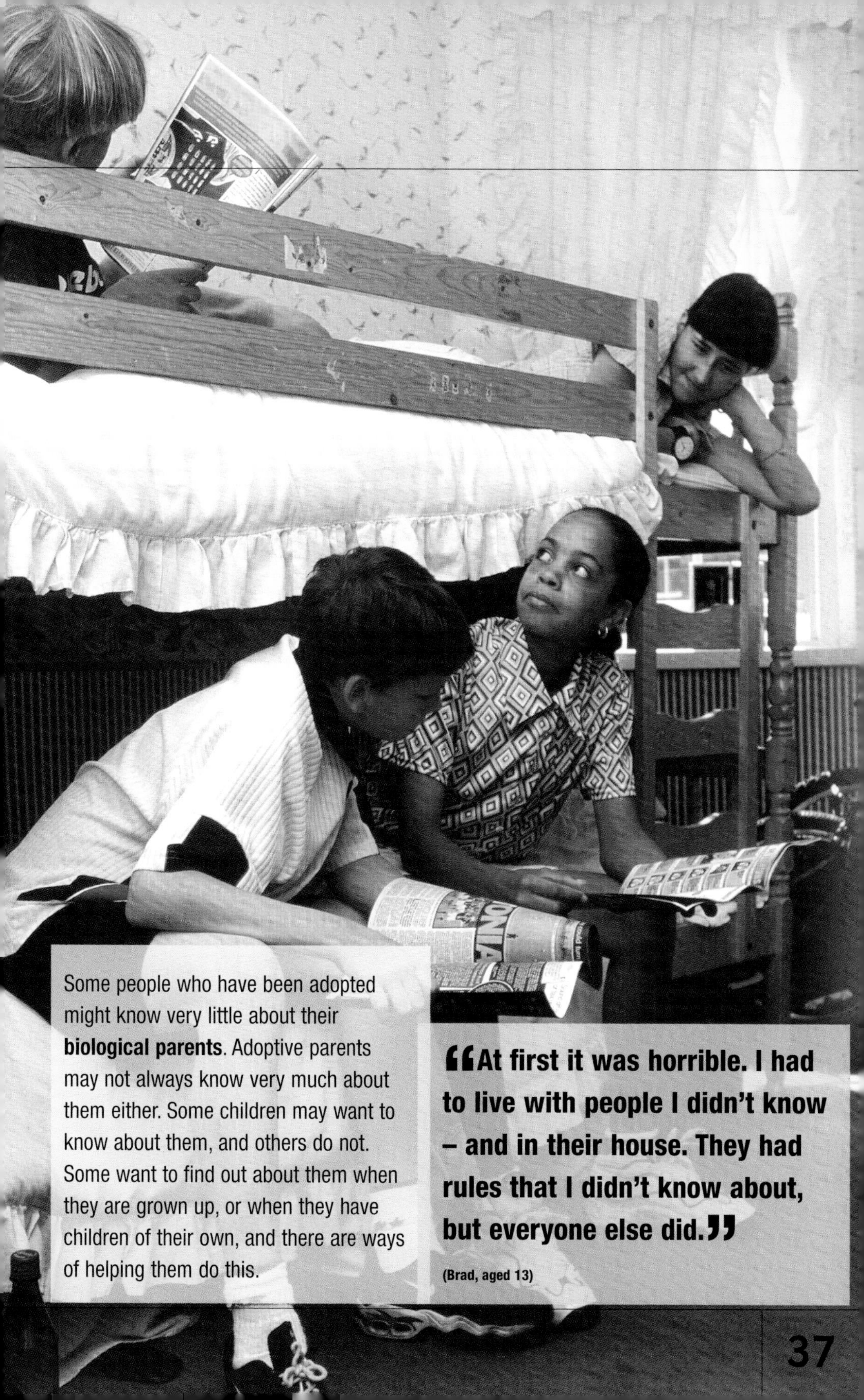

Some people who have been adopted might know very little about their **biological parents**. Adoptive parents may not always know very much about them either. Some children may want to know about them, and others do not. Some want to find out about them when they are grown up, or when they have children of their own, and there are ways of helping them do this.

“At first it was horrible. I had to live with people I didn’t know – and in their house. They had rules that I didn’t know about, but everyone else did.”

(Brad, aged 13)

Keeping in touch

Family break-up can mean that one household becomes two, and children see less of the parent they no longer live with. The official name given to the times when children see their **absent parent** is '**contact**' or '**visitation**'.

Many young people say that regular contact with both parents helped them deal with the emotional upheaval surrounding family break-up. Continued contact helps them to understand that a parent still loves them even if they live somewhere else.

Ways of keeping in touch

Separated families keep in touch in all sorts of ways. It might be through weekly visits, or going to stay every weekend or once a month. Some people keep in touch through phone calls, emails and letters. Some families use web pages and web cams, while others regularly exchange videos and photographs.

Why does contact help?

Children who do not have regular contact with one of their parents can grow up with an unrealistic view of what that parent is really like. They might come to imagine them as all good, or all bad. Few parents really fall into these two categories, and a child in regular contact with both its parents will be able to see the true picture.

Continuing contact with an absent parent helps children feel part of a loving family, even if all the members of it do not live together. Staying in touch means that

family members can continue to share experiences and keep each other up-to-date with what is happening to them. It is especially important if brothers or sisters – or maybe even grandparents or other family members – are now living with the absent parent.

Saying 'goodbye' at the end of a visit can be difficult, but usually gets easier over time.

When contact is difficult

When parents separate or **divorce**, they may find it hard to agree on when, where and how children and the absent parent are to see each other. Difficulties in arranging contact times usually have more to do with the parents' relationship with each other than anything children do. Even when an agreement has been reached, some parents find it hard to stick to it. One parent may feel so angry with the other that they cannot encourage and support their child's relationship with them. Another may be so upset by what has happened that they cannot bear their children to go anywhere near their former partner. Some children find themselves passing messages between their parents because the adults find it so hard to talk directly. This changes over time, but is common to begin with.

Kids-in-the-middle

In this kind of situation, children may hear one parent say all sorts of critical things about (or to) the other – almost as if they think the child is deaf, or not there. 'Of course, she's always late!' and 'You'd rather go out with your friends than see the children anyway' might be some of them. Other comments may be directly addressed to the children – 'Your father was never any good at keeping his promises!', for example. This kind of talk can often sound to children as if one parent is trying to turn them against the other. Sometimes this is true, but more often it is an expression of how hurt and angry the parent feels.

Sometimes children feel as if one parent is trying to get them to spy on the other, and be unwilling to say anything about what they do when they are with them for fear of causing an argument or upsetting anybody. Children can end up feeling like ping-pong balls bouncing between separated parents. There may be nothing they can do to keep them both happy at this stage, but many children try.

No contact

There may be times when it is impossible for children to see one of their parents – if they are at risk of violence or other harm, for example, or if either parent finds it too difficult. As the child gets older, though, it may become possible again.

“Before contact was sorted, I spent my weekends on the train travelling between my parents ‘cos I didn’t want to upset anyone.”

(Jack, aged 15)

Religious views

It is becoming more common for people to have children without being married, but most of the world's major religions think that marriage is the best way of making sure that children are born into stable and long-lasting families. Within every religious community, however, there are some who believe that parental separation and **divorce** are always wrong, and others who think that it depends on individual circumstances.

In most countries, a legal marriage can be ended by divorce if certain conditions are met. These vary from place to place. Religious marriages can usually be ended, too, but those who belong to some religious communities can find themselves rejected – even by their families – if they divorce.

Christians

Customs vary from country to country, and between the different Christian churches. For example, legally divorced members of the Church of England were unable to re-marry in church for many years, while those who belonged to the Church of Scotland could. Now ministers look at individual cases before making a decision. In the USA, some ultra-strict churches expel **divorcees** who marry for a second time. A Roman Catholic marriage can only be dissolved under certain rare conditions. The Greek Orthodox Church disapproves of divorce, but does not forbid it.

Although more and more couples are choosing not to marry, most religions still believe that marriage is the best way of ensuring that children are properly cared for. But will a marriage last? Nearly half of them now end in divorce.

Muslims

Customs and ideas vary between one branch of Islam and another, and from country to country. There are strict rules about how property should be divided up, and children looked after. Divorcees are not prevented from marrying again, but in some cultures women who do so are frowned upon.

Jews

Within each branch of Judaism – as in all religions – there are ultra-strict and more liberal groups. All recognize divorce, and there is no bar on remarriage.

Hindus

Marriage is an unbreakable holy bond for Hindus, rather than a legal contract as it is for Muslims and Jews. Most communities recognize legal divorce, but some find it hard to believe that a divorced woman – or even a woman whose husband has died – could even think of marrying again.

Sikhs

Like Hindus, Sikhs see marriage as a holy bond but recognize divorces granted in accordance with the law of the land.

Ethical questions

Ethics are the moral values on which nearly all civilizations, societies and communities are based. They provide people with answers to questions like 'What is right?', 'What is wrong?', 'What is good?' and 'What is bad?' It is often very difficult to come up with the 'right' answer to this kind of question.

Are two parents always better than one?

Some children are born to mothers and fathers who are committed to raising their offspring together. Some live happily with both their parents, others with one of them. Some parents successfully bring up their children outside a traditional family structure, either by themselves or with a **partner** of the opposite – or their own – sex.

A two-parent family may not automatically be a good thing. If one parent beats up the children, for example, or spends money on drugs or gambling rather than food, the family may be better off without that person.

Should families always stay together?

At one time, a family stayed together whatever happened and no matter how miserable its members were. Women and children were the property of their husbands and fathers, and men could treat them as they saw fit. If wives and children were **abused** or neglected, there was often nowhere else for them to go. Two hundred years ago, a woman married at 18 might have given birth to 10 children by the time she was 30, and seen most of them die in infancy. She might not even have reached 30.

Things are very different today, and some people argue that rules and customs should not remain fixed when people's lives have changed so dramatically. Medical advances, reliable **contraception**, better nutrition and better housing have all meant that people are living longer and having fewer children than they used to. Women are no longer expected to spend their whole lives raising children and looking after the home. Some earn far more money than the men they choose to have children with, and some are choosing to have no children at all.

Is there such a thing as a 'proper' family?

Trends in **Westernized societies** worldwide show that families are now much more likely to break up than they were even 20 years ago. They also re-form into different shapes. Today's babies may grow up happily within a number of different family groups, or with a single parent. A hundred years ago, family change might only have happened when a parent died.

Even royal families experience family break-up. The future king of England, HRH The Prince of Wales, is divorced and so is his current partner, Camilla Parker-Bowles. Public opinion in the UK is divided as to whether they should marry, and about whether she should become his queen if they do.

Help during family break-up

A family at risk of breaking up, or one that has broken up already, is going through a very difficult time. People may be feeling guilty, or **depressed**, or frightened – sometimes a mixture of all these emotions and more. They may be very short of money. Some may be homeless, others physically hurt or mentally ill. Some feel that what happens to their family is nobody's business but their own, and are unwilling or unable to ask for help from outside. Others – especially children – often don't know where to get help.

Friends and relations

Young people whose family is breaking up can feel very alone. They may be able to talk to an aunt, uncle or grandparent about what's happening at home, but sometimes worry that they are being disloyal. They might also be afraid that what they say will lead to trouble – for them, or for another family member. Often they find that talking to someone they know and trust helps them feel less lonely and more able to cope.

When people don't agree, an outsider can sometimes help.

Outside help and advice

Children may find it easier to talk to someone completely outside their family. A trusted teacher or youth worker may be able to offer advice, or put them in touch with someone who can help. Schools and community workers have information about a whole range of support services available to children and families in difficulties. In the USA, schools offer assistance through special support groups, **counsellors** or student-assistance programs.

There are organizations that give emotional and practical support to children and adults dealing with family problems, and contact details for some are listed on pages 52–53.

Counselling and support

Health centres and doctors' surgeries can also put people in touch with someone who will listen to their problems and help them work out what to do next. These counsellors work face-to-face with individual children or parents, with couples, and with families – and sometimes larger groups – depending on what kind of help is needed.

Support groups, sometimes organized and run by local parents or members of religious communities, can also be helpful. Their meetings may be listed in local newspapers or advertised on local radio stations.

Legal help

Some people will never reach agreement without help – perhaps because their situation is complicated, or they are hostile to each other. Many people today have the chance to use the services of a **mediator** – someone who is not on anybody's side, who knows the law, and who can help the couple work together rather than fight things out.

If a couple cannot agree about what should happen to their children, their house or their money, they can each instruct **lawyers** to negotiate for them and speak for them in **court**. A **judge** or **magistrate** listens to both sides of the argument, and comes to a decision for them.

People often turn to grandparents for help during family break-up. Grandchildren often find them easier to talk to than their parents.

Family break-up and the law

Throughout the world, special laws protect the rights of family members. Details vary from one country to another, and one state's family law may be different from another within the same country. Family law covers situations when the police or **welfare services** can step in to protect children and young people thought to be in danger, and can be used to prevent an **abusive** person making contact with other family members. It also covers **divorce**.

Divorce

Divorce is the legal ending of a marriage. In order to get a divorce, a couple has to meet certain conditions and follow a set legal procedure. Conditions and procedures vary. Divorcing couples with children have to show that the children's needs for a

Children's thoughts and feelings are taken into account by the law courts when families break up.

home, financial support, education and **contact** with the parent they will not be living with have all been taken into account. The views of the couple's children are also heard. Some couples agree all the arrangements concerning their children's future, and these are included as part of their divorce.

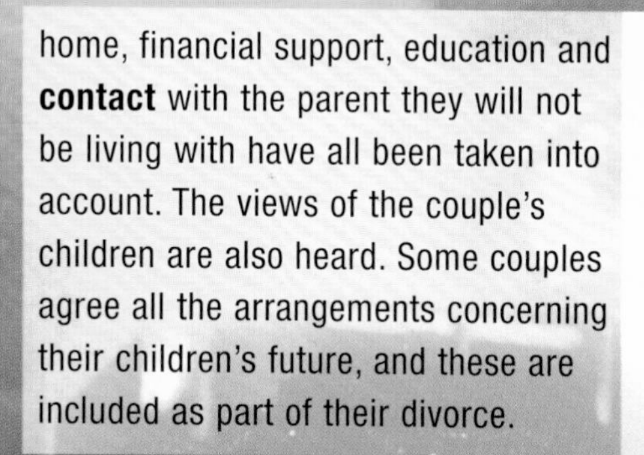

What if parents cannot agree?

Judges or **magistrates** have the power to make decisions for any parents – not just those who are divorcing – who cannot agree about things to do with their children. These decisions are **court orders**. They may say who the children will live with, and cover arrangements for visiting, phoning and having contact with an **absent parent** or other family members. Judges can also make decisions about how much money one parent should give the other.

If one parent is violent or abusive, a judge can make them leave the family home and not come back, or forbid them from being abusive again. Adults who do not do what the judge orders can be punished.

Information and advice

Contacts in the UK

Telephone helplines

All 0800 numbers are free of charge, and do not show up on a phone bill.

ChildLine
Tel: 0800 1111
www.childline.org.uk
Freephone 24 hours a day, offering free advice to children about a range of family and personal problems.

Children's Legal Centre
Tel: 01206 873820,
www.childrenslegalcentre.com
Although calls have to be paid for, the advice line is open 10 a.m.–12.30 p.m. and 2–4.30 p.m. on weekdays. A free, confidential information service for children and young people – and anyone else wanting legal advice on matters relating to them.

Cruse Bereavement Care
Tel: 020 8332 7227
Help, advice and support if a relative or a friend has died. Lines are open every day, including weekends.

National Youth Advocacy Service
Tel: 0800 616101
Freephone 9 a.m.–9 p.m., Mon–Fri, 2–8 p.m. weekends. Information, advice and someone who can speak for young people needing legal representation.

NSPCC Helpline
Tel: 0800 800500
Freephone 24 hours a day. Counselling, information and advice from the National Society for the Prevention of Cruelty to Children for children at risk of abuse.

Samaritans
Tel: 08457 909090
Freephone 24 hours a day. Advice and support for anyone who is really unhappy or depressed.

Who Cares? Linkline
Tel: 0500 564570
Freephone 3.30–6 p.m., Mon, Wed, Thurs. Advice and support for young people who are or have been in care.

Youth Access
Tel: 020 8772 9900
9.30 a.m.–5.30 p.m. Mon–Fri. Information on where to get help nearby.

Websites

www.carelaw.org.uk
Legal information for young people in care.

www.justask.org.uk
Information, help and advice on legal services.

www.nacab.org.uk
National Association of Citizens Advice Bureaux – advice for everybody about everything.

www.parentlineplus.org.uk
Information and advice on all sorts of family issues. Mainly for parents.

www.thesite.org.uk
Information, help and advice for 15–24 year-olds.

Contacts in the USA

School **counsellors** have information about resources for young people in their local areas.

Contacts in Australia

Child and Youth Health
Tel: 1300 364 100
www.cyh.com.au
Click on Youth Health Link, then Relationships, for information on family break-up and how to deal with it.

Kids Help Line
Tel: 1800 55 1800,
www.kidshelp.com.au
Free helpline for under-18s in difficult situations. Website has lots of useful links to ways of getting help and advice on all sorts of topics.

National Children and Youth Law Centre
www.lawstuff.org.au
Legal rights for under-18s explained, searchable by state and territory.

Reach Out!
www.reachout.com.au
Self-help kit and local contacts.

Further reading

Caught in the Middle: Teenagers Talk about their Parents' Divorce, by Alys Swan-Jackson; Piccadilly Press, 1997

Children Don't Divorce, by Rosemary Stones; Happy Cat Books, 2002

My Family is Splitting Up – A Guide for Young People, Lord Chancellor's Department leaflet (current version available on LCD website – go to **lcd.gov.uk/family/leaflets** and follow the link)

Parent Problems! Children's Views on Life When Parents Split Up, by Bren Neale and Amanda Wade; Young Voice, 2000

The Suitcase Kid, by Jacqueline Wilson; Corgi Yearling, 1993

Torn in Two, by Matthew Whyman; Hodder Children's Books, 1997

Understanding the Law – A Teen Guide to Family Court and Minors' Rights, by Anne Bianchi; Rosen Publishing Group, 1999

Voices of Children of Divorce, by David Royko; St Martin's Press, 2000

Glossary

absent parent
mother or father who does not live with their child

abuse
ill-treatment of someone – by hurting them (physical abuse), forcing them to have sexual contact against their will (sexual abuse), not looking after them properly (neglect), or harming them emotionally (emotional abuse)

adoption
legal process leading to a child being raised by people who are not its biological parents

biological parent
mother or father of a child – that is, the mother who conceived and gave birth to it or the man whose sperm helped create it

blended families
families formed when a parent goes on to have children with a new partner, who may also have children from a previous relationship

commune
alternative to traditional family life, where unrelated people and their families live and work together as a closely-knit group based on shared ideas or goals

contact
child's right or opportunity to stay in touch with an absent parent, or an absent parent's right or opportunity to communicate with its child

contraception
artificial or natural means of preventing pregnancy

counsellors
people trained to give advice and help to others

court
body with the power to hear and make decisions on legal matters

court order
official decision made by a court, with penalties for anyone who does not abide by it

depression
long-lasting mental state that brings with it feelings of deep sadness and worthlessness

divorce
legal ending of a marriage

divorcees
people who are legally divorced

extended family
family members less closely related to someone than their mother, father, brothers
and sisters – for example cousins, uncles, aunts, grandparents

fostered
when a child is housed and cared for temporarily by a family not its own

illegitimate
child born to parents who were not married to each other at the time of its birth

judge
legally qualified public official with the power to preside over legal cases and make decisions (court orders)

lawyer
trained professional who can advise people on legal matters and speak for them in court

legitimate
child born to parents legally married to each other

magistrate
(UK) a non-legally qualified public officer who works in a magistrates' court or family proceedings court to determine the outcome of some family cases

mediators
people who help those involved in disputes to reach agreement

nuclear family
someone's closest relations – for example parents, brothers, sisters

nurturing
encouraging the development of a child

paedophiles
criminal adults who befriend young children because they want illegal sexual relationships with them

partner
either member of a couple in a relationship

step-families
families formed when one or two adults with children form a lasting relationship

visitation
(USA) the child's right or opportunity to stay in touch with an absent parent, or an absent parent's right or opportunity to communicate with his or her child

welfare services
people employed by local or central government to provide help that ensures the well-being of individuals and families in need

Westernized societies
societies that share the kind of customs, laws and values common in the Western – as distinct from the Asian or African – world

Index

Mastering e-Business

e-Business – business collaborations enabled through information and communication technologies – is an essential activity for any business organization and constitutes a significant and growing sector. This textbook presents an innovative teaching framework to help students gain a thorough understanding of the principles of this vital aspect of business and management.

Casting aside the over-complicated and narrow introductions of other textbooks, Grefen presents, analyzes and explains the principles of e-business with refreshing clarity. The book covers both the business and technology aspects of this topic, using a unique framework integrating:

- Business – focuses on why a specific e-business scenario exists and how an organization can profit from it;
- Organization – analyzes how organizations and their processes are structured to achieve strategic e-business goals;
- Architecture – explains the high-level design of advanced information systems to describe how e-business functions;
- Technology – examines the technological implementation of e-business scenarios using a wide variety of ingredients from ICT.

Mastering e-Business offers a well-structured overview of all aspects of e-business and is an essential read for all students and professionals interested in this central aspect of modern, global business.

Paul Grefen is a Professor at the School of Industrial Engineering at Eindhoven University of Technology, the Netherlands. He has a rich background in research in information systems and e-business, cooperating with industry and academia. He has published many international journal and conference papers and several books.

Mastering e-Business

Paul Grefen

Routledge
Taylor & Francis Group
LONDON AND NEW YORK

First published 2010 by Routledge
2 Park Square, Milton Park, Abingdon, Oxon, OX14 4RN

Simultaneously published in the USA and Canada
by Routledge
270 Madison Avenue, New York, NY 10016

Routledge is an imprint of the Taylor & Francis Group, an informa business

Typeset in Amasis by
Swales & Willis Ltd, Exeter, Devon
Printed and bound in Great Britain by
TJ International, Padstow, Cornwall

British Library Cataloguing in Publication Data
A catalogue record for this book is available from the British Library

Library of Congress Cataloging in Publication Data
Grefen, Paul.
Mastering e-business/Paul Grefen. – 1st ed.
p. cm.
Includes bibliographical references and index.
1. Electronic commerce--Management. I. Title.
HF5548.32.G745 2010
658.8'72–dc22 2009052238

ISBN: 978–0-415–55785–6 (hbk)
ISBN: 978–0-415–55787–0 (pbk)
ISBN: 978–0-203–84912–5 (ebk)

Contents

Illustrations

FIGURES

TABLES

Preface

This book provides a view on e-business that is different from views found in other textbooks on the subject. The core of this view consists of two observations. The first is that e-business is a complex, multi-faceted field in which it is most important to understand its structure in terms of essential conceptual elements and relations between these elements. By understanding the overall structure, it is easy to understand further details of the field, as well as cases and developments in the field. The second observation is that e-business can only be completely understood by having a well-balanced (and well-structured) treatment of the entire spectrum from business elements to information technology elements.

This preface explains the background and intended audience of this book – thereby also further explaining its view and its aim. After that, a short reading guide is presented.

ABOUT THE BACKGROUND OF THIS BOOK

This book has been written on the basis of a framework reader for the *Electronic Business Architectures and Systems* (EBAS) course taught at the School of Industrial Engineering at Eindhoven University of Technology (TU/e, Netherlands). The EBAS course at TU/e is the successor of the *e-Commerce* course previously taught at the University of Twente (UT, Netherlands). The author of this book was responsible for the design of both courses. As such, there is a substantial amount of teaching experience behind this book. Although the material was developed in the Netherlands, it was given an explicit international orientation from the very beginning.

The EBAS reader has also been used at the Department of Supply Chain and Information Systems of Pennsylvania State University (PSU, USA), at the Economics and Management School of Beijing University of Technology (BJUT, China) and in collaboration with industry.

This book is a substantial improvement on the EBAS reader. Where the reader mainly provided a skeleton text, this book provides fully elaborated texts. Also, the selection of topics has been heavily extended. Integration of topics has been brought to a far more structured level. Further, two case studies have been added that run through all main chapters of this book. They provide an integral illustration and further explanation of the topics discussed in the chapters.

Although the book is much more elaborated than its predecessor, the general aim in writing it was to provide a relatively short book that focuses on the main concepts and structures of the e-business field, covering all major topics from business aspects to technology aspects in a well-balanced way and paying explicit attention to relations and mappings between these topics. Through this approach, the book provides a way to understand the e-business domain without touching too many volatile details – hence, it is less susceptible to the erosion of time than a book containing many details of specific e-business cases or technologies. Note that real-world examples are given throughout the book, details of which may of course change in the course of time. However, because they are examples only, this will not affect the main contents of the book.

INTENDED AUDIENCE AND SETTING

This book has been developed primarily to be used in M.Sc. courses (or advanced B.Sc. courses) in programs like Industrial Engineering, (Business) Information Systems, Management Science and Computer Science. The book is, however, also well suited for professionals in the field of e-business and managers of organizations engaging in e-business, as it provides a structured treatment of the field that is a good basis for developing e-business models and their supporting infrastructure.

To understand the book, only a basic level of prior knowledge of business structures and information technology is required. This makes the book equally suitable for readers with a technical background who want to broaden their view on business aspects and for readers with a business background who want to delve further into the technical aspects of e-business.

As explained before, this book provides a general framework for the field of electronic business in which a complete spectrum of topics is discussed with explicit attention for their interrelationships – ranging from business to information technology aspects. As such, the individual topics are not treated at the highest possible level of detail – the aim is to provide a complete and cohesive overview of the domain. The reader is expected to find more detailed material himself or herself based on the framework offered (the reference list at the end of this book provides a first point of entry into the literature about e-business and related fields).

READING GUIDE

The first three chapters of the book lay the conceptual framework for the rest of the book. After these, the structure of the book follows the structure of the BOAT framework, which is introduced in Chapter 3 – this framework is used to analyze the world of e-business in a structured way. The BOAT framework distinguishes four aspects to e-business: business, organization, architecture and technology. Each of these four aspects is treated in a separate chapter. Chapter 8 provides additional material with respect to the analysis and design of e-business scenarios. Chapter 9 ends the book with concluding remarks. The structure of the book is depicted in the figure below.

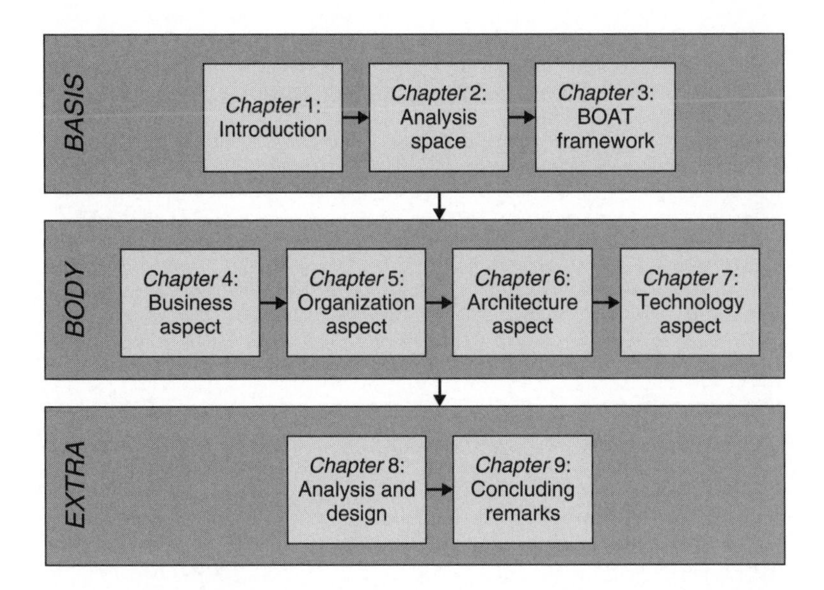

To get the most benefit from the approach of this book, the reader should read the chapters in the sequence in which they are organized. The chapters discussing the four BOAT aspects contain sections that summarize the relationships between these aspects, thereby paying explicit attention to dependencies between aspects. Also, references between elements in the chapters are explicitly included in the text.

It is possible, however, to focus on one or more individual aspects of the BOAT framework when reading this book. In this case, the reader is advised to start with the first three chapters, then continue with the chapter(s) of interest. To appreciate the last two chapters best, one should read all other chapters first.

Each chapter starts with a set of learning goals that serves as an advanced organizer for the reader. Each chapter (apart from the last) ends with a summary of the chapter and a set of questions and exercises to apply the knowledge gained from the chapter.

To enable this book to also be used as a reference guide, a list of figures and tables is included at the beginning and an extensive index is included at the end of the book, providing easy access to the discussion and illustration of major concepts.

The reader is wished a good deal of reading pleasure in the dynamic domain of electronic business.

Acknowledgments

A number of people have contributed in an important way to making the book into what is in front of you now. Samuil Angelov of TU/e is thanked for his feedback on the draft versions of the reader on which this book is based, his feedback on the draft version of this book and the collaboration in presenting the material to students at TU/e in the EBAS course. Akhil Kumar of Pennsylvania State University is thanked for his suggestions with respect to extensions of the material covered in this book and his detailed feedback on the draft version of the book. Ria Marinussen of the University of Twente is thanked for her feedback on the draft and pre-final versions of this book. Rob Kusters, Ricardo Seguel and Egon Lüftenegger of TU/e are thanked for their feedback on the draft version of the book. The (anonymous) reviewers of the initial book proposal are thanked for their feedback and suggestions. The publishing team at Routledge is thanked for their pleasant cooperation in realizing this book. Last but not least, Ilonka is thanked for being such a positive influence on my mood during the period of writing this book.

Paul Grefen
Eindhoven, 2010

1

Introduction

Learning goals

By the end of the chapter you should:

- Be able to precisely define and explain what e-business is;
- Know the essentials of the history of e-business;
- Be able to explain the relation of e-business to related concepts;
- Understand the role of business and technology in e-business.

1.1 INTRODUCTION

Electronic business (or e-business for short) is all around us nowadays. As consumers, we buy all kinds of things through electronic channels: books, music, electronics, airplane tickets, complete holidays, etc. We receive more and more information from a broad spectrum of organizations in 'the digital way'. Companies collaborate more and more using automated systems that exchange information digitally. They also engage in digital business networks that become increasingly dynamic and complex. Government organizations are moving to digital business processes, creating *e-government* initiatives. The Internet and the Web are the default means of communication for many – be it for professional or private goals. We all live and work in the *global village* that has been enabled by the advance of the Internet.

Although the extreme e-business hype (also referred to as the *Internet Bubble* (Perkins and Perkins 1999) of the turn of the century has passed, it is clear that the combination of computers, networks and business has a high impact on how the modern economy (and the entire society, for that matter) operates (Pieper *et al.* 2001). Some argue that this is actually *the* most important development of the past decades. But when one takes a more thorough look around, the question 'what exactly is e-business?' quickly comes to mind. Clearly, not any combination of computers and business constitutes e-business – if this were the case, we would have had e-business back in the 1960s, when business organizations started using computers to support basic administrative tasks.

In the first section below, we deal with the question what e-business is and try to provide some clarity. Next, we briefly discuss the history of e-business. In the third section, we compare the term e-business to a number of related terms. Then, we take a closer look at the relation between business and technology in the e-business context. In Section 1.6, we explain the purpose and structure of our exploration of e-business and hence the structure of this book. We end this chapter with the introduction of the running case studies that we use throughout this book for illustrative purposes, the chapter summary and a few questions and exercises related to the contents of this chapter.

1.2 WHAT EXACTLY IS E-BUSINESS?

As we have stated above, e-business is not just any combination of computers and business. A company that only uses a computer to perform its salary administration clearly does not constitute an e-business. Below, we first work towards a basic definition that distinguishes e-business from non-e-business. Next, we extend this definition to identify an interesting subset of e-business, which we address later in this book.

1.2.1 Towards a basic definition

To start, we must observe that we do not use the term *e-business* to denote an organization form or information technology. The term *e-business* denotes specific kinds of business activities performed by one or more organizations with the use of information technology. To call a combination of business activities and information technology *e-business*, a number of criteria have to be met to make sure that we deal with a truly important combination of business and information technologies:

1 The activities must be *core activities* (also called *primary activities*) for the business, i.e., they must be directly related to the reason of existence of the organization(s) involved. For example, for an airline company, selling tickets and transporting people are core activities, but bookkeeping and cleaning their offices are not.
2 The use of information technology must be essential for the way the activities are performed, i.e., the activities must be *IT-enabled*. Activities for which efficiency or effectiveness are only improved by the use of IT are called *IT-supported* activities – hence, they do not qualify for e-business.[1]
3 The information technology must be used in an *integrated fashion* for both processing and communication of information. In other words: information must be both transformed and transported digitally. If only one of these two aspects is enabled by IT, we do not call it e-business.

The above criteria lead to the following basic definition of e-business that we use in this book (we extend it in the next subsection):

Electronic business is conducting core business activities in a way that is enabled by the integrated use of information technology for processing and communication of information.

If you prefer ultra-short definitions, you may use the following abbreviation:

E-business is IT-enabled business.

Given the above definition, the use of IT is the discriminating factor in distinguishing e-business from 'traditional' business. As we will see later in this book, this discriminating use of IT can either be realized by using 'general' IT in a way that is specific for e-business, or by using new types of IT in a *technology push mode* – we revisit this issue in Section 1.5.

1.2.2 Towards an extended definition

The above definition separates e-business from non-e-business by stating the minimum requirements that have to be met. Using minimum requirements implies including quite a lot, the interesting as well as the not-so-interesting cases. To distinguish the not-so-interesting cases from the really interesting cases, we have to discuss two aspects: *scope of activities* and *dynamism of relations.*

The *scope of activities* determines whether activities are executed entirely within the boundaries of a single organizational (intra-organizational) or are executed across the boundaries of organizations (inter- or cross-organizational). If activities are inter-organizational, they are part of collaboration between organizations. Inter-organizational e-business helps in transforming the nature of collaboration in business markets. Inter-organizational e-business has much greater consequences than intra-organizational e-business, making it more complex but also more interesting.

The *dynamism of relations* determines how dynamic the relations are between organizations that engage in e-business activities together. e-Business can help in decoupling dependencies between organizations because it enables new forms of collaborations, thereby enabling highly dynamic partnerships. Dynamism of relations is obviously only of interest to inter-organizational e-business. Highly dynamic partnerships are clearly more interesting than static partnerships, as they have to rely to a larger extent on specific characteristics of e-business.

Given the above discussion, we provide an extended version of the basic definition of e-business given above, which delineates the *interesting* field of e-business:

Electronic business is conducting inter-organizational core business activities in dynamic collaborations, such that these activities are enabled by the integrated use of information technology for both communication and processing of information.

In our terminology, e-business is conducted in *e-business scenarios.* An e-business scenario is a setting in which two or more parties engage in e-business to achieve a specific business goal. This implies that one organization can be involved in more than one e-business scenario (to achieve more than one business goal).

In this book, we concentrate on e-business conforming to the above definition.[2] We start the discussion of the e-business domain below with a brief discussion of the history of e-business.

1.3 A BRIEF HISTORY OF E-BUSINESS

Although e-business is not per se coupled to the use of the Internet (as we have seen in the definitions of the previous section), its development is closely related to the development of the Internet. Therefore, the development of the Internet plays an important role in the history of e-business. Below, we first briefly look at e-business before the Internet era. Then, we discuss how the Internet became the communication platform of choice for e-business. After that, we pay attention to two important periods after these initial developments: the e-business hype and the 'steady times' that we have witnessed after the hype.

1.3.1 Before the Internet

The use of information technology to allow companies to collaborate in business goes way back into the previous century. In the early days of this development, we find dedicated systems for very specific business activities. An example is the SABRE airline booking system, which was used from the early 1960s to connect airline ticketing offices to a central data center[3] (Wikipedia 2009a). Another example is electronic business between banks, which has been supported by the SWIFT network since the 1970s (Wikipedia 2009b).

Before the rise of the Internet, high-volume e-business scenarios typically relied on dedicated digital communication channels, i.e., communication channels that were created for specific business activities between specific pairs of business partners. Low-volume e-business typically relied on using existing phone lines and modems to connect computers to each other.

Often, dedicated channels were dedicated both conceptually and physically, i.e., both in their logical design and in their realization in hardware (physical wires). With these channels, standards like Electronic Data Interchange (EDI) (Sokol 1995) and Electronic Funds Transfer (EFT) (Kirkman 1987) were supported to allow business organizations to perform business transactions in an electronic fashion.

The dedicated channels were usually very expensive and time-consuming to set up (and maintain). Therefore, they typically only supported long-term, stable business collaborations between pairs of large organizations. This implies that e-business was only available to a small set of business organizations. Also, it then only conformed to our basic definition of e-business as discussed before in this chapter, as e-business relations were far from dynamic. The rise of the Internet was to change the e-business landscape dramatically.

1.3.2 The rise of the Internet

The history of the Internet goes way back to the 1960s (Wikipedia 2009c), long before the days of modern e-business. The predecessor of the Internet, ARPANET, was established as a research network at the end of the 1960s, linking only a few research institutions in the USA. ARPANET grew both in size and in technology and was linked to NSFNet in the late 1980s. Around that time, the name Internet started to be used for a global network based on TCP/IP technology (we discuss this technology in Chapter 7). At the same time, this global network started to rapidly grow in size.

We show the growth in the size of the Internet in Figure 1.1. In this figure, the vertical axis shows the number of Internet hosts, i.e., the number of computers connected to the Internet. The curved line gives a rough indication of the number of hosts through the years. Note that the vertical axis has a logarithmic scale: the figure shows that the Internet has undergone an exponential growth since the early 1980s. It is this growth that has enabled the pervasiveness of Internet computing. Currently, the Internet is 'always everywhere' – making 'ubiquitous' rather literally true.[4] It is hard to find places in the 'civilized world' that do not have Internet access.

With the advent of the Internet, a ubiquitous and inexpensive infrastructure became available for business transactions. Figure 1.1 shows two important technology milestones: the definition of HTML as a standard Web markup language in 1989 and the release of Mosaic (Raucci 1995) as the first Web browser in 1993. Together, these two milestones enabled the development of the World Wide Web or WWW, one of the technology cornerstones of modern e-business (we revisit the technology of the World Wide Web in detail in Chapter 7). Its presence has become so generally accepted that it is commonly referred to as 'the Web' – without anybody asking which web.

Figure 1.1 also shows that commercial use of the Internet was only allowed from the early 1990s. Among the first large commercial parties taking advantage of the

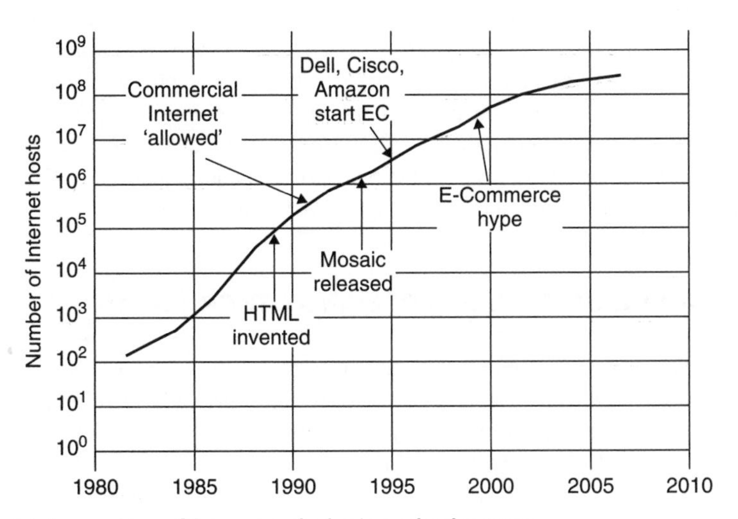

Figure 1.1 An overview of Internet and e-business developments

Internet possibilities were Dell (Dell and Fredman 2006), Cisco (Paulson 2001) and Amazon (Marcus 2005). The fact that two of these three are IT companies is not a coincidence, as using e-business was still highly technology-dominated in those days. A few years later, however, many business organizations were venturing commercially onto the Internet, leading to the *Internet hype* or *e-commerce hype*.

1.3.3 The e-commerce hype

Towards the turn of the century, e-business (then often labeled 'e-commerce') got into a hype of tremendous (if not ridiculous) proportions. Many were convinced that prefixing any business idea with an 'e' would lead to immediate success and of course wealth of the inventor. As prefixing a business idea with an 'e' usually led to setting up a Web site with an address ending in '.com', the e-commerce hype is also known as the *dot-com hype*. During the hype period, the number of e-business companies grew at an exponential rate, not unlike the Internet that provided the technical infrastructure for them.

The hype period though lasted a few years only, until people realized that not all that shines (or appears to shine) is gold. Many Internet startups went bankrupt after very short operating periods. Or, to use a coined phrase: the Internet bubble burst. Many were disillusioned, thinking that the days of e-business were over. But this wasn't the case at all: digital castles in the air were simply separated from realistic e-business developments – and these realistic developments were actually doing well, moving into steady times for e-business.

1.3.4 Into steady times

Since the burst of the Internet bubble, e-business has been growing steadily and has taken a solid position in the global economy. In many domains, e-business has become the primary way of doing business, like in the banking, insurance and travel industries. Other domains are currently in a transitional phase, like the music, television and publishing industries – here we observe a growing use of digital communication media, interactivity, and *on-demand* services. Anything can be traded using e-business nowadays, from simple pencils to complete islands (see Figure 1.2). It is this mature version of e-business that we deal with in this book.

1.4 E-BUSINESS, E-COMMERCE AND OTHER TERMS

The term e-business is used (and misused) in many different ways, as are quite a few related terms. We have defined our use of the term in Section 1.2. In this section, we place our interpretation of the term e-business in the context of a number of related terms to obtain clarity in terminology.

A term that is often used as a synonym of e-business is *e-commerce*. We, however, see e-commerce as a subset of e-business, i.e., all e-commerce is e-business but not

Figure 1.2 (Almost) anything can be traded using e-business

the other way around. In our use of the word, the term e-commerce implies explicit trading of objects (physical or non-physical objects, see Section 2.4). So, we have the following definition of e-commerce:

> Electronic commerce is e-business in which objects are explicitly traded between participating parties.

e-Business may include trading, but it doesn't have to. Collaborative product design through electronic channels is an example of e-business in which there is no explicit trading. One may argue, however, that there is implicit trading in collaborative design as parts of designs are exchanged between organizations. Note that other visions on the relationship between the terms e-business and e-commerce exist in literature. According to one view, e-business refers to intra-organizational activities and e-commerce to inter-organizational activities (Van Hoose 2003). Obviously, this latter view conflicts with that of this book.

The term e-business does not imply anything about the nature of the digital communication channel used to communicate between involved organizations. If we restrict the channels to wireless channels, we restrict electronic business to *mobile business* or *m-business*. As such, m-business is a subset of e-business. So, we have the following definition of m-business:

> Mobile business is e-business in which a substantial part of collaboration between participating parties is realized through wireless channels.

If m-business is about explicit trading of objects, we speak of *m-commerce.* As such, m-commerce is a subset of both m-business and e-commerce. Worded more precisely, m-commerce is the intersection of m-business and e-commerce.

The subset relations between e-business, m-business, e-commerce and m-commerce are shown in Figure 1.3.

Apart from the terms introduced above, many other related terms have been invented, like *internet commerce* or *i-commerce, digital commerce, cyber-commerce* and *cyber-business, virtual commerce, online commerce* and *online business,* etc. To make matters worse, these terms are used differently in different places. Hence, we will not try to discuss and define them all here. In this book, we stay with the terms and relationships shown in Figure 1.3.

1.5 BUSINESS VERSUS TECHNOLOGY

In the developments in the e-business field, business and technology aspects are very strongly interwoven. In many other fields, business developments create new requirements on technology. In other words: technology follows business. In the field of e-business, however, many business developments have taken place because the enabling technology created the opportunity. A well-known and very clear example is the development of the use of the Web for retailing applications: the Web was not developed because business had demanded this, but the mere existence of the Web has pushed business into new directions.

So, the developments in e-business are driven by two concurrently operating forces that reinforce each other: a market pull (also called requirements pull) force and a technology push force (see Figure 1.4). Both forces are strong in the sense that they are driven by rapid developments. Developments are very easily observable for the technology side,[5] but they can also be observed on the market (business) side. These developments cause e-business to change at a pace that is sometimes hard to keep up with.

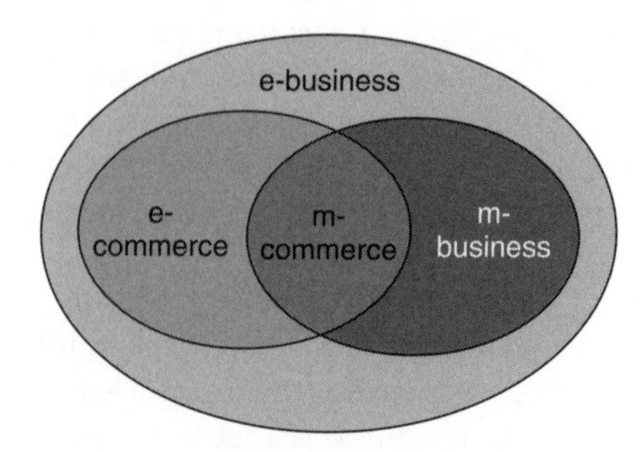

Figure 1.3 Subset relations between some terms

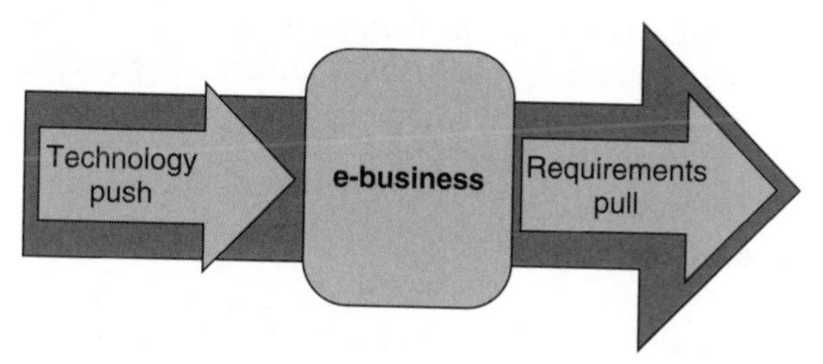

Figure 1.4 Technology push and requirements pull

In trying to understand the fast developments in e-business, we must always be aware of the dual force field shown in Figure 1.4. Focusing only on technology may mean that one forgets to understand what the market wants. Many e-business initiatives have died this way. Focusing only on the market side may mean that one forgets to adequately use new technological possibilities. Many traditional business organizations have lost large market shares by disregarding technological developments.

1.6 GOAL AND STRUCTURE OF THIS BOOK

Now that we have a first impression of the domain of e-business, it is time to see what and how this book contributes to our further understanding of this domain. To do so, we discuss the goal and the structure of this book below.

1.6.1 Goal of this book

The goal of this book is to explain the domain of e-business in a well-structured way, covering the complete spectrum from business to technology. Note that many explorations of the domain do already exist, but in isolation most are not fit for our purposes. Often, they have a more narrow main focus, e.g. mainly on business aspects (Phillips 2003, McKay and Marshall 2004), sometimes explicitly with a case-based orientation (Elliott 2002, Jelassi and Enders 2008), or mainly on technology aspects (Van Slyke and Bélanger 2003). Often, they do not follow a well-defined structure that indeed helps to clearly and unambiguously chart the e-business territory. To achieve a clear structure, we introduce a three-dimensional analysis space and a four-aspect framework in the next two chapters of this book.

Note that the purpose of this book is to provide a time-independent framework for the e-business domain. This implies that the focus is not so much on lots of rather volatile technical details or case studies – for this, the reader is referred to the heaps of related material (the list at the end of the book provides many references for the reader). The focus is on concepts and relations between concepts.

The book is aimed both at students at the graduate or senior undergraduate levels and at professionals operating in the e-business field. Understanding this book requires only basic prior knowledge of business structures and information technology, so that it is useful for both readers with a technology-oriented background and readers with a business-oriented background.

1.6.2 Structure of this book

In this chapter, we have given a first introduction to the field of e-business. In the rest of this book, we explore this field in a systematic way.

We start in Chapter 2 by identifying a space of three description dimensions for classifying scenarios in the e-business field. In Chapter 3, we extend these three dimensions with a fourth for the structured analysis or design of e-business scenarios. This dimension uses the *BOAT framework* to distinguish aspects of e-business scenarios. This fourth dimension is chosen as the leading dimension for the structure of the rest of this book (as the text in a book is in principle one-dimensional, one leading dimension is clearest).

The BOAT framework distinguishes between four aspects of e-business (one for each letter in the acronym): *business*, *organization*, *architecture* and *technology*. These aspects are each discussed in more detail in Chapter 4 to Chapter 7. As BOAT is also explicitly concerned with relating aspects to one another, we pay explicit attention to mapping the discussed aspects to the other aspects in Chapter 5 to Chapter 7.

In Chapter 8, we provide an approach to use the classification space and the BOAT framework as an analysis instrument for the assessment of existing e-business scenarios and a design instrument for the design of new e-business scenarios. Chapter 9 concludes this book by presenting some final observations.

Throughout the book, we use two running example cases to illustrate the introduced concepts and models. These cases are introduced in the next section. Each chapter is concluded by a section which includes a short chapter summary and a set of questions and exercises to actively apply the knowledge gained in that chapter.

1.7 RUNNING CASES

In this book, we use two example cases to illustrate most of what we introduce in the various chapters. We use two case studies to show how e-business can be different depending on the business domain and the business goals of an organization. The case studies are based on fictional companies to allow full freedom in their discussion. They are described in such a way, however, that they conform to real-world e-business as much as possible.

The first case study is centered on the Perfect Office Solution House (POSH), a company specializing in office solutions. POSH is making the move from the 'old economy' to the 'new economy' by introducing e-business concepts. The second case study is TalkThroughUs (TTU), a newly established company specializing in interpretation and translation between various languages via the Internet. For reasons of clarity and brevity, the discussion of the cases throughout the book is simplified with respect to real-world scenarios – the complete and detailed description of one e-business scenario elaboration could easily fill a book by itself.

1.7.1 POSH

The Perfect Office Solutions House (POSH) is a chain of stores that supplies complete office solutions, consisting of supplies like simple pens and notepads to complete sets of office equipment and office furniture, complemented by professional service and advice. POSH supplies to both consumers and companies, focusing on the high-end market (that is why they are happy with the abbreviation of their name) – they do not compete on price, but on quality. POSH has been in the market for several decades now.

POSH has five large stores and three smaller branch offices around the country. The large stores have most of their products physically on display. The smaller branch offices work mostly with catalogs. POSH's head office and central warehouse are co-located with one of the large stores. POSH has a turnover of about $800 million per year and employs about 750 staff. Currently, they sell both out of their own stores and branch offices, and through selected retailers (third parties to whom they act as a wholesaler).

Seeing that e-business can bring new business opportunities, POSH decides to launch a new business master plan for the company to open new opportunities. They have two major directions in which they want to go:

1. To sell directly to all customers nationwide without the intervention of third-party retailers, in order to increase their profit margin or be able to make more compelling offers to larger companies by lowering their prices.
2. To offer a more complete spectrum of services to their customers, like office design advice and inventory management (so that their customers can look up what they have exactly bought at POSH and easily adapt new purchases to this).

We analyze these new business goals in Chapter 4 after we have discussed the theory of business aspects in e-business.

1.7.2 TTU

TalkThroughUs (TTU) is a recently established company that aims at offering language services in the context of the global economy. With companies more and more doing business across country boundaries, language boundaries become more and more a problem in the global economy. Though many speak English around the globe, this is not yet common in many countries – and where it is common, their mastery of the English language is often too poor to be a basis for conducting business. This holds both for written and spoken communication. Therefore, TTU wants to provide translation and interpretation services through the internet. They call this the *IT² concept*: interpretation and translation through information technology. TTU tries to offer language services between any pair of major languages around the globe.

TTU as a relatively new company is still in an expanding phase. They have one central head office combined with their research and development (R&D) division. The R&D division is responsible for both the development of new business models and for the introduction of new information technology into TTU's operation. Apart from the head office, TTU currently has five international offices around the world (they have plans to expand this number). Currently, they employ about 150 staff, of which almost two-thirds work at their central location. Apart from their staff, they have an extensive network of more than 1,000 freelance interpreters and translators all over the world. TTU's turnover has been growing rapidly since the company started and is currently about $63 million per year.

TTU interpretation services allow customers to have TTU interpreters support electronic business meetings between parties that do not share a common language in an adequate way. Interpretation services are based on interpreters engaging live in electronic meetings using digital conference systems – both telephone- and video-conferences. As TTU aims at the business market where confidential matters may be discussed in meetings, explicit confidentiality of their services is of utmost importance.

TTU translation services allow customers to send documents in one language to TTU to be translated into another language. Translation services are preferably based on electronic exchange of documents: customers send input document in digital format and TTU returns the output the same way. For electronic documents, TTU strives for very short turnaround times: short documents can typically be translated within one hour. To comply with more traditional markets and historic documents, TTU also offers translation of physical documents. These translation services can be ordered through the Internet. Obviously, transport of physical documents (typically by post) implies that turnaround times are much longer here than in the electronic document case, but TTU guarantees quick responses. For urgent, high-priority orders concerning physical documents, they employ a high-quality, third-party courier service for document transport.

We will further consider and analyze the business goals of TTU in Chapter 4.

1.8 CHAPTER END

Below, we present a brief chapter summary containing the 'main messages' of this chapter. Next, we provide a set of questions and exercises to apply the concepts from this chapter.

1.8.1 Chapter summary

e-Business is the type of business that is enabled by the use of information technology. In e-business, information technology is used both for processing and for communication of information. This book focuses on dynamic, inter-organizational scenarios for e-business. e-Business (following this focus) is a relatively new area, which started around 1995.

e-Commerce is the subdomain of e-business that explicitly aims at trading objects. *m-Business* is the subdomain of e-business that relies on mobile devices for communication between business parties. *m-Commerce* is the intersection of e-commerce and m-business.

e-Business develops fast as a consequence of the sum of technology push and requirements pull forces, which reinforce each other.

1.8.2 Questions and exercises

1 What are the major differences between POSH and TTU (as described in Section 1.7) from an e-business point of view? Formulate your answer both in terms of their current business operations and their business innovation characteristics. Take both the individual companies and the markets in which they operate into account. Make assumptions where necessary.
2 In Section 1.3, we have sketched the history of e-business and pointed out that this is still a short history with rapid developments (given the ubiquitous nature of e-business nowadays). Compare the history and development of e-business with those of other areas that have had a development with technology push elements, like railroad transport or telecommunication.
3 Try and make an 'educated prediction' of the further growth of the Internet (in terms of number of Internet hosts), beyond the graph shown in Figure 1.1. Are there parameters or factors constraining its future size? Note that there are not only 'traditional computers' connected to the Internet, but also other devices (both in the business world and in the personal world).
4 Select a well-known e-business organization and reconstruct its development. Establish whether it is a new organization (a so-called greenfield operation) or a pre-existing organization that (partly) converted to e-business.
5 Try and get numbers on the 'size' of e-business in terms of the total turnover of e-business transactions per year. Note that the numbers obviously depend heavily on the exact definition of the term e-business.

2

An e-business classification space

Learning goals

By the end of the chapter you should:

- Understand the goal of classifying e-business scenarios;
- Know the main dimensions for classification of e-business scenarios;
- Be able to classify an e-business scenario in terms of participating parties;
- Be able to classify an e-business scenario in terms of traded objects;
- Be able to classify an e-business scenario in terms of time scopes.

2.1 INTRODUCTION

The e-business domain is a complex field in which many elements and aspects play a role and in which many interrelationships exist. To explore e-business scenarios in this domain in a well-structured, systematic way, we need an instrument to clearly organize the relevant characteristics of these scenarios. In other words, we need a tool enabling us to clearly classify specific e-business scenarios. In this chapter, we introduce such a tool: a three-dimensional classification space of e-business characteristics. In the first section below, we describe the nature and structure of this three-dimensional space. In the next three sections, we go into the details of each of the three classification dimensions identified.

In the next chapter, we will see how the three classification dimensions are complemented by a fourth, which is the analysis dimension that we use as the basis for the structure of the rest of this book. The classification space of this chapter is also an ingredient for the analysis and design approach that we discuss in Chapter 8.

2.2 STRUCTURE OF THE CLASSIFICATION SPACE

When exploring the complex field of e-business, it is important to distinguish various dimensions in which an e-business scenario can be described. Having multiple dimensions allows us to use a clear separation of concerns in classifying an e-business scenario. Each dimension describes specific characteristics of an e-business scenario. A proper classification of a scenario is the basis for subsequent analysis or design of a scenario.

When thinking about the characteristics of e-business scenarios, the questions '*who?*', '*what?*', and '*how?*' are rather obvious. These questions pertain to the performers of a scenario, the objects that are handled by them and the way they perform the scenario. There are many aspects to the *how*, not all of which can be easily classified. One thing that e-business scenarios have in common, however, is that the *time aspect* is very important in the *how*, as e-business changes the relative importance of time.[1]

Based on the above observations, we use an e-business classification space consisting of three dimensions that describe the basic characteristics of e-business scenarios:

1 *Parties in e-business*: this dimension contains the options for the combinations of parties that perform the e-business activities, i.e., engage together in an e-business scenario. This dimension is further elaborated in Section 2.3.
2 *Objects of e-business*: this dimension contains the options for the type of object that is primarily manipulated (traded, for instance) by e-business activities in a scenario. We further discuss this dimension in Section 2.4.
3 *Time scopes of e-business*: this dimension is used to classify e-business scenarios with respect to the time scope of e-business activities, i.e., the duration of relationships between e-business parties. The time scopes dimension is discussed in Section 2.5.

The three above dimensions describe characteristics of e-business scenarios that are in principle mutually independent. In other words, the three dimensions are orthogonal.[2] Consequently, we can depict the e-business classification space that they create as a three-dimensional space, as illustrated in Figure 2.1. Each e-business scenario can be positioned along each of the three dimensions (axes), giving it a position in the three-dimensional space. In the figure, this is shown for an abstract e-business scenario labeled *Scenario A*.

As we will see in the sequel of this book, many e-business developments are related to shifts of a business domain in the classification space of Figure 2.1. For example, time scopes may change (typically, business relations become more dynamic) or the nature of objects may change (physical objects may be replaced by digital objects, such as digital media objects).

The *parties*, *objects* and *time scopes* classification dimensions of e-business are discussed in detail in the following three sections. At the end of this chapter, we apply the classification to our two running cases, POSH and TTU, to have concrete examples.

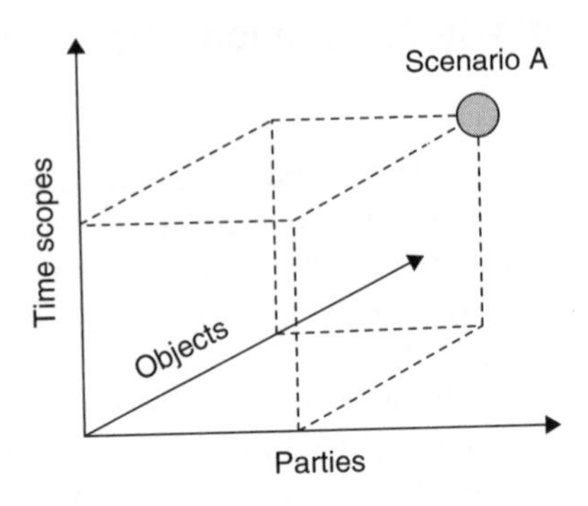

Figure 2.1 e-Business classification dimensions

2.3 PARTIES IN E-BUSINESS

In the previous section, we have seen the three dimensions that are the basis for the e-business analysis space. In this section, we elaborate the *parties* dimension by analyzing which combinations of parties can engage in e-business relationships. We perform a general analysis of the dimension first, then discuss the most important values in it.

2.3.1 Values in the parties dimension

In general, the following three types of parties can be involved in an e-business collaboration:

1 *Business party*: a commercial organization of any size and any type, ranging from a multi-national to a one-person company.
2 *Consumer party*: an individual acting as a private person (note that this is different from an individual acting on behalf of a business).
3 *Government party*: (a part of) a government organization (such as a tax office or a municipality office) or a related non-profit organization (such as a public educational organization).

By combining the three types of parties in all possible ways, we get the combinations shown in Table 2.1. In this table, the vertical dimension indicates the *initiator* of an e-business activity, i.e., the party that starts the activity. The horizontal dimension indicates the *responder*, i.e., the party that responds to the initiative by participating in the activity. By having three values along each axis, we find nine pairs of interacting party types that form the values along the *parties* dimension of the e-business analysis space.

The most common combinations in the table are shown in bold. The combinations B2B and B2C are usual terms in the e-business world – they form the main classes of e-business. Although B2C may be more familiar to many, B2B is by far the most important class when it comes to 'turnover'. C2C is the class where consumers

Table 2.1 Overview of e-business types in *parties* dimension

	Responder ⟶		
↓ *Initiator*	Business	Consumer	Government
Business	**B2B**	**B2C**	*B2G*
Consumer	*C2B*	**C2C**	*C2G*
Government	**G2B**	**G2C**	*G2G*

perform transactions among one another (we discuss examples in the sequel). Although this class is less important from a large-scale economic perspective (i.e., in financial volumes), it is interesting from an e-business point of view. G2C and G2B are the classes in which government bodies are the main players. These classes get quite a bit of attention in specific circles too (often termed *e-government*). We discuss the five important classes in more detail below. The four less important combinations are printed in italic in Table 2.1. Examples can also be found of these – we leave this as an exercise to the reader.

Note that we do not include intermediaries as parties here, although they can be very important for the implementation of e-business processes. Typical intermediaries are search engine and catalog providers, payment service providers and transport service providers. In principle, intermediaries can also be of business, consumer or government type. One e-business scenario may include multiple intermediaries for various intermediary roles (payment handler, goods transporter, etc.). Therefore, including intermediaries in the dimension would make this dimension overly complex. We address intermediaries when we discuss e-business organization structures in Chapter 5.

2.3.2 B2B e-business

Business-to-business (B2B) e-business is, from an economic perspective, by far the most important form of e-business in the parties dimension. On a daily basis, many transactions worth enormous amounts are conducted between companies through e-business channels, trading all kinds of objects and performing all kinds of collaborations.

B2B e-business can be found in a wide range of business domains. A few example B2B scenarios are:

- supply chains in industry, where e-business systems are used to orchestrate the operation of the links in the chain;
- industry-level market places through which industrial goods are traded; an example in the oil and gas industry is shown in Figure 2.2;
- complex logistics scenarios, where e-business applications are used to place logistics orders, monitor their progress, and synchronize parties involved in transportation;
- inter-bank financial traffic, where e-business is the basis for the execution of business transactions between banks all around the globe.

We discuss more examples later in this book.

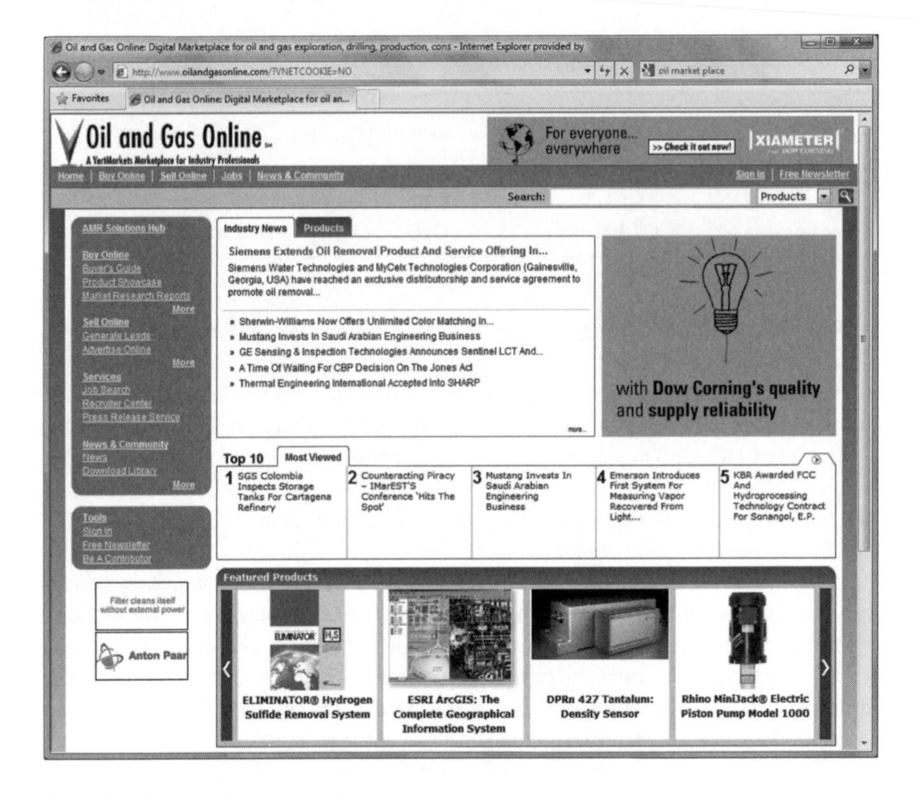

Figure 2.2 Example industry-level market place

In B2B e-business, we often find a certain level of symmetry when it comes to the complexity of a scenario. This means that the complexity of business processes and supporting automated systems for realizing e-business is divided between two business parties. The situation is not necessarily completely symmetric, but it can be so. As we will see below, this symmetry is not equally applicable to all values in the parties dimension.

2.3.3 B2C e-business

Business-to-consumer (B2C) e-business is the form of e-business that most of us are familiar with. Many of us use Web shops on a regular basis to buy a wide variety of goods – this is the e-retailing business model (which we discuss in more detail in Section 4.6.1). But B2C e-business is more than e-retailing – another B2C application that most of us use on a very regular basis for example is e-banking. B2C e-business is actively used in many domains – we see an example from the travel industry domain in Figure 2.3.

Characteristic for the B2C scenario is asymmetry in the realization of the scenario between the B party and the C party. The complexity of the scenario arises within the B party: this is where the main part of the business processes takes place and

Figure 2.3 Example B2C application

the complex e-business information systems reside. The C party typically has simple processes and a very limited information system infrastructure (usually, a standard Web browser suffices).

2.3.4 C2C e-business

Consumer-to-consumer (C2C) e-business is the situation where two customers (individual persons) engage in a business transaction through an electronic channel. Typical examples for the C2C class are electronic marketplaces at which individuals sell or barter[3] (second-hand) goods.

In most C2C scenarios, a third party is involved that facilitates the C2C transactions. This is obvious, as individual consumers do not have the means to realize an e-business information system (and if they do, they typically do not have the volume of business to make this cost-effective). The electronic marketplace mentioned above is typically set up by such a third party. This third party may have income from advertising or from fees with respect to the transactions conducted through the market place. From the third party's point of view, the C2C scenario may also be seen as a B2C scenario – although this also changes the main objects traded (see the next section). A well-known example of a marketplace facilitating both C2C and B2C e-business is eBay[4] (as shown in Figure 2.4). Many similar marketplaces exist, often with a regional or national character.

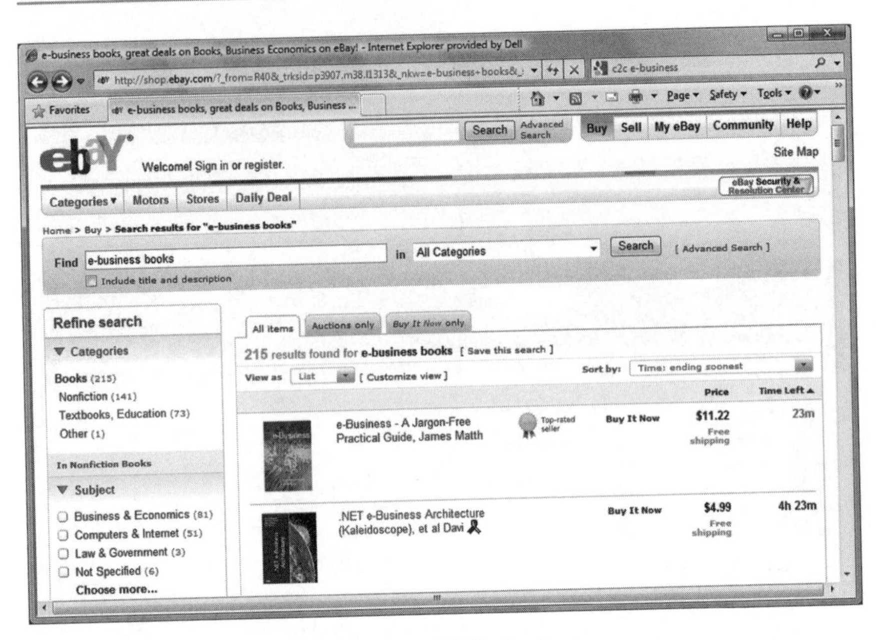

Figure 2.4 Example marketplace for C2C and B2C e-business

2.3.5 G2C and G2B e-business

Government-to-consumer[5] (G2C) and government-to-business (G2B) scenarios include a government body as one of the parties. Example government bodies are municipality offices, tax offices, and bureaus that give out documents, licenses and permits. Typical G2C examples are electronic tax statement handling and the use of electronic portals through which municipalities serve their citizens in various ways. An example B2C e-government service is shown in Figure 2.5, which is part of an e-government portal of a municipality in the United Kingdom (perhaps not the most appreciated part of their portal . . .). Comparably, G2B examples are digital handling of business taxes and portals through which business organizations can obtain various kinds of permits.

A special case of e-business scenarios that we can classify as G2C/G2B are the scenarios of charity organizations, which commonly use Web-based information systems to inform people, attract members and raise funding. A well-known example is shown in Figure 2.6. Although we classify charity scenarios as G2C/G2B, they typically also have characteristics of B2C or B2B scenarios (for example, they often try to make money). However, the fact that the scenarios are controlled by public organizations and have a non-profit character puts them closer to G2C/G2B.

In many respects, G2C and G2B scenarios are like B2C and B2B scenarios when it comes to operational issues – this is why we do not pay them much dedicated attention in the rest of this book. Obviously, the objects traded in G2C and G2B scenarios are typically not of a commercial nature. And obviously, the G side in these scenarios is often bound with many more regulations than a typical business

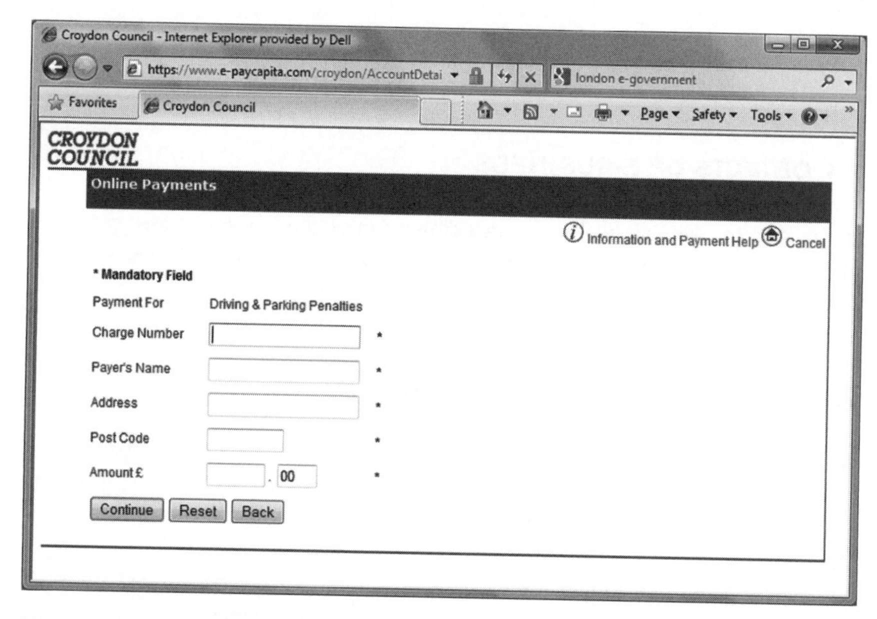

Figure 2.5 Example G2C e-government service

Figure 2.6 Example charity institution application

organization. These characteristics imply that G2C and G2B e-business scenarios are usually not as dynamic as B2B or B2C scenarios.

2.4 OBJECTS OF E-BUSINESS

In this section, we elaborate the *objects* dimension of the e-business analysis space (see Figure 2.1). As with the *parties* dimension, we first establish the values in the dimension, then discuss the interesting values in more detail.

2.4.1 Values in the objects dimension

As we have seen before, the type of objects that are manipulated (for example, traded) in e-business is important to characterize an e-business setting. We distinguish the following basic classes of e-business objects:

- *physical goods* are tangible goods which are physically exchanged between e-business parties, such as books, clothing or aircraft engines;
- *digital goods* are intangible goods which are electronically exchanged between e-business parties, such as electronic reports or music in MP3 format;
- *services* are activities that one party in an e-business relation performs for another party, taking relevant characteristics of this other party into account, such as transport or maintenance of physical goods;
- *financial goods* are sums of money or specific forms of guarantees for the later delivery of a sum of money;
- *hybrid objects* are combinations of the above, e.g. a physical device combined with a maintenance contract for that device.

The boundaries between the above classes are not always 100 percent clear. For example, one might argue that a music CD is a hybrid object consisting of a physical information carrier and digital content. The line between digital information and digital services is sometimes hard to establish. An example of an e-business object that fits into two classes is a personalized holiday weather information service. These examples are illustrations of the fact that e-business can erase boundaries that used to be clear – and proper classification of scenarios thus becomes even more important to keep things as much as possible in the clear.

Note that in e-business scenarios involving trading, typically two kinds of objects are exchanged. Most often, one of the two is a financial good for the payment, the other one the actual product being bought or sold. An exception is when trading takes the form of bartering (as mentioned in the previous section), in which non-financial goods are exchanged.

We discuss the first three of these classes of goods in more detail below to analyze their characteristics in e-business. Financial goods are rather straightforward and hybrid objects possess the composition of the characteristics of their constituents.

2.4.2 Physical goods

Physical goods are the kinds of goods that have always been traded in 'traditional' business. When trading them in e-business, we usually get a combination of electronic business and 'physical' business. The electronic business part is focused on the actual selling (or buying) of goods, i.e., finding a business partner, reaching an agreement on a transaction and making a payment. The physical business part is involved because the goods typically need to be transported in some way from seller to buyer. As we will see later when discussing business models, these business parts may be allocated to different organizations (logistics may be outsourced, for example).

We can distinguish between the following subclasses of physical goods:

- *discrete goods*: goods that are exchanged on a per piece basis, e.g. books, music CDs, office furniture;
- *bulk goods*: goods that are exchanged in large quantities on a per volume or per weight basis, e.g. crude oil or bulk food like unprocessed grain.

Discrete goods (or discrete merchandise) are traded both in B2C and B2B scenarios. They are also traded in C2C scenarios, for example in second-hand goods markets such as e-Bay (see Figure 2.4). Bulk goods are typically relevant in B2B scenarios only. Physical goods hardly play a role in G2B and G2C scenarios.

2.4.3 Digital goods

Digital goods are a 'new' class of goods that has actually come into existence through the advent of e-business. Digital goods have a number of characteristics that distinguish them from physical goods. First, they can be copied in arbitrary numbers (almost) without cost to the producer (if not protected by some kind of digital rights management mechanism). Second, they can be transported (almost) instantaneously and (almost) without cost from seller to buyer (using the Internet). This enables the creation of business models that are simply impossible for physical goods. We will see this when discussing the business aspects of e-business in Chapter 4.

We can distinguish between the following subclasses of digital goods:

- *digital content*: copies of published and cataloged (multi-media) content,[6] e.g. e-books, digital music (often in the MP3 file format), on-demand movies – an example is shown in Figure 2.7;
- *digital information*: on-demand produced informational data, e.g. electronic weather forecasts, on-demand stock analyses;
- *software*: copies of software products, such as word processors, multi-media players of bookkeeping systems; often accompanied by a usage license.

The subclasses of digital goods determine the organization of the business that provides these goods. Digital information is often produced in reply to a specific

Figure 2.7 Example digital contents provider

customer request (in an on-demand fashion), where digital content is often produced for entire markets. Software usually requires a service organization to provide support for software users, where this is usually less required for digital content and digital information.

The exact lines between the subclasses of digital goods are not always clear. Software may include digital information, for example, or digital information is sold with software to access it. Digital information exists that is actually published, making it similar to digital content.

2.4.4 Services

Services are different from goods. When services are traded, there is no actual product exchanged between two parties, i.e., no object (either physical or digital) is sold by one party to the other. Instead, one party performs a process on behalf of the other (or the two parties do this mutually) such that the other achieves a certain goal.

We can distinguish between the following subclasses of services:

- *physical services*: activities that involve manipulation of physical objects that are not exchanged goods, e.g. air transportation (where the goal is to get someone or something to a specific destination), or car washing (where the goal is to have a clean car).

- *digital (non-physical) services*: activities that do not involve manipulation of physical objects, e.g. financial services, shopping advice, agenda management (where the goal is to be better informed).

As with physical objects, physical services require some physical business activities for their delivery. Digital services can in principle be completely delivered through electronic means. An important example of the digital services class is electronic banking, where services are offered for making electronic payments or electronic money transfers. Clearly, hybrid forms of physical and digital services exist too.

Financial services are a special kind of digital services as they can be used for reimbursement of other e-business objects. Note that direct payment (by plain money, physical or electronic) is not considered a service. Loan and leasing services can replace direct payments however.

2.5 TIME SCOPES OF E-BUSINESS

In this section, we elaborate the *time scopes* dimension introduced in Section 2.2. We first give an overview of the values we identify in this dimension, then discuss each of these values in more detail.

2.5.1 Values in the time scopes dimension

The time scope of an e-business scenario determines how long a typical e-business collaboration lasts. When analyzing the time scope of an e-business scenario, it does not make much sense to use a dimension scaled in absolute time units, like weeks, days or minutes. Obviously, time scales differ immensely depending on the nature of an e-business scenario. When we are talking about a stock exchange e-business scenario, things have a different scale of time than when we are talking about trading real estate with e-business support (we have seen an example in Figure 1.2). Therefore, we use a relative time scale coupled to *e-business orders*, i.e., the exchange of individual objects as discussed in the previous section.

We identify the following time scope values:

- *A static time scope* means that e-business collaboration between the parties in a scenario is of a long-lasting (or even permanent) character, which is not related to individual e-business orders. The selection of parties is performed at a strategic decision level.
- *A semi-dynamic time scope* means that e-business collaborations between business parties are changed periodically, but not on the basis of individual orders. The selection of parties is performed at a tactical decision level.
- *A dynamic time scope* means that e-business collaborations are determined for each individual e-business order. Selection of parties is an operational decision.
- *An ultra-dynamic time scope* means that collaborations are changed even during the execution of an individual e-business order. Selection of parties is a small-scale operational decision.

The durations of the four time scopes are illustrated in Figure 2.8. The four scopes are shown in the middle row. In the top row, we see the duration of an e-business order. In the bottom row, we see a very coarse indication of the time periods in abstract time units (the concrete time unit depends on the application domain). Note that the time scale is logarithmic because the scopes often vary by orders of magnitude.

Given our definition of e-business (see Section 1.2), it is clear that scenarios with the more dynamic time scopes are the more interesting ones. If a collaboration has a permanent character (the extreme version of a static time scope), it is even excluded by our definition of *interesting* e-business.

2.5.2 Static time scope

In the static time scope case, the nature of the collaboration between e-business parties is defined by the relationship between the parties, not by the execution of individual e-business orders. That means that e-business is primarily based on a relational collaboration setting, not on a transactional collaboration setting. The static time scope is typically applicable in three kinds of situations.

The first situation is that of very stable markets. This means that the players in a market are well-known and don't often change the way they do business. This also means that the objects traded in the market (as discussed before in this chapter) have stable characteristics, both in terms of function and price.

The second situation is determined by the fact that specific parties are tied to each other because of an infrastructure they have invested in. This can be a business infrastructure (such as a long-lasting contractual relation), an organizational infrastructure (such as a business process that was very costly to implement), or a technical infrastructure (such as a shared information system or a shared communication facility). A typical example of a technical infrastructure in 'old-fashioned' e-business is a dedicated Electronic Data Interchange (EDI) connection between two organizations.

The third situation is determined by the fact that one or more parties in the market are unique, such that there simply is no alternative to choose from in a collaboration scenario. A party is unique because it has unique characteristics, such as unique capabilities (e.g., as a consequence of highly specialized production facilities) or

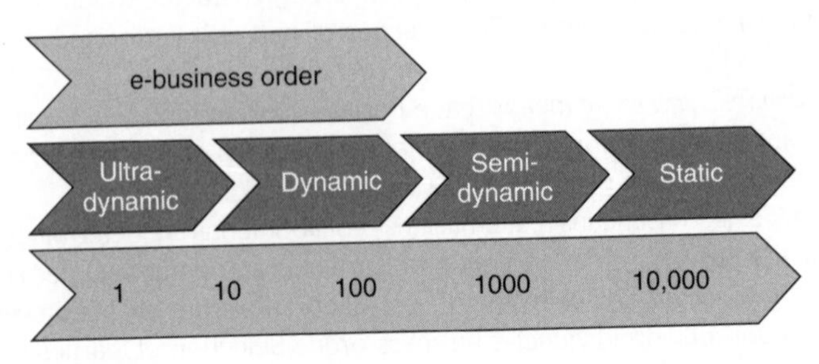

Figure 2.8 e-Business time scope durations

unique branding (it is the owner of a trade mark with a highly special position in a market).

2.5.3 Semi-dynamic time scope

In the semi-dynamic time scope, the nature of the collaboration is defined both by the relation between parties and current market circumstances. Executed batches of e-business orders or predicted batches of orders to be executed may lead to the re-selection of partners; however, individual orders do not lead to a need for partner selection.

The semi-dynamic time scope is typically used in scenarios where parties engage in collaboration for some period of time. The length of the period can be fixed, such that parties reselect their partners on a regular basis. A period may also end because some specific market characteristic reaches a threshold value.

As partners are selected more frequently than in the static case, effective means for partner selection are important. Efficiency of these means is of less importance, because the frequency of partner selection is typically low.

2.5.4 Dynamic time scope

In the dynamic time scope case, selection of parties is based on the characteristics of a single e-business order and current market circumstances – therefore, an e-business collaboration is based on a single e-business order. Typically, partner selection has a just-in-time character: a partner is selected only at the moment that its activities are actually needed. Because partners are selected very frequently and at the last possible moment, partner selection mechanisms must be both effective and efficient.

The well-known Web shop scenario[7] is a typical example of e-business with a dynamic time scope. Consumers decide per e-business order (i.e., per object to purchase) at the last moment where they will buy this object. Comparison Web sites further stimulate this dynamic, just-in-time behavior.

2.5.5 Ultra-dynamic time scope

In the ultra-dynamic time scope case, the collaboration parties may change even during the completion of a single e-business order. This can happen for two reasons.

First, a party requesting an e-business object may decide to switch the delivery of that object to another provider during the execution of the order for that object. In other words: an e-business order may be chopped up into pieces. An example is a scenario where holiday packages are sold consisting of several elements, like flight, hotel and rental car. During an e-business order, a customer may decide not to proceed with the purchase of one or more elements, and to obtain them through a different provider.

Second, the execution of an e-business order initiated with one partner may be aborted to be restarted with another partner. This is possible with low or zero transaction cost scenarios, for example in search engine transactions where a customer may switch to another search engine when search results are not satisfactory (or the engine is simply too slow).

Obviously, the ultra-dynamic time scope is used only in extreme e-business scenarios.

2.6 RUNNING CASES

In this section, we revisit the two case studies, POSH and TTU, that we introduced in the first chapter. Using these cases, we apply the concepts of this chapter respectively to the worlds of online furniture retail, and online translation and interpretation.

2.6.1 POSH

When we look at the e-business *parties* dimension, we classify POSH as both B2B and B2C: they sell both to individual consumers and to business organizations. Note that we do not include B2G: even if POSH sells furniture to government organizations, the government organization is a 'normal business organization' to POSH in such a transaction.

The *objects* that POSH trades are mainly physical goods, more precisely discrete goods (office supplies, equipment and furniture). But POSH also provides services around these physical goods, so we identify an aspect of hybrid objects as well. In the POSH scenario, we also see financial goods, as customers have to pay for bought goods.

In the *time-scope dimension*, POSH typically works in semi-dynamic and dynamic scenarios. The semi-dynamic time scope is related to project-based collaborations in which a number of individual but related e-business orders are placed by the same business customer – here, a sequence of business transactions is performed in the context of a longer lasting business relationship. The dynamic time scope is applicable to individual purchases, usually by non-business consumers.

2.6.2 TTU

In the *parties* dimension, TTU is a typical B2B case: they are a business organization that interacts with other business organizations. They might incidentally work for consumers as well, but this is not the basis for their business model.

In the *objects* dimension, TTU sells digital services. One might argue that TTU sells digital content (translated documents). Producing new content of documents is not their main activity, however, but transforming existing content – which is a clear service functionality. Financial goods play a role for the payment of the services provided by TTU.

Time scope wise, TTU works in both semi-dynamic and dynamic fashions. As customers have to be registered with TTU to use their services, the e-business relationship has semi-dynamic characteristics. But it is also possible to use TTU for individual activities, creating dynamic characteristics. When working in a real-time fashion, ultra-dynamic elements may slip in: interpretation sessions may be ended (and diverted to another service provider) before they are completed.

2.7 CHAPTER END

We end this chapter on the e-business analysis space with a brief summary of the main observations in this chapter and a few questions and exercises to apply the concepts of this chapter.

2.7.1 Chapter summary

e-Business scenarios can be classified using a structured, three-dimensional framework. The three dimensions specify the *parties* that collaborate in e-business, the *objects* that are traded or handled in e-business, and the *time scopes* of e-business.

In the *parties dimension*, we find combinations of business (B), consumer (C) and government (G) parties. These combinations make for nine possible values, of which B2B, B2C, C2C and G2C/G2B are the most important.

In the *objects dimension*, we find physical goods, digital goods, services, financial goods, and hybrid objects. The physical object class can be subdivided into discrete goods and bulk goods, the digital object class into digital content, digital information, and software, and the service class into physical services and digital services.

The *time scope dimension* ranges from static via semi-dynamic and dynamic to ultra-dynamic. The time scope depends on the relation of e-business collaborations to e-business orders – not on absolute time periods.

These three dimensions are summarized in Figure 2.9.

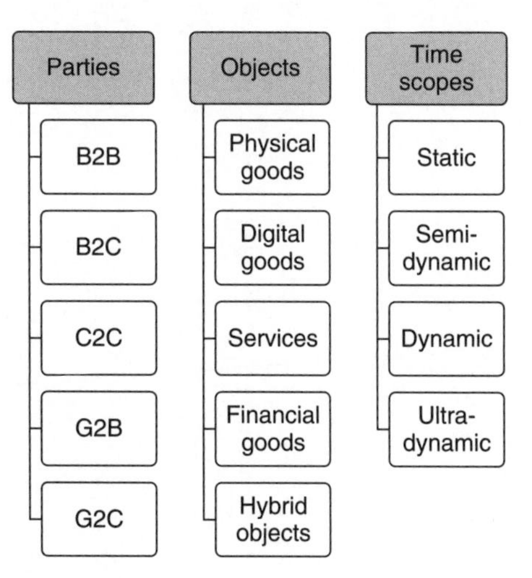

Figure 2.9 Overview of e-business classification dimensions

2.7.2 Questions and exercises

1 Are *all* combinations of values in the three-dimension classification practical? Explain your answer.
2 We have shown a number of business examples in this chapter. Try to find a competitor in the e-business domain for each example shown.
3 Try to find practical examples of each of the four values in the parties dimension that have not been discussed in detail in this chapter: C2B, B2G, C2G and G2G (see Table 2.1).
4 Find examples of objects traded in e-business that are hybrid objects consisting of physical good(s), digital good(s) and service(s). Establish for each example whether the object needs to be traded by one party, or whether each of the components might be traded by separate parties.
5 Find examples of business scenarios that have moved from a static time scope in the 'traditional' business days (i.e., in the past) to a dynamic time scope in the e-business days (i.e., in the present). In other words: find example scenarios where the introduction of e-business has dramatically changed the time scope towards the dynamic end of the dimension.

3

The BOAT framework

Learning goals

By the end of the chapter you should:

- Understand the fact that an e-business scenario has multiple aspects;
- Know the aspects of the BOAT framework and the possible ways in which they are related to each other;
- Understand the relation between the classification dimensions of Chapter 2 and the BOAT framework;
- Understand the relation of the BOAT framework to models for strategic alignment of business and information technology.

3.1 INTRODUCTION

In the previous chapter, we introduced a three-dimensional space for the classification of e-business scenarios. Of this space, the three classification dimensions (*parties*, *objects* and *time scopes*) have been explored. In this chapter, we investigate the additional dimension that we use for the analysis and design of e-business scenarios: that of the *aspects* of e-business.

In Section 3.2, we describe the four e-business aspects that we find along this analysis dimension, making up the BOAT framework. In Section 3.3, we discuss how we can organize the BOAT aspects with respect to each other. Section 3.4 places the BOAT framework in the context of *strategic alignment*. As usual, we end the chapter with our two running case studies, a summary and questions and exercises.

In the rest of this book, we use the BOAT framework as the main structure for the further exploration of the e-business domain: Chapter 4 to Chapter 7 discuss each of the four BOAT aspects in detail.

3.2 ASPECTS OF E-BUSINESS

e-Business is always a mix of business-oriented elements and technology-oriented elements – for the simple reason that e-business is IT-enabled business (as we have seen in Chapter 1). When we want to perform a good analysis of an existing e-business scenario or design a new e-business scenario, we need to make a clear separation between elements to arrive at well-structured choices: the *what* and the *how* are not the same thing and can be seen from different perspectives. For this reason, we introduce the *aspects* dimension to separate these elements in an e-business scenario. Below, we first discuss the basics of this aspects dimension. Then, we relate this dimension to the three classification dimensions that we introduced in the previous chapter.

3.2.1 Values in the aspect dimension

The *aspects* dimension of e-business is the dimension that covers the spectrum from very business-oriented aspects to very technology-oriented aspects. As this is a broad spectrum including business goals, people, organizational processes, software structures and concrete information technology, we need more than two aspects. For this reason, we distinguish four aspects in the dimension that together form the BOAT framework:[1]

- *Business (B)*: the business aspect describes the business goals of e-business. As such it answers the question *why* a specific e-business scenario exists or should exist or *what* goal should be reached. Topics can be access to new markets, reorientation of interaction with customers, leverage of efficiency levels, etc. *How* things are done is not of interest in this aspect. The B aspect is treated in detail in Chapter 4.
- *Organization (O)*: the organization aspect describes *how* organizations are structured and connected to achieve the goals defined in the B aspect. Organization structures, business processes and business functions are the main ingredients here. Automated e-business systems to support these structures, processes and functions are not part of the scope of this aspect. The O aspect is elaborated in Chapter 5.
- *Architecture (A)*: the architecture aspect covers the conceptual structure (i.e., the architecture) of automated information systems required to make the organizations defined in the O aspect work. As such, it describes *how* automated systems support the involved organizations in a conceptual way. Specific technology is not within the scope of the A aspect. The A aspect is discussed in Chapter 6.
- *Technology (T)*: the technology aspect describes the technological realization of the systems whose architecture is specified in the A aspect. In other words, the T aspect describes *from what ingredients* an e-business system is built. The T aspect covers the concrete ingredients from information and communication technology, including software, languages, communication protocols, and hardware where relevant. It is treated in detail in Chapter 7.

Before we go further, we need to add a small explanation. The term *architecture* in general relates to the *structure* of arbitrary things. As such, it is in principle applicable to all four BOAT aspects. One may, for example, speak about *business architecture*. In the BOAT framework, however, the A aspect is dedicated to the structure of automated e-business systems. As such, it coincides with the concept of *information system architecture*.[2]

3.2.2 Aspect dimension and classification dimensions

In the previous chapter, we saw three classification dimensions for e-business: the *parties*, *objects* and *time scopes* dimensions. As shown in Figure 2.1, each e-business scenario can be positioned in the three-dimensional space created by these three dimensions. In other words: each e-business scenario has in principle *one* value in each of the classification dimensions (though sometimes a combination of values is possible to indicate a hybrid situation).

In the BOAT aspects dimension, each e-business scenario can be described with respect to four aspects. The aspect descriptions combined constitute the full description of that scenario. In other words: each e-business scenario has in principle *all* 'values' in the aspects dimension. As we will see in the next chapters, the four BOAT aspects do not contain simple values of characteristics (as in the classification dimensions), but complex sets of elements (such as models) describing e-business scenarios.

The classification dimensions and the BOAT aspect dimension are orthogonal with respect to the e-business characteristics they describe, as each value in a classification dimension can be described with respect to all four BOAT aspects. This orthogonality of classification dimensions on the one hand and the aspect dimension on the other is illustrated in Figure 3.1.

Note, however, that the classification dimensions describe the 'outside' of an e-business scenario (i.e., they describe the scenario as a whole), whereas the BOAT aspects describe the 'inside' of a scenario (i.e., they describe the internal organization of a scenario).

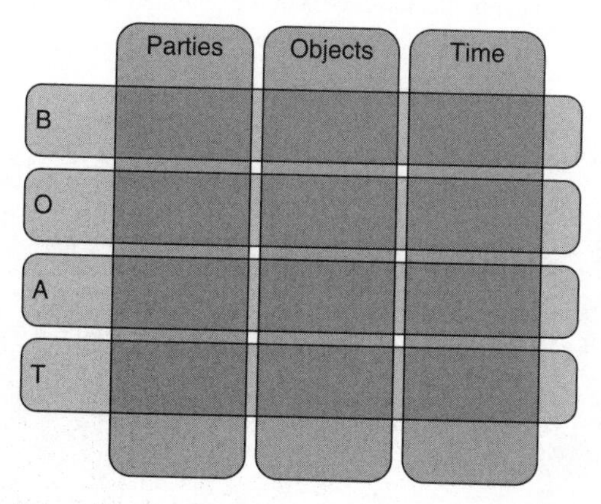

Figure 3.1 Classification and aspect dimensions

3.3 STACK OR WHEEL MODEL?

In the previous section, we introduced the four aspects of the BOAT framework, which range from the business to the technology side of e-business scenarios. Given this framework as a tool, we can make an analysis or design of a scenario. However, to do so, we have to decide how we will traverse the BOAT framework. In other words, we have to decide in which order we will treat the BOAT aspects in analyzing or designing a scenario.

In traditional information system design practice, analysis and development of a system proceeds in a linear way from the business to the technology side. This is the order from requirements analysis to system implementation, which is commonly referred to as the *waterfall model* of information system design (Wikipedia 2009d). A simple waterfall model with four *stages* (also called *phases*) is shown in Figure 3.2.[3]

Using a waterfall approach with the BOAT framework would mean starting from the B aspect and working stepwise to the T aspect, where the description of each preceding aspect defines the requirements that must be fulfilled in the succeeding aspect.[4] This leads to a design process as depicted in the left-hand side of Figure 3.3, which we call the *stack model* for BOAT: the aspects are stacked on top of each other defining a linear ordering.

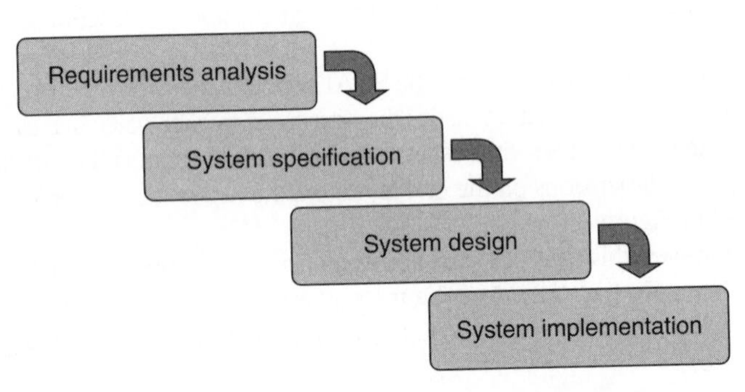

Figure 3.2 A simple waterfall model for information system development

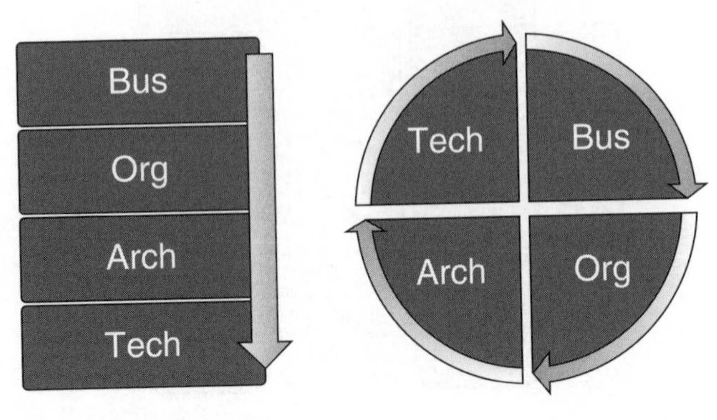

Figure 3.3 BOAT – stack or wheel?

But in the e-business field, the relation between business and technology is not so linear. As we have seen in Section 1.5, business 'pulls' technology development by stating new requirements, but technology also 'pushes' business by offering new opportunities (see Figure 1.4). In other words, sometimes the business aspect is the starting point of analysis or design, sometimes the technology aspect. Likewise, the organization or architecture aspect can be the starting point. The choice often depends on changes in the context related to an aspect, which trigger new possibilities.

To model the fact that we can start at each BOAT aspect, we need to organize the BOAT aspects such that we get a more cyclical dependency between the aspects. This results in the picture shown at the right-hand side of Figure 3.3, which we call the *wheel model* for BOAT. With the wheel model, we can make two important observations:

1 An analysis or design process of an e-business scenario can – in principle – start at each aspect of the model (although the B and T aspects may be most common). A new organization structure in the O aspect, for example, may be the trigger for a new e-business scenario.
2 The wheel model suggests a lasting cyclical process. An e-business development process does not end after one cycle around the wheel, but keeps 'spinning'. It is a continuous process of adjustment to new business and technology contexts. As we have observed, these contexts change fast and often in the e-business world.

3.4 BOAT AND STRATEGIC ALIGNMENT

The BOAT framework provides a structure to relate business to technology in the analysis and design of e-business scenarios. Strategic alignment models are used in business engineering to model and analyze the interplay between strategic design of business and use of information technology. Therefore, the BOAT framework and strategic alignment models have in some respects similar goals and hence can be related to each other.

We explore this relation in this section. Below, we first explain a well-known strategic alignment model. Next, we discuss its relationship to the BOAT framework.

3.4.1 The Henderson and Venkatraman model

Probably the best known strategic alignment model is that of Henderson and Venkatraman (1993). They base their model on two basic assumptions. First, the performance of an organization is determined by the *strategic fit* between the position of that organization in a market and its internal administrative structure. Second, the strategic fit is dynamic, i.e., it changes over time as a consequence of market developments.

The strategic alignment model is shown in Figure 3.4 in a simplified form. The model is defined in terms of four domains of strategic choice in an organization:

- the *business strategy* describes the general strategy that an organization has for developing its business;
- the *IT strategy* describes the general strategy an organization that has for developing the way it uses IT;
- the *organizational infrastructure and processes* describe how an organization is organized in terms of 'people' structures and processes;
- the *IT infrastructure and processes* describe how an organization is organized in terms of IT structures and processes.

The alignment model focuses on the integration in two dimensions. The *strategic fit* considers the interplay between the strategy and operational aspects of an organization (the vertical dimension in Figure 3.4). The *functional integration* considers the interplay between the organizational and information technology aspects of that organization (the horizontal dimension in the figure). This results in four relations between the cells of the model[5] (indicated by the arrows in the figure).

3.4.2 Henderson and Venkatraman versus BOAT

As indicated before, the strategic alignment model of Henderson and Venkatraman can be related to the BOAT framework. We briefly explore this relation in this subsection.

The strategic alignment model contains four quadrants (cells), and the BOAT framework four aspects. There is a clear relation between quadrants and aspects, but it is not completely one-to-one. We can relate the quadrants of the alignment model to the BOAT aspects as summarized in Table 3.1 and explained below.

The business strategy quadrant relates to the business (B) aspect of BOAT. The organizational infrastructure and processes quadrant is reflected in the organization (O) aspect of BOAT. The IT strategy quadrant pertains to both the architecture (A)

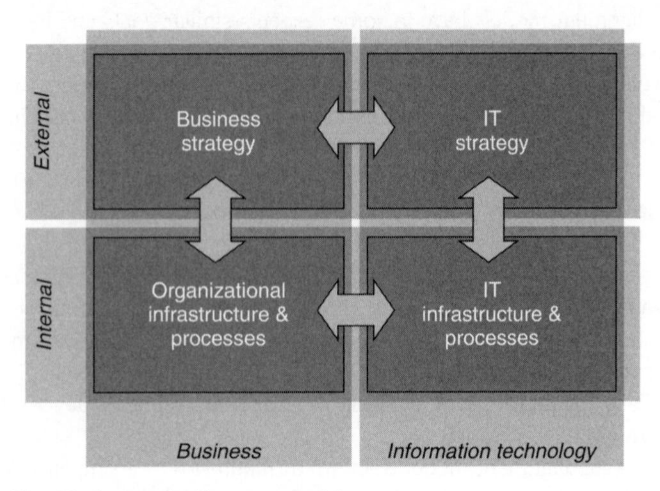

Figure 3.4 Simplified strategic alignment model

Table 3.1 Strategic alignment model and BOAT framework

	B	*O*	*A*	*T*
Business strategy	X			
Organizational infrastructure and processes		X		
IT strategy			X	X
IT infrastructure and processes			X	X

and technology (T) aspects of BOAT: strategic choices are made both with respect to architecture structures employed and technology classes used. The same goes for IT infrastructure and processes: this quadrant can be mapped to both the architecture (A) and technology (T) aspects of BOAT: internal architectural choices and details of the technology used belong to this quadrant.

Note that the Henderson and Venkatraman model considers architecture only at the internal level (in the IT infrastructures and processes quadrant). As we will see in Chapter 6, we use architecture also to shape support for inter-organizational relations in e-business scenarios, hence clearly use it at the external level too.

The dynamic character of strategic fit as described by the strategic alignment model can be easily related to the wheel model of BOAT: relations between elements in both models are not static, but have to be reconsidered over and over again.

3.5 RUNNING CASES

Below, we apply the concepts of the BOAT framework to the two running cases of this book: POSH and TTU.

3.5.1 POSH

The e-business designers of POSH recognize that getting into e-business is not a one-time affair, but requires constant evolution. Although the office supplies market may not be the most dynamic market objects-wise, the market is relatively new to the e-business field and players in the market will therefore need to pay attention to changes.

As POSH realizes that their e-business design will have to evolve in future, the organization embraces the wheel model of BOAT. In the POSH case, e-business development is clearly driven by the quest for new business opportunities. The elements in the other BOAT aspects follow from business requirements. Hence, the B aspect is the trigger for e-business developments (as shown in Figure 3.5).

3.5.2 TTU

TTU realizes that going into e-business implies constant innovation. The online translation business is a new business domain, requiring adaptations to follow the

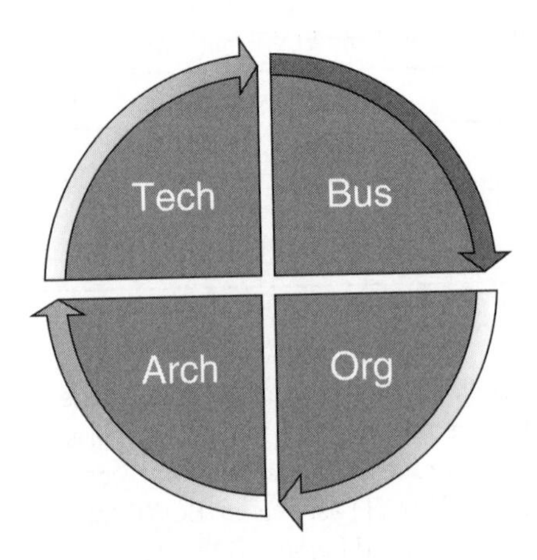

Figure 3.5 BOAT wheel model for POSH

market. Also, the business model relies on advanced communication technology when it comes to real-time translation (certainly when video or even telepresence is required – we discuss this technology in Chapter 7). As this technology is developing fast, it induces changes to the business model or the way TTU is organized.

Hence, TTU uses the wheel model of BOAT. In their application of the wheel model, the T aspect is the trigger for e-business developments (as illustrated in Figure 3.6): the technical possibility to provide online translation services leads to the identification of new business opportunities. In other words, the business goals are defined on the basis of the availability of new technologies.

3.6 CHAPTER END

We end this chapter with the chapter summary and a set of questions and exercises to put the theory to the test.

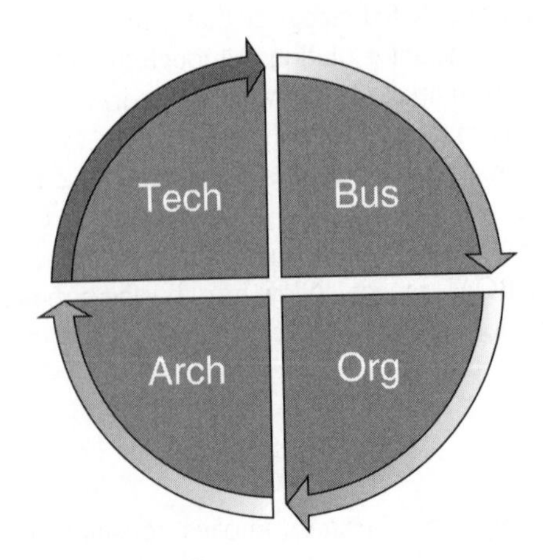

Figure 3.6 BOAT wheel model for TTU

3.6.1 Chapter summary

e-Business scenarios should be analyzed (or designed) with a clear and structured separation of concerns by distinguishing aspects of those scenarios. The *BOAT framework* provides a set of aspects: *business, organization, architecture* and *technology*. The *business* aspect deals with the *what* and *why* of e-business. The *organization* aspect deals with the *how* from an organizational perspective, i.e., without taking automated systems into account. The *architecture* aspect deals with the *how* from an abstract automation perspective, working out the blueprint of e-business systems. The *technology* aspect finally provides the technological details for the realization of concrete e-business systems.

The four BOAT aspects have important interrelationships. These can be placed in a linear *stack model*, or a cyclical *wheel model*. The stack model represents a one-shot approach from business requirements to technological implementation. The wheel model represents a cyclical approach, where the trigger can be in any of the four BOAT aspects. For most e-business scenarios, the wheel model is preferable.

The BOAT framework relates different aspects of e-business. As such, it can be compared to *strategic alignment models* (e.g. the model of Henderson and Venkatraman) that align the role of business and organization on the one hand and the use of information technology on the other hand. Architecture in BOAT terms is a strategic issue.

3.6.2 Questions and exercises

1. Take the wheel model of BOAT. For each of the four BOAT aspects, find an existing, real-world e-business example scenario for which that aspect was indeed the trigger for the development of the scenario.
2. Are there e-business situations where the stack model of BOAT may be preferable over the wheel model? If your answer is *yes*, give a convincing example of such a situation. If your answer is *no*, explain why the wheel model is *always* preferable over the stack model.
3. The wheel model of BOAT implies a cyclical development approach to e-business scenarios, in which the four BOAT aspects are traversed over and over again. The question is what determines the frequency of 'cycling' through the BOAT aspects. In other words: one may ask what determines how long one cycle lasts. To investigate this, take a few concrete e-business scenarios and discuss for each scenario which main factors may influence the cycle time. Take into account that there is a likely relation between development triggers in the BOAT model and the factors that influence the cycle time.
4. Find and get the paper on the strategic alignment model of Henderson and Venkatraman (1993). Each of the four quadrants of the model has three ingredients (as shown in Figure 1 of the paper). Discuss how each ingredient relates to the BOAT aspects.
5. Find information on the Zachman framework for enterprise architecture (2002). Try to relate the elements in the framework to the aspects of the BOAT framework.

4

Business aspect

Learning goals

By the end of the chapter you should:

- Understand the set of main business ingredient concepts of e-business and their relation to each other;
- Know and understand the main business drivers for e-business;
- Know and understand the main business chain operations related to e-business;
- Understand business directions and business structures for e-business;
- Understand business models for e-business and be able to analyze them in a structured way.

4.1 INTRODUCTION

In the previous chapter, we introduced the BOAT framework as the basis for structuring the discussion of e-business in this book. In this chapter, we explore the main elements of the first aspect of the BOAT framework: the *business aspect*.

The exploration in this chapter is performed in a structured setting following the integrative character of this book. We do this by starting from elementary characteristics of business in the e-business domain and working our way to typical e-business models. The business models are the basis for the achievement of an organization's business goals. We take four steps in consecutive sections before arriving at business models:

1 We first take a look at the main business characteristics that are redefined through the use of e-business – the *business drivers* for the e-business case from the viewpoint of an organization.

2 Next, we see how e-business can be used to change *business chains* that contain collaborations between organizations.
3 Then, using the discussed elements, we identify a number of new *business directions* that an organization can take.
4 These new directions enable new *business structures* between organizations, which we discuss next.

As such, we 'hop' between the single organization view (in steps 1 and 3) and business collaboration view (in steps 2 and 4). Finally, the characteristics, restructuring possibilities, directions and structures are used as the ingredients for new business models for e-business (illustrated in Figure 4.1), which are discussed in Section 4.6. We end the chapter with our running case studies, summary and questions.

Obviously, not all imaginable business topics can be discussed in full detail in one chapter. One topic that we do not discuss, for example, is the set of legal implications of e-business. Further topics and details can be found in other publications that focus on business aspects of e-business (for example, Evans and Wurster 1999, Perkins and Perkins 1999, Pieper *et al.* 2001, Turban *et al.* 2002, VanHoose 2003, Jelassi and Enders 2008, Holden *et al.* 2009).

Note that we do not discuss generic business models or the way they are conceived in general in this chapter – there are other publications that have this as an objective (e.g. Mitchell *et al.* 2003, Chesbrough 2006, Osterwalder and Pigneur 2009). In this book, we focus on the impact of e-business elements on business models.

4.2 BUSINESS DRIVERS

As discussed in Section 1.2, business is e-business if it is different from other types of business through the essential use of information and communication technology. Using this technology, there are two important elements in which e-business can be different from traditional business in achieving its business goals: *reach* and *richness*

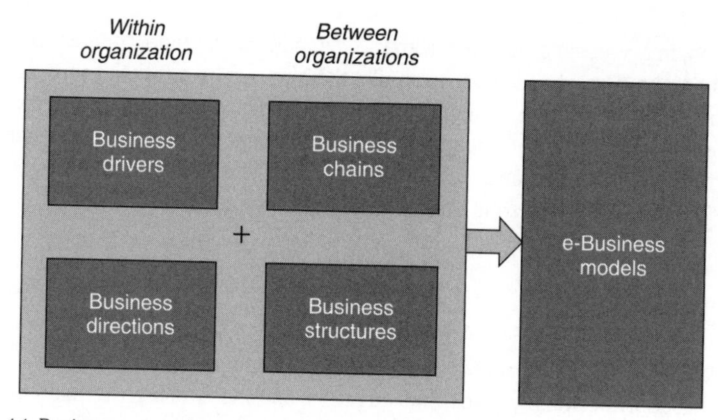

Figure 4.1 Business aspect ingredients as input for business models

(Evans and Wurster 1999). These elements are *drivers* for the development of e-business. They are essentials for contacting (potential) business parties, engaging into business with them, and retaining them as business partners. As such, they are major parameters in the way an organization creates value.[1]

Below, we first discuss these elements individually. Then, we combine them into a two-dimensional space. As the use of information and communication technology often also has an efficiency goal, we discuss this characteristic too in the context of e-business.

4.2.1 Reach

The *reach* of an e-business scenario defines which set of business parties can be included in that scenario. The aim of the use of information and communication technology can be to increase the reach of a scenario, i.e., to enable the inclusion of more potential parties. A party can be any type of individual or organization with whom business activities can be conducted: customers, providers, collaborators, etc.

We distinguish between three types of reach:

- *Geographic reach* determines where potential business parties are geographically located, i.e., where they are physically based. Increasing geographic reach means attracting parties that are further away. Reach may for instance be increased from regional to national, from national to continental, and from continental to global.
- *Temporal reach* determines during what times potential parties can be active in a scenario. Increasing temporal reach means opening up business more hours a day and/or more days a week. Very often, e-business scenarios are active continuously, typically indicated as *24/7* (all hours of the day, all days of the week).
- *Modal reach* determines through which channels business parties can collaborate, i.e., what communication means can be used between partners. Increasing modal reach means opening new channels in an e-business scenario. New channels can be the World Wide Web, email, instant messaging, text messaging, virtual environments, etc.

Obviously, in a specific e-business scenario, the aim can be (and often is) to address more than one type of reach: for example, the aim can be to reach more parties at more moments. Note that changing one type of reach can imply the necessity of considering another type of reach as well. Increasing the geographic reach from national to global, for instance, can imply the necessity of increasing the temporal reach – to deal with time zone differences around the globe.

4.2.2 Richness

The *richness* of an e-business scenario is determined by the intensity of the communication between parties that engage in business, using the main business communication channel. Intensity of communication can be interpreted both in a quantitative and a qualitative sense (as we discuss below). We refer to the main communication channel (such as a Web site in e-business) because in traditional business, extended richness in communication is often realized outside the main communication channel (such as paper-based mail), e.g. by personal contact. Information and communication technology can be used to increase richness by allowing more intense communication without having a substantial efficiency or cost penalty.

Richness has a number of sub-aspects:

- *Frequency* of communication determines how often parties have contact. In traditional business scenarios, frequency may be low because of cost of communication or lack of speed of the channels used (like physical mail). In e-business, more frequent communication can often easily be established.
- *Level of interactivity* in communication determines how much interaction there is in communication sessions. Where traditional, paper-based communication allows very little interaction, internet-based communication allows much more by having the possibility of instantaneous action-response coupling.
- *Level of detail* in communication determines how many details about the manipulated objects (as discussed in Section 2.4) or the manipulating processes (as discussed in the next chapter) are communicated between parties. Using higher levels of interactivity allows providing higher levels of details about traded objects without flooding a party. Higher frequencies of communication allow higher levels of details about processes.
- *Used media* in communication determine which media types are used in communication between business parties. In e-business, a richer medium selection can be used than in traditional business without getting into excessive costs. Media types used in e-business range from traditional types like text, graphics and photos to more advanced types like animations, audio and video. Recent developments even enable the use of virtual 3D environments:[2] business activities are common in a virtual world like Second Life (Terdiman 2007).
- *Adaptation to party* determines how much the communication is adapted towards specific individual business parties or specific groups of them. Adaptation means tuning the content of communication (and possibly the delivery process) so that it best fits the specific characteristics of a party. The presentation of a catalog of a Web shop may for instance be tuned to individual customers, based on prior shopping behavior. This is commonly referred to as *customization*. In B2C scenarios, the term *personalization* is also used.

Note that *modal reach* and *used media* have a strong connection: the available communication means heavily determine what media types can be used. Though connected, they are different things: *modal reach* is about communication infrastructure, whereas *used media* is about communication content.

4.2.3 Increasing reach and richness

Designing new e-business scenarios is often based on increasing reach, increasing richness, or increasing both. In other words: an e-business transformation often implies moving a business scenario further into the reach and/or richness dimensions. This is illustrated in Figure 4.2, where we show reach and richness in a two-dimensional grid. The arrow in the figure indicates an example increase in reach and richness from a traditional business scenario (at the tail of the arrow) to an e-business scenario (at the head of the arrow).

Clearly, when designing a concrete e-business scenario, a simple sketch like the one in Figure 4.2 does not suffice. Changes in reach and richness have to be carefully operationalized, i.e., specified concretely. In doing so, the types of reach and the sub-aspects of richness discussed in this section provide a basis for the operationalization.

4.2.4 Efficiency

A desired increase in the efficiency of conducting business is often a reason for the use of information and communication technology. If the increase of efficiency is used only to reduce the costs related to existing business models without altering the essence of these models, we do not consider this e-business: in this case, technology is supporting business, not enabling business (remember our definition of e-business in Chapter 1). Replacing a paper-based personnel administration in a company by an automated system is not e-business according to our definition (though some authors may not share this vision).

When efficiency of conducting business is increased dramatically, however, this may induce the possibility of new business models. An example is enabling the cost-effective handling of far smaller transactions (micro-transactions) than possible in traditional business, thereby moving to entirely different sales models. If this is the

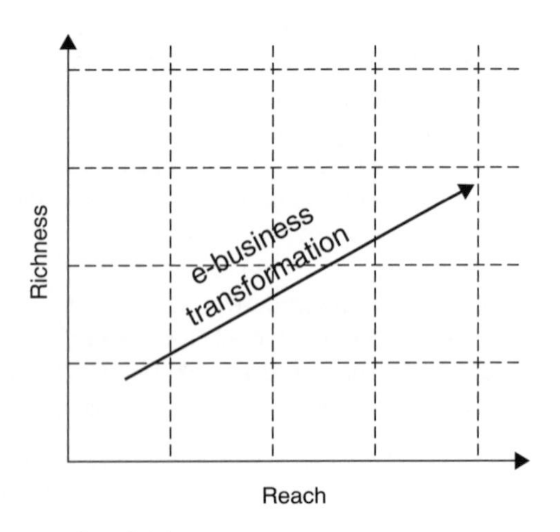

Figure 4.2 Increasing reach and richness

case, we do speak of e-business, as information technology is indeed an enabler of new ways of doing business, and hence of new business models. In other words: efficiency alone is an e-business characteristic in extreme cases only – otherwise, it can be a 'nice extra' as an addition to the other e-business drivers (i.e., increased reach and richness).

A business control view on increasing efficiency

We can take a closer look at increasing efficiency by viewing a business organization as a three-level control structure:

- the *operational level* performs the primary business process, making transaction-scale decisions;
- the *tactical level* controls the operational level, making medium-term, medium-scale decisions;
- the *strategic level* controls the tactical level, making long-term, large-scale decisions.

In a traditional business organization, the sizes of the levels in terms of personnel count are as shown in the left-hand side of Figure 4.3: the operational level is the largest, accounting for the pyramid shape. Increasing efficiency often boils down to highly automating business functionality at the operational level: routine tasks are automated and human effort mainly goes into exception handling. This changes the pyramid shape into a diamond shape as shown in the right-hand side of the figure, making the tactical layer the largest. In this case, an important task of the tactical layer is to set the parameters for the automated systems that perform the operational processes.

4.3 CHANGING BUSINESS CHAINS

In the previous section, we have seen that business characteristics like reach and richness can be changed by the use of e-business. These new characteristics are

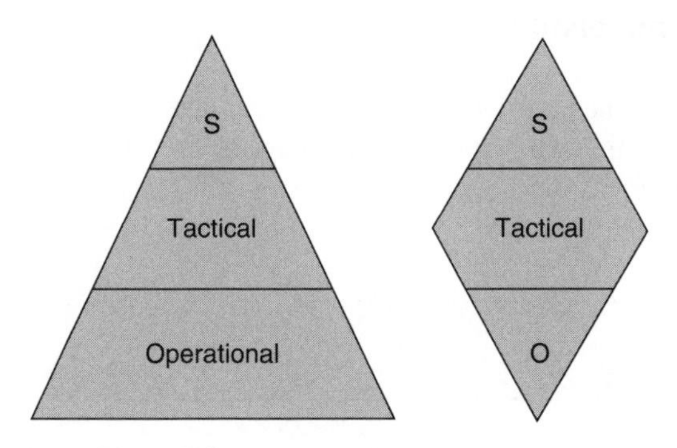

Figure 4.3 Pyramid and diamond business control structures

implemented in business models (which we will see later in this chapter) that are based on new forms of business collaboration, enabled by the use of information and communication technology. In other words, e-business changes business relations by restructuring business collaborations.

These business collaborations take place in business chains like production chains, service chains and supply chains. A chain consists of a number of links. Each link is an organization that provides a specific part of the functionality of the overall chain. Note that we will show simple chains with a linear structure in this section for the sake of simplicity. The principles discussed below apply similarly to chains with a more complex, networked structure.

In these chains, restructuring collaboration is implemented through the two basic forms of *disintermediation* and *reintermediation*. We discuss these two 'operations' on chains below. When we take restructuring business collaboration to the extreme, we get the forms *deconstruction* and *reconstruction*. We discuss these at the end of this section.

4.3.1 Disintermediation

In typical 'traditional' business chains, links often exist that have a function between other links that is heavily based on 'traditional' communication patterns or media. *Disintermediation* is the removal of such a link from a business chain (as illustrated in Figure 4.4) because it has become 'superfluous' through the use of e-business technology that allows increase of reach (and sometimes richness) (Evans and Wurster 1999, Turban *et al.* 2002).

Typically, disintermediation applies to a link in a chain that has some kind of intermediary function between other parties in the chain. A typical B2C example is disintermediation in supply chains for consumer products where the retailer is removed because the producer (or distributor) of the goods has direct contact with the individual consumers through digital channels (typically, Web sites). In the B2B world, we can find comparable examples, where suppliers of professional products (e.g. office or computing equipment) sell directly to user organizations.

4.3.2 Reintermediation

Reintermediation is the insertion of a new link in an existing business chain (Turban *et al.* 2002), as illustrated in Figure 4.5. The new link provides new functionality (i.e., new added value) to the chain that is enabled by the use of information and

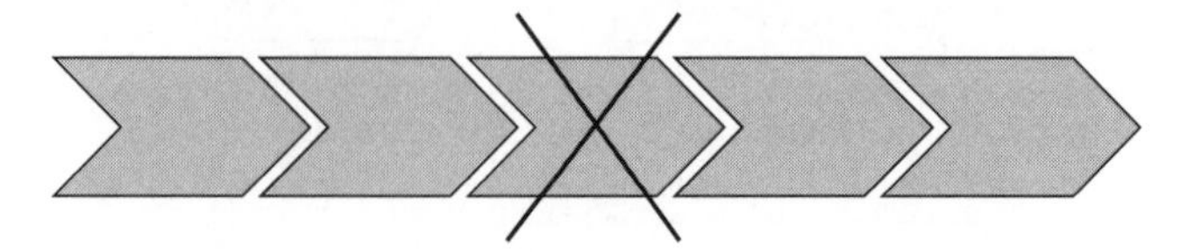

Figure 4.4 Disintermediation

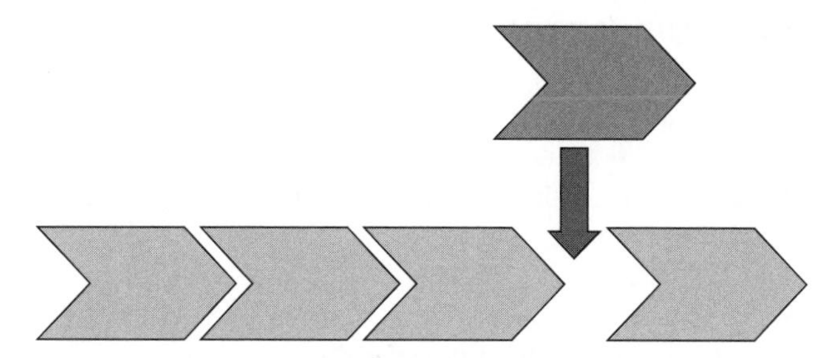

Figure 4.5 Reintermediation

communication technology. As such, reintermediation can be seen as the 'opposite' of disintermediation.

Reintermediation often applies to organizations with a new kind of intermediary function. Common B2C examples can be found in the retail world, where product comparison or integration sites take a new place as a broker in a supply chain between producers and consumers. A B2B example of reintermediation is the creation of electronic market places where products (or services) are traded between communities of suppliers and consumers, instead of pairs of partners.

4.3.3 Deconstruction and reconstruction

In disintermediation and reintermediation, a business chain is modified by manipulating one single link (as shown in Figure 4.4 and Figure 4.5). If we take the approach to the extreme, we deconstruct a complete chain into its constituent pieces (links). Next, we evaluate the added value of each piece, perhaps throw away a few, combine a few and add a few. From the results of this, we finally reconstruct a completely new chain (Evans and Wurster 1999). This new chain may follow a completely different business model than the old chain, yet provide the same functionality to a market.

Clearly, deconstruction and reconstruction can most easily be applied in chains that are not so 'physical' in nature, e.g., information-intensive chains. A typical example is the travel world, in which the chains between providers (airlines, hotels, etc.) and consumers (the travelers) have been completely changed by the introduction of e-business. In the traditional economy, most transactions were channeled through large travel organizations with many travel agencies close to the consumers (both private and professional travelers). In the electronic economy, we see that the role of travel offices is decreasing, that providers sell directly to consumers (some low-fare airlines only use direct sales), that product integration and product comparison services have emerged, that physical travel documents (tickets, vouchers) are disappearing and hence the role of postal services is fading, and so on.

4.4 BUSINESS DIRECTIONS

Based on redefined business characteristics and chain modifications as discussed in the previous sections, various new business directions can be distinguished in the e-business domain. In this section, we discuss a number of important directions – there is no aim to be complete, however.

4.4.1 True on-time and online capability

The 'old economy' relies heavily on slow and asynchronous communication channels, like the old-fashioned postal service. This means that direct interaction between business parties is very limited and 'time margins' are built into business processes to accommodate this. In e-business, we can have direct interaction between partners using electronic channels like the Internet. This paves the way for online business, i.e., business where parties interact directly using digital means. Online business allows much tighter synchronization between partners, which enables 'true on-time' processes – also referred to as *real-time* business processes. In various business domains, this real-time character is very important, for example the stock exchange domain. As a consequence, business structures can be built with much tighter coupling (leading to *just-in-time* business operation) or scenarios are enabled with smaller time scopes (see Section 2.5).

In the early days of e-business, being 'truly on-time and online' was a major goal to be achieved. A Web interface did not necessarily imply fully online transaction handling behind it: often, the Web interface was only a façade to manual handling behind it. This means that 'true online' was not achieved. Nowadays, it is more and more taken as a default setting for e-business models that transactions are completely performed in an online and real-time fashion. An example is the travel industry, where actual bookings for air travel and hotels are usually made completely interactively and automatically.

4.4.2 Enriched customer relationship management

In the 'old economy', the nature of communication media typically enforces infrequent, coarse-grained communication between partners. The cost of off-line, manual data processing prevents the management of detailed, up-to-date partner information. This makes customer relationship management (CRM) rather limited. In e-business scenarios, interaction between partners can be fast and frequent. Online data gathering allows the management and use of very detailed and up-to-date information about partners. This opens the door to complete new forms of CRM.

Examples can be found in electronic retail applications that dynamically compose offers for customers, based on their current and past behavior. Note that in traditional retail, typically only transactions (sales) are recorded, leading to rough pictures of client behavior. In electronic retail, the complete behavior of customers can be recorded in great detail, e.g. their catalog browsing history, even when this does not lead to any transactions. Obviously, privacy of clients in a digital environment (Acquisti *et al.* 2008) is an important issue in this context.

4.4.3 Integrated bricks and clicks

Many business organizations already have an established foothold in the 'old economy'. Recognizing that e-business offers new possibilities does not necessarily mean doing completely away with this established presence – as this might imply a substantial loss of customer base. So, an integration of 'old' and 'new' business is necessary, referred to as *integrated bricks and clicks*.[3]

In this integration, two aspects are of utmost importance. In the first place, there should be synergy between the bricks and the clicks, such that the one offers added value to the other (for example, by offering additional services to business partners). In the second place, the demarcation between bricks and clicks should be flexible, such that both customers and business activities can be moved from the one to the other without disturbing business operation. Usually, the move is from bricks to clicks, but not necessarily so (if a clicks scenario fails, a bricks backup should be available in some business segments).

An integrated bricks and clicks direction is – obviously – often coupled to a multi-channel business design as discussed below.

4.4.4 Multi-channel business design

The introduction of e-business often means that multiple communication channels come into existence through which an organization can be accessed. This is certainly the case with integrated bricks and clicks as discussed above, where traditional communication channels (e.g. physical post, telephone) are operated alongside digital communication channels (e.g. a Web site). But in pure e-business also, more than one channel may exist, e.g. e-mail, Web-based forms, digital voice response systems, etc.

From a business point of view, two aspects are of paramount importance when using multiple channels: flexibility and synchronization. Flexibility should allow business partners to change channels without disturbing business relations. Synchronization must be taken into account into the business design to make sure that transactions conducted over more than one channel still provide consistent results.[4] We refer to e-business setup taking this into proper account as *multi-channel business design*.

A multi-channel business design may be necessary for several reasons. One important reason is the existence of different customer groups, each of which prefers a different channel. We see this for example with general mail order companies, where older customers may prefer traditional channels and younger customers may prefer digital channels. Another reason is the use of different kinds of communication devices. We see this for example in m-business settings, where different kinds of mobile devices are used depending on the context of a user.

4.4.5 Completely automated business

In an extreme case of e-business, one may strive for business operation (at the operational level) without human intervention at all – thus, human effort is only required for management tasks (at the tactic and strategic levels). We call this business direction the *completely automated business*. This business direction is an extreme version of efficiency increase as discussed in Section 4.2.4 – actually 'erasing' the operational business control level as shown in Figure 4.3.

Complete automation is typically only achievable if there is no manipulation of physical objects (see Section 2.4). This implies that only digital objects or services are manipulated *or* physical handling is completely outsourced to an external service provider.

Often, automation of operational processes cannot be pursued in its full completeness: humans may be needed to deal with exception handling. But for highly standardized digital objects or services, complete automation is *in principle* achievable. Note that even the operation and maintenance of the required computing infrastructure can be outsourced, such that a business organization can completely focus on tactical and strategic activities.

4.4.6 Time-compressed business

By integrating elements of the true on-time and online business and completely automated business directions, one can obtain the *time-compressed business* direction. This means that e-business models can be used that are based on transactions that are executed in a fraction of the time needed by traditional business models. This is caused by the fact that reaction by business partners can always be almost instantaneous (as they are always online and they can automate decision tasks). This business direction enables business models with high levels of just-in-time behavior and short-lived partnerships. Note that this is related to the *time scopes* dimension that we have discussed in Section 2.5: moving towards time-compressed business means moving business models to the 'short-lived' end of the *time scopes* dimension.

Examples can be found for example in stock and currency markets, where fast-moving players obviously have their advantages over slow-moving players. Note that extreme examples of time-compressed business are typically found in e-business scenarios with digital objects only (see Section 2.4) – this because of the fact that handling physical objects requires time as dictated by physical constraints (for instance, goods have to be shipped).

4.5 BUSINESS STRUCTURES

Based on the ingredients discussed in the previous sections of this chapter, new business structures can be defined that rely heavily on e-business characteristics. In this section, we introduce several important classes of such business structures.

4.5.1 Demand chains

Traditionally, the operation of many supply chains is producer-controlled, i.e., the producer decides what to produce when and 'pumps' it into a supply chain where at the end, the consumer decides what to buy. A disadvantage of this business design is that production may not meet consumer wishes qualitatively or quantitatively:

- Consumers may want products with different characteristics (for instance, with a different color) than available at the purchasing moment.
- There may be too few or too many products on the market at a given moment. The former may lead to loss of market, the latter to substantial waste.

Hence, this business design may be suboptimal in markets where consumer behavior is fast changing and unpredictable. Traditionally, more direct coupling between consumer behavior and producer activities was hard to realize because the necessary synchronization channels did not exist (or were far too costly or slow).

To cope with these problems, one may go from a supply chain business design to a *demand chain* business design. In the pure demand chain design, a producer only produces a product after a consumer has ordered it, i.e., the operation of the chain is consumer-controlled (see Figure 4.6). This is a form of just-in-time business operation, enabled by the fact that electronic channels allow fast and cheap synchronization between consumer and producer (even if there are many consumers), and enable the efficient orchestration of the intermediate links in a chain. Moving from a supply chain to a demand chain business design often implies moving in the time scopes dimension (see Section 2.5): a static time scope is exchanged for a dynamic time scope.

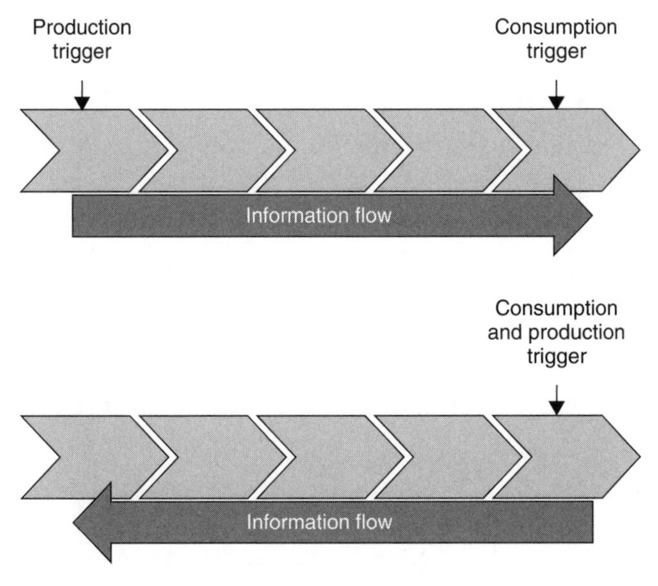

Figure 4.6 Supply chain (top) and demand chain (bottom)

A demand chain business design allows mass customization: producing large volumes of products, each of which can be customized to meet the requirements of an individual buyer. An example of this business design is Dell,[5] a computer supplier that produces personal computers to customer order in a demand chain fashion (Dell and Fredman 2006).

In a hybrid supply/demand chain design, we have a well-defined *customer order decoupling point*. At the producer side of this point, the chain operates in supply mode (referred to as *produce to stock*), producing products that can be configured to customer demands. At the consumer side of this point, the chain operates in demand mode (referred to as *produce to order*). At the customer order decoupling point, the configuration of products takes place. This is illustrated in Figure 4.7.

Where traditional business scenarios do allow hybrid chain designs, e-business allows designs in which the decoupling point is moved much more towards the producer (i.e., a larger part of the chain is operating in demand mode – illustrated in Figure 4.7). As for pure demand chains, this is enabled by more efficient and richer communication and synchronization between links in a chain.

This hybrid supply/demand chain business structure also allows mass customization of products (although at a lower level than a pure demand chain) – we see this for instance in the automotive domain, where cars are configured to buyers' specifications.

4.5.2 Dynamic partnering

The flexibility of e-business technology allows the 'on-the-fly' establishment of business collaborations between autonomous business organizations. This can differ

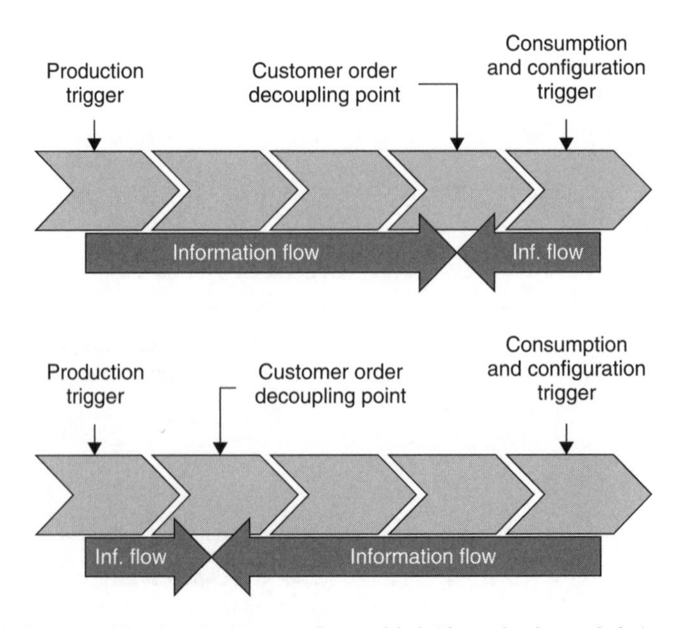

Figure 4.7 Traditional (top) and e-business (bottom) hybrid supply/demand chain

radically from traditional collaboration forms. In the traditional forms, collaborations are typically set up before the actual business operation starts. Given the cost of such set-up, these collaborations are often forged for prolonged spans of time (e.g., several years or even indefinitely). In the e-business form of collaboration setup, the partnership is created during business operation at the time that the functionality of a partner is actually needed. We call this *dynamic partnering*. In an extreme form, we have *just-in-time* partnering: choosing and binding a partner at the last possible moment in order to be able to use as much context information (for example market conditions or case characteristics) as possible in choosing the best partner.

Clearly, this business structure is related to the *time scopes* classification dimension discussed in Section 2.5.

4.5.3 Highly dynamic supply chains

Traditionally, supply chains have limited flexibility with respect to the partners involved in a specific supply chain. An organization in a chain typically obtains a specific type of input object from one or a small set of providers. Similarly, it typically delivers a specific type of output object to one or a small set of consumers. This inflexibility is related to the slowness and cost of traditional communication and collaboration channels. In other words: so-called *switching costs* are typically high in traditional business scenarios, leading to *switching barriers.*

e-Business allows the design of supply chains with much more 'routing flexibility', i.e., the dynamic selection of input and output partners in a chain. Standardized and inexpensive digital communication and collaboration platforms (we discuss these in Chapter 7) can lower switch costs considerably. In a highly dynamic chain, both types of partners may be selected completely on-the-fly, based on selection processes conducted on real-time electronic market places. This is illustrated in Figure 4.8, where the focus organization is shown in the center and both input side and output side of this organization are connected to an electronic market (EM) providing connections to many business partners.

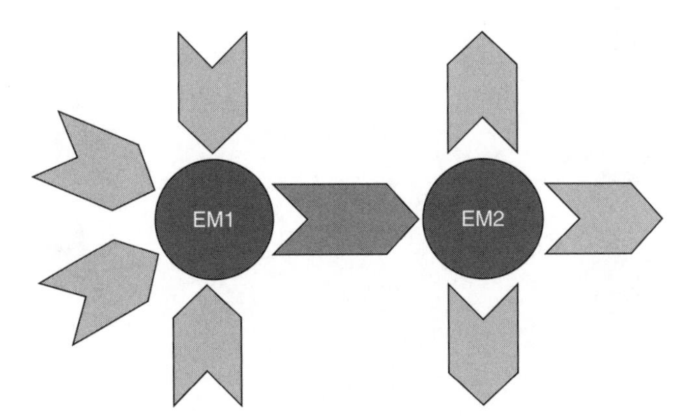

Figure 4.8 A highly dynamic supply chain with two electronic markets

The highly dynamic supply chain business structure is a specialization of the dynamic partnering business structure discussed before: partners are chosen dynamically, but for a specific reason: providing goods or buying goods (as discussed in Section 2.4).

4.5.4 Dynamic service outsourcing

Another specific structure of dynamic partnering is *dynamic service outsourcing* (Ströbel 2000). In this business paradigm, an organization chooses parts of its business process that it does not consider to be its core competence and decides to outsource these subprocesses to specialist provider organizations. For these organizations, the outsourced subprocesses are core competence, such that they can perform these in a better way than the outsourcer. The decision as to which service provider actually to outsource a specific piece of work at hand is taken dynamically – preferably just-in-time. Clearly, just-in-time outsourcing requires fast communication channels. Service providers can be selected using electronic markets in which they advertise their services.

Dynamic service outsourcing is schematically illustrated in Figure 4.9. In the middle of the figure, we see an organization with five business activities. Three are core competences (indicated by stars), two are non-core (indicated by circles). The non-core activities are dynamically outsourced to external parties, for whom these activities are core competence. For one activity, there is a choice of three service providers, for the other a choice of two. In practical situations, these numbers may be (much) greater.

Dynamic service outsourcing can improve the competitiveness of the outsourcer in a number of ways. It can enhance the efficiency of its processes, as the provider can perform the outsourced subprocesses faster and/or cheaper. It can enhance the effectiveness of its processes, as the provider can perform the tasks it specializes in qualitatively better. Finally, it can greatly enhance the flexibility (also called agility)

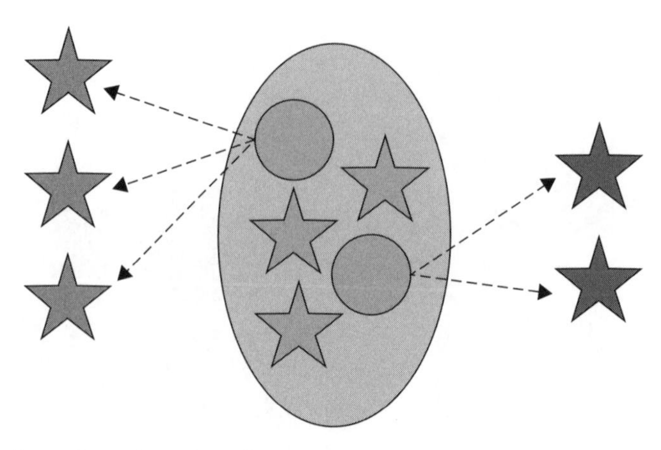

Figure 4.9 Dynamic service outsourcing

of the outsourcing organization, as the provider can be chosen dynamically, depending on both the case (e.g. customer order) at hand and the current market circumstances.

In an extreme case, an organization can outsource *all* its operational business processes, such that it only coordinates the operation of other organizations (and the business model of the organization is indeed based on agile synchronization of its service providers). This is where the *integrator-only* business model comes into play, which we discuss in the next section.

4.6 BUSINESS MODELS

In this section, we combine all elements of the previous sections of this chapter to arrive at the definition of business models for e-business – or business models of the 'new economy'. As new business models are 'invented' continuously, obviously we cannot be complete here. Therefore, we describe a number of typical e-business models.

Each business model we discuss is summarized in a table, which combines a classification in the three dimensions of Chapter 2 and an identification of the B aspect ingredients as treated in the previous four sections of this chapter. This leads to seven rows in a table, as illustrated in Table 4.1.

4.6.1 e-Retailing

Probably the best known business model in the e-business domain is *e-retailing* – simply because we as consumers are often confronted with it. e-Retailing in its basic form is the bringing of traditional consumer shopping to the internet – therefore it is very typical B2C.

The business drivers behind e-retailing are typically twofold. First, the use of the internet typically provides an extreme reach increase when compared to traditional shops – both in geographical and in temporal reach (see Section 4.2.1). Second, pure e-retailing may provide a substantial cost reduction because physical shops are not necessary – and hence a substantial efficiency increase. Note that e-retailing may imply other costs, though, like the maintenance of an elaborate Web site and to-

Table 4.1 Business model summary table ingredients

Business model summary	
Parties	Section 2.3
Objects	Section 2.4
Time Scope	Section 2.5
Drivers	Section 4.2
Chains	Section 4.3
Directions	Section 4.4
Structures	Section 4.5

customer shipping. The richness aspect in e-retailing depends very much on the type of product being traded. On the one hand, customer experience is typically low in a Web shop compared to a physical shop, as products cannot be physically examined. The lack of physical examination possibilities can be compensated to some respect by providing actual user reports for the products offered. On the other hand, Web shops do allow more elaborate product presentations, both in numbers of products and in the way these are presented to the customer. For example, electronic catalogs allow showing many product variants (e.g. many different colors) and allow showing usage pictures or videos of offered products.

In Table 4.2, we summarize the e-retailing business model in terms of the classification dimensions and in terms of the ingredients introduced in the previous sections of this chapter (corresponding sections are indicated in the table for easy reference). Note that we show the most common choices for all ingredients – obviously, other choices are possible too. In the third column, we provide additional remarks with respect to chosen ingredients.

There are many, many examples of e-retailing. One of the earliest and best-known examples is Amazon.com, which started business in 1995 as an online book store – one of the pioneers of this business model.

4.6.2 Integrator-only

An integrator-only organization is an organization that only integrates products of other companies, i.e., does not produce product ingredients itself. As such, it either buys product elements from other organizations or forms a virtual organization with other organizations that provide product elements to it. As such, an integrator-only has no production facilities (unless you view integrating as a form of production, of course).

Table 4.2 Summary of the e-retailing business model

Business model: e-Retailing			
Parties	*(2.3)*	B2C	B2B also possible
Objects	*(2.4)*	Physical goods Digital goods	Services can be offered too, but less common
Time Scope	*(2.5)*	Dynamic	
Drivers	*(4.2)*	Increasing reach Increasing efficiency	Geographic and temporal
Chains	*(4.3)*	Disintermediation	
Directions	*(4.4)*	On-time and online Integrated bricks and clicks	 (If physical goods)
Structures	*(4.5)*	Highly dynamic supply chains Demand chains	 (In specific domains)

Integrator-only organizations typically provide digital goods or digital services (see Section 2.4) – integrating physical objects or services would imply production facilities. The added value of an integrator is providing the right combination of digital objects or services to the right customers at the right time. Hence, customer relationship management is often important for this business model.

The integrator-only model can for instance be applied in the financial domain. Here, an integrator can combine the financial products of other financial service providers to obtain integrated financial products that are tailored to specific customers (either of the business or the consumer type). Ingredients can be banking accounts, savings accounts, mortgages, stock portfolios, insurances etcetera, which are combined into highly customized financial packages.

A summary of the integrator-only business model is shown in Table 4.3.

4.6.3 Dynamic virtual enterprise

Dynamic partnering and dynamic service outsourcing as discussed in the previous section can lead to the establishment of *dynamic virtual enterprises*. Virtual enterprises are business collaborations that have a formal character (typically based on a contractual agreement) and that present themselves to third parties as a single business entity. Dynamic virtual enterprises are virtual enterprises that have a dynamic character, i.e., that are established on-the-fly when opportunities arise and are dismantled again when the opportunity disappears.

Whereas the life cycle of a traditional virtual enterprise usually spans multiple years, the life cycle of a dynamic virtual enterprise may be as short as several days or even less. Also the business scope of a dynamic virtual enterprise may be small, i.e., it may be set up to accomplish a very specific, relatively small business goal. In the CrossFlow project (Grefen *et al.* 2000), for example, extreme prototype scenarios

Table 4.3 Summary of the integrator-only business model

Business model: Integrator-only			
Parties	*(2.3)*	B2C B2B	
Objects	*(2.4)*	Digital goods Digital services	
Time scope	*(2.5)*	Static, Semi-dynamic Dynamic	Depends on the integrated object and the market
Drivers	*(4.2)*	Increasing richness	
Chains	*(4.3)*	Reintermediation	
Directions	*(4.4)*	Enriched CRM	
Structures	*(4.5)*	Dynamic supply chain Demand chain	In dynamic markets

were developed where a dynamic virtual enterprise is established for the fulfillment of an individual customer order. In the telecom and logistics domain, a scenario was developed for the sale and delivery of one single mobile phone in which a telecom operator and a logistics provider form a dynamic virtual enterprise. In the car insurance domain, a scenario was developed for the handling of a single insurance claim, where the dynamic virtual enterprise is formed between an insurance company and a damage assessment bureau.

Clearly, such short life cycles and small scopes require extremely efficient support for setup and management of the collaboration to deal with time and cost conditions – hence the entrance of e-business. In some domains, so-called *breeding environments* are created, which provide the infrastructure for setting up virtual environments. These environments offer, for instance, electronic marketplaces in which potential partners can find each other and standard communication channels for the operation of virtual enterprises. Electronic contracting and automated business process support are typical ingredients of dynamic virtual enterprises to deal respectively with the formal collaboration character and the required efficiency (Grefen *et al.* 2000, Hoffner *et al.* 2001).

Again, we summarize the business model, in Table 4.4.

The term *instant virtual enterprise* is also used to indicate a virtual enterprise that is created dynamically. For example, in the CrossWork project (Grefen *et al.* 2009, Mehandjiev and Grefen 2010), an approach was developed to create instant virtual enterprises semi-automatically based on explicitly specified business goals. The approach was prototyped in the automotive industry to massively reduce time and effort in setting up and managing virtual enterprises for car production. The time scope for this scenario is semi-dynamic, dictated by the 'physical' of the automotive industry (a strong *bricks and clicks* combination).

Table 4.4 Summary of the dynamic virtual enterprise business model

Business model: Dynamic virtual enterprise			
Parties	*(2.3)*	B2B	
Objects	*(2.4)*	All	Tight collaboration is required to deliver a product
Time scope	*(2.5)*	Semi-dynamic Dynamic	
Drivers	*(4.2)*	Increasing richness	In collaboration
Chains	*(4.3)*	Reintermediation	If a controller party is used for the dynamic VE
Directions	*(4.4)*	Time-compressed business	Both in set-up and execution of the dynamic VE
Structures	*(4.5)*	Dynamic partnering Dynamic supply chain Dynamic service outsourcing	

4.6.4 Crowdsourcing

Crowdsourcing (Howe 2008) is a business model in which the 'power of the masses' is used to address business problems. The increase in reach of an organization enabled by e-business means (see Section 4.2.1) is used to enable outsourcing to a very large number of 'business partners' (which can be individual people), each of which contributes a small element to the overall outsourcing task. In crowdsourcing, the 'business partners' are typically individuals with whom the outsourcing organization has no official relation (i.e., they are not employees of the organization in any form), but who may be part of some virtual community. As such, crowdsourcing can be considered a 'reversed B2C' business model – reversed as the C side provides input to the B side (contrary to typical B2C models like e-retailing).

We can distinguish between various types of crowdsourcing, depending on the kind of task outsourced to the 'crowd':

- *Crowdcasting*[6] is a business model in which the crowd is used to generate ideas by answering specific questions, for example ideas for new products or product variations. An example of a company employing crowdcasting is InnoCentive,[7] which uses a crowd of researchers to try and solve problems of companies. Crowdstorming is a variation on crowdcasting in which the crowd forms a brainstorming power to generate completely new ideas without very clear questions as a basis.
- *Crowdproduction* is a business model in which the crowd is used to actually produce a product or a collection of products. Often, these products are of a digital nature (see Section 2.4). A well-known example where a crowd produces a product is Wikipedia,[8] where large numbers of people collaboratively build a digital encyclopedia (we actually use Wikipedia as a reference source in this book). An example where a set of products is produced is iStockPhoto,[9] where individual photographers offer their photos to media users.
- *Crowdfunding* is aimed at having a crowd fund a venture for which 'regular' funding channels are not available. A good example is Sellaband,[10] which operates as an alternative business model in the music industry. In the Sellaband model, bands (and individual artists) in the music scene show their work on the Sellaband Web site and try to sell 'parts' to people who believe the band has potential. When a band has sold a specific number of parts,[11] it has enough funding to record and publish a music album in a professional way. A part gives specific rights to a part owner (called a 'believer' in the Sellaband model), like a copy of an album by the artist and a share in profits.

A number of issues have to be taken into account to use crowdsourcing effectively. One important issue is handling the crowd efficiently. In crowdcasting for example, an efficient filtering mechanism must be employed to separate the few usable ideas from the many unusable ones. Another important issue is the 'reimbursement' of the crowd, i.e., the way the individuals in the crowd get something in return for their contribution and thus stay motivated to continue contributing (this is related to the

Figure 4.10 Sellaband as a crowdsourcing example

exchange of e-business objects as discussed in Section 2.4). In a crowdfunding scenario, this may be easier, but in a crowdcasting scenario, it is not always obvious.

Below, we show the summary of the crowdsourcing business model. Depending on the type of crowdsourcing – as discussed above – the table can be further specialized. We leave this as an exercise for the reader.

Table 4.5 Summary of the crowdsourcing business model

Business model: Crowdsourcing			
Parties	*(2.3)*	B2C	Reversed object flow
Objects	*(2.4)*	Digital goods	Can include money
Time scope	*(2.5)*	Dynamic Ultra-dynamic	
Drivers	*(4.2)*	Increasing reach	Reach on 'input side'
Chains	*(4.3)*	Reconstruction	
Directions	*(4.4)*	On-time and online	
Structures	*(4.5)*	Dynamic service outsourcing	Extreme B2C scenario

4.7 RELATING B ASPECT ELEMENTS

In this chapter so far, we have analyzed the B aspect element classes of e-business following a path from basic ingredients to business models. These element classes can be used for B aspect design or analysis by relating them in a structured way. This can be done in several ways.

The most common way is the one illustrated in Figure 4.11. One starts characterizing an e-business scenario using the reach and richness (R&R) business drivers (and if applicable, the extreme efficiency characteristic). Based on that, the disintermediation and reintermediation (D&R) principles can be discussed (deconstruction and reconstruction in the extreme cases) to see how business chains are affected. Based on the business drivers, one can also find new business directions. The combination of business directions and choices with respect to business chains leads to the identification (or definition) of business structures. All these elements combined lead to the definition of business models.

The element classes can also be analyzed in different orders. For example, one may use a linear order from drivers to chains, to directions and on to structures, as illustrated in Figure 4.12. One may even work backwards, starting from structures, and analyze how a specific structure in a specific situation affects the choice of the other three element classes. The four element classes and their ordering are intended to be a thinking structure, not a rigid recipe.

As shown in Figure 4.11 and in Figure 4.12, combinations of the elements in the four classes lead to the definition of new business models (or the application of existing models in a new context). We have seen a number of these business models in this chapter: e-retailing, integrator-only organizations, dynamic virtual enterprises, and crowdsourcing. New business models are designed continuously – e-business is a dynamic domain.

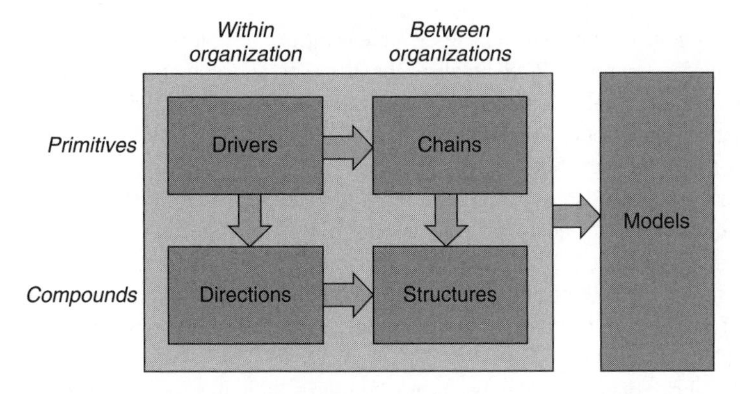

Figure 4.11 Common relation between B aspect elements

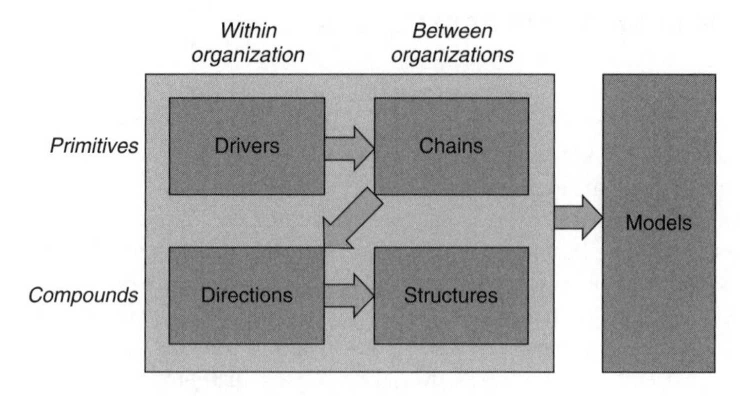

Figure 4.12 Alternative relation between B aspect elements

4.8 RUNNING CASES

In this section, we turn again to our two running cases – POSH and TTU – and discuss their business aspect.

4.8.1 POSH

As we have seen in Section 1.7, POSH has embraced two new business goals:

1 Sell to all customers in the country directly, without intervention of third-party retailers;
2 Offer a broader spectrum of advisory services to their customers.

Business goal 1 is typically a case of increasing geographical reach. When thinking about increasing reach, POSH realizes that they should also increase temporal reach, as owners of smaller companies may want to do business with POSH outside regular business hours. Removing the intervention of third-party retailers is a typical case of disintermediation.

Business goal 2 is a case of increasing richness: POSH wants to have more interaction with its customers to tie them in more strongly to the company. Disintermediation or reintermediation does not play a role here.

In terms of new business directions, enriched CRM is most applicable to the POSH scenario. In terms of business models, POSH uses a combined B2C and B2B e-retailing model.

The above discussion can be summarized in a table like we used to describe the business models in Section 4.6, but augmented with a *business model* row. The result for POSH is shown in Table 4.6.

Table 4.6 Summary of the business model ingredients of the POSH case study

Case study: POSH			
Parties	*(2.3)*	B2B B2C	
Objects	*(2.4)*	Physical objects	
Time scope	*(2.5)*	Semi-dynamic Dynamic	
Drivers	*(4.2)*	Increasing reach	Mainly geographical, temporal secondary
Chains	*(4.3)*	Disintermediation	
Directions	*(4.4)*	Enriched CRM	
Structures	*(4.5)*	None	POSH does not use typical e-business structures as discussed in this chapter
Model	*(4.6)*	e-Retailing	

4.8.2 TTU

The main business driver for TTU is increasing reach: through e-business channels they can reach more potential customers than a traditional translation service (offering either document translation or 'physical' interpretation services) would. TTU aims to increase reach in the geographical, the temporal and the modal sense. The modal sense pertains most clearly to providing online, real-time translations in video conferencing sessions. Increasing richness is not a major point for TTU, though they will use any opportunities 'on the side' here. We can thus modify Figure 4.2 for TTU into Figure 4.13.

In terms of business chain restructuring, the TTU case belongs in the reintermediation category: they provide services that did not exist in the TTU form in the 'traditional economy'.

The main e-business direction is on-time and on-line business: the strength of the TTU approach is the fact that they can be contacted through the internet at the time

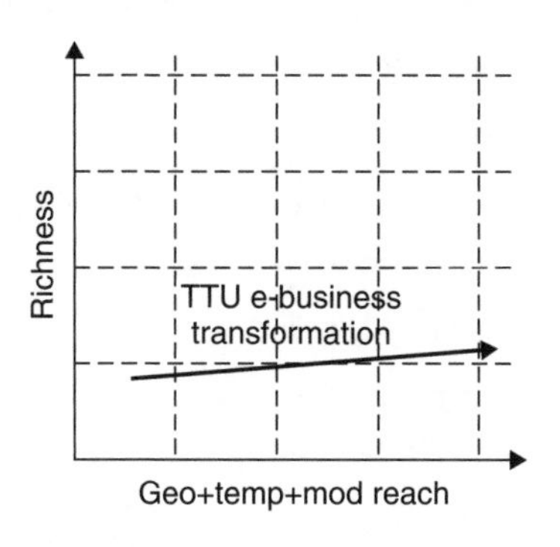

Figure 4.13 Increasing reach for TTU

when needed. In terms of e-business structure, the TTU case is a form of dynamic service outsourcing: a party needing a translation service in its business process outsources this part of the process to TTU instead of getting a translator 'on board'.

None of the business models presented before in this chapter fits the TTU case. This illustrates that it is hard – if not impossible – to provide a comprehensive set of business models for e-business.

As for the POSH case study, this discussion is summarized in a table (Table 4.7).

4.9 CHAPTER END

We first provide a summary of the most important elements of the business aspect of the BOAT dimension. Then, we provide a few questions and exercises to apply the contents of this chapter to.

4.9.1 Chapter summary

In this chapter we have seen the basic business aspect ingredients of e-business in five classes:

- *e-Business drivers* are the basic reasons to engage into e-business. Two important drivers are increasing *reach* and increasing *richness*. A third driver is increasing *efficiency* – we consider this an e-business driver only when efficiency is dramatically increased.
- *e-Business chain operations* are the basic ways to manipulate a business chain based on new opportunities offered by e-business. *Disintermediation* and *reintermediation* are respectively the basic operations to remove a link from a chain or to insert a

Table 4.7 Summary of the business model ingredients of the TTU case study

Case study: TTU			
Parties	*(2.3)*	B2B	B2C possible too, but not main aim
Objects	*(2.4)*	Digital services	
Time scope	*(2.5)*	Dynamic	
Drivers	*(4.2)*	Increasing reach	Geographical + temporal + modal
Chains	*(4.3)*	Reintermediation	
Directions	*(4.4)*	On-time and online	
Structures	*(4.5)*	Dynamic service outsourcing	
Model	*(4.6)*	Dedicated	Does not conform to 'standard' models discussed in this chapter

new link. *Deconstruction* and *reconstruction* are the extreme forms, in which complete business chains are redesigned.

- *e-Business directions* are the directions in which a business scenario can be developed to achieve drivers or facilitate chain operations. Example directions are *multi-channel business design, integrated bricks and clicks* and *completely automated business.*
- *e-Business structures* are the 'abstract structures' that form business models. Example structures are *demand chains* and *dynamic service outsourcing.*
- *e-Business models* are the 'complete template structures' for e-business in the business aspect. Example business models are *e-retailing, integrator-only,* and *crowdsourcing.*

The above ingredients can be related in various ways in analyzing or designing e-business scenarios. An overview of the ingredients is presented in Table 4.8.

4.9.2 Questions and exercises

1 Take an existing B2C e-business scenario – preferably a real-world case that is not a standard e-retailing scenario. Analyze its B aspect using the elements of this chapter and describe it in a summary table (as for POSH and TTU in Tables 4.6 and 4.7). Explicitly choose an approach as discussed in Section 4.7.

Table 4.8 Overview of business aspect ingredients

Business Drivers	*Business Chain Operations*
Reach	Disintermediation
Richness	Reintermediation
Extreme efficiency	Deconstruction
	Reconstruction
Business Directions	*Business Structures*
True on-time and online	Demand chain
Enriched CRM	Dynamic partnering
Integrated bricks and clicks	Highly dynamic supply chain
Multi-channel business	Dynamic service outsourcing
Completely automated business	
Time-compressed business	
Business Models	
e-Retailing	
Integrator-only	
Dynamic virtual enterprise	
Crowdsourcing (crowdcasting, crowdproduction, crowdfunding)	

2 Take an existing B2B e-business scenario. Analyze its B aspect and describe it in a summary table (like done for TTU in Table 4.7). Explicitly choose an approach as discussed in Section 4.7.
3 Which of the business models discussed in Section 4.6 is also applicable to e-government, i.e., to G2C or G2B (see Section 2.3.5), scenarios? Provide an example for each model chosen.
4 In Section 4.5, we have seen the business structures *demand chain* and *highly dynamic supply chain*. Can these two business structures be combined to arrive at a *highly dynamic demand chain* structure? If you think so, give an application example of a highly dynamic demand chain.
5 As noted before, the list of e-business models presented in this chapter is not exhaustive. Find an e-business model that is not discussed in this chapter, analyze it and describe it in a summary table (as for the crowdsourcing business model in Table 4.5).
6 Specialize the summary table for the crowdsourcing business model (see Table 4.5) for the crowdfunding business model. Pay special attention to the objects dimension, as discussed in Section 2.4.
7 Analyze the TTU business model and generalize it to obtain a general business model that can be reapplied for other scenarios (like those discussed in Section 4.6).
8 Many companies use *off-shoring* nowadays in their business model. Find out what this exactly entails. Then discuss whether this is e-business conforming to the definitions in this book. Analyze the relation to the B aspect elements discussed in this chapter.

5

Organization aspect

Learning goals

By the end of the chapter you should:

- Understand hierarchically organized organization structures for e-business;
- Know a set of e-business functions and understand its organization based on a business framework;
- Understand business processes in an e-business setting and be able to specify them;
- Understand the role of operations management and change management in an e-business setting;
- Understand the mapping of business aspect elements (as discussed in Chapter 4) to organization aspect elements.

5.1 INTRODUCTION

In the previous chapter, we discussed the business aspect of the BOAT framework. In this chapter, we continue with the organization (O) aspect. Again, the aim is to provide an overview of relevant issues – for more elaborate discussions, the reader is referred to more detailed material.

Below, we first turn our attention to e-business organization structures. Using a top-down approach, we first discuss structures between organizations (called inter-organizational structures) and structures within organizations (called intra-organizational structures). Then, we focus on a systematic treatment of e-business functions appearing in these structures. Next, we discuss how business processes can be placed in the context of these organization structures and functions.

We continue with an explanation of how operations management is required to keep processes running, and change management is required to keep organization structures and processes aligned with new developments, for instance changes in the business aspect or in the technology aspect.

In Section 5.7, we show how concepts from the B aspect can be mapped to the O aspect. Here, we show how concepts discussed in the previous chapter like reach, richness, disintermediation and reintermediation can be operationalized in organization aspect terms. We further develop our running cases and conclude the chapter with a summary and a set of questions and exercises.

5.2 E-BUSINESS INTER-ORGANIZATION STRUCTURES

A good understanding of organization structures is important for every type of business domain (see e.g. Mintzberg 1992). In e-business, however, we generally deal with complex scenarios, in which a clear structure of the business organization is essential for a decent understanding of the scenario. The dynamic nature of many e-business scenarios further increases the need for clear structure: one needs to understand what is subject to change and what is not.[1]

In this section, we explore the structure of e-business collaborations in a stepwise, top-down manner: we start with a very high-level picture and then refine this in two steps. In the next section, we continue the refinement within organization boundaries.

5.2.1 Parties in an e-business scenario

As we have seen in Section 1.2, we focus in this book on inter-organizational e-business scenarios, i.e., scenarios in which two or more autonomous business parties are involved that collaborate in an e-business market. So the most trivial structure of an e-business scenario is just the market, as shown in Figure 5.1. Obviously, this organization structure is not very informative – therefore, we label it *level 0*. It gets more interesting when we open it up – in other words, refine or explode it.

When we refine an e-business market, we typically identify three roles of parties collaborating in that market:

- *consumer*[2] (a party that requires a product or service);
- *provider* (a party that offers a product or service); and
- *intermediary* (a party that has an auxiliary role in getting a product or service from provider to consumer).

Figure 5.1 e-Business organization structure (level 0)

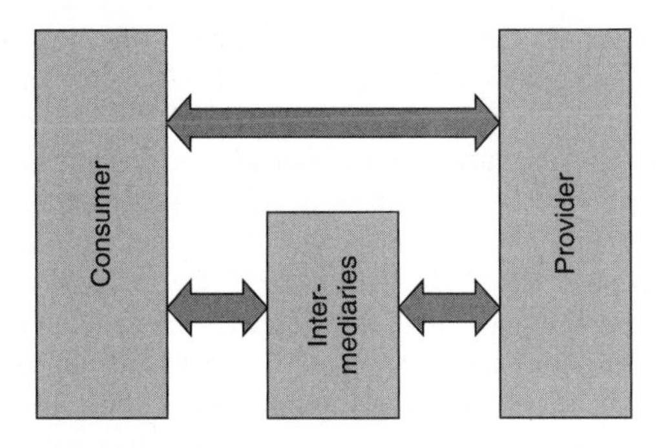

Figure 5.2 e-Business organization structure (level 1)

When we put the three roles of parties and their relations in a diagram that refines Figure 5.1, we get Figure 5.2. This figure shows an e-business organization structure at *level 1*. Each of the three parties can be of a different type, as explained in Section 2.3.

For reasons of simplicity, we use only one consumer and one provider in this diagram (and the rest of this chapter). Although this one-to-one scenario is common in practice, scenarios exist in which multiple consumers and multiple providers may interact in an e-business collaboration, forming an e-business network. Extension of the one-to-one scenario to one-to-many or even many-to-many is straightforward though.

Note that *consumer* and *provider* are roles – one organization can be a provider in one e-business relationship but at the same time a consumer in another relationship. Note also that the role of *intermediary* is to some extent relative to an e-business scenario. When analyzing an e-retailing scenario, for example, a credit card organization is an intermediary. In a payment handling scenario, however, the same organization can act as a provider. Typically, an intermediary is characterized by the fact that it does not produce or consume primary objects (as discussed in Section 2.4) in an e-business scenario.

The structure in Figure 5.2 may be clear, but it contains too little structure to be of help in a detailed design or analysis of e-business scenarios. Therefore, we further refine this figure in the sequel.

5.2.2 Refining intermediaries and channels

In Figure 5.2, there is no distinction between different types of intermediaries. Often, however, an e-business scenario requires more than one type of intermediary. Examples are:

- a broker that helps parties find and identify each other in an e-business market (for instance through a mechanism like the Yellow Pages);
- a financial intermediary that arranges the execution of payments between parties;
- a transport intermediary that arranges for the transportation of physical objects between parties.

The set of intermediaries needed depends on the classification of the e-business scenario. If the e-business scenario does not involve exchange of physical objects (see Section 2.4), a transport intermediary may be unnecessary. In a pure bartering scenario, a finance intermediary is unnecessary. Other scenarios may require other intermediaries, e.g. for trust establishment or service aggregation.

The multi-intermediary situation is shown in Figure 5.3, illustrating an e-business organization structure at *level 2*. For reasons of clarity, only two intermediaries are shown, labeled *Inter1* and *Inter2*. In practice, this can be an arbitrary number.

The second extension shown in Figure 5.3 is the identification of multiple communication channels between consumer and provider through which information or e-business objects can be passed. Multiple channels may each serve a different business function (as explained in the rest of this chapter) or may serve the same business function in different ways (e.g. by means of different physical communication channels, like telephone or internet). The latter is commonly referred to as *multi-channeling* (this is related to the *multi-channel business design* discussed in Section 4.4.4). The figure shows two channels for reasons of clarity. In practice, the number can be arbitrary.

5.3 E-BUSINESS INTRA-ORGANIZATION STRUCTURES

In the previous section, we have refined an e-business market, but left the internal organization structure of the collaborating parties opaque – they have stayed black boxes. In this section, we further refine the organization structure by opening up this internal structure, exploring intra-organization structures.

5.3.1 Front-end versus back-end

In Figure 5.3, the business functionality of both consumer and provider are shown as a black box, i.e., without any internal detail. To completely design or analyze an e-business organization structure, we need to open up this black box.

The interaction between parties in an e-business context changes frequently, both as a consequence of changing business models (as discussed in Chapter 4) and of

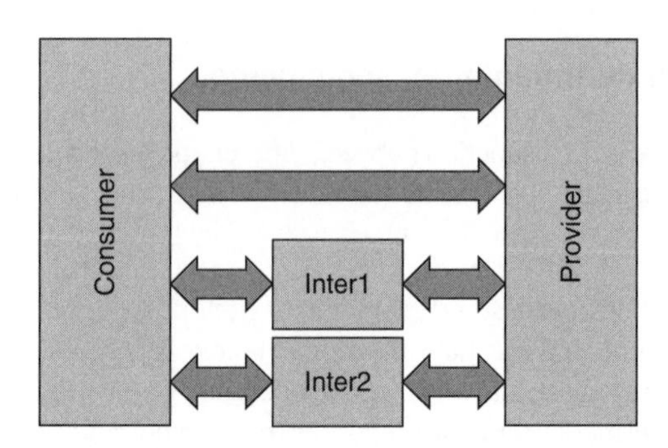

Figure 5.3 e-Business organization structure (level 2)

changing technology (as discussed in Chapter 7) – remember the joint forces of requirements pull and technology push as discussed in Chapter 1. The core activities of organizations typically do not change that frequently, however. Take for example a telephone company selling its services over the internet. The interaction with its clients, for instance in the form of subscription packages offered, changes continually. The core activities, providing infrastructure for phone calls and accounting its use, change only slowly over time.

The fact that internal business functionality and externally oriented business functionality change at different paces implies that we have to make a clear decoupling between these two types of functionality. Without a clear decoupling, we cannot change the one without affecting the other. In other words: we need a separation of concerns implemented in the organization structure.

We see the result of the decoupling in Figure 5.4 (the organization structure at *level 3*). The core business functionality that is of an intra-organizational nature (i.e., not exposed to the outside world) is commonly referred to as *back-end functionality*. The business functionality that is in contact with external parties (hence of an inter-organizational nature) is commonly referred to as *front-end functionality*. In administrative organizations, both types of functionality are often called *back-office* and *front-office* respectively.

Decoupling front end and back end means that in a concrete situation, it should be very clearly defined what is part of the back-end, what is part of the front-end, and how the two ends interact.

5.3.2 Front-end functionality and channels

The final refinement we make here is the identification of individual functionalities in the overall front-end functionality. A party (with a consumer or provider role) has a number of distinct business functionalities that it requires to collaborate with external parties, such as advertising for the objects that it offers on a market, negotiating about prices or delivery conditions, buying objects and paying for bought objects (and typically quite a few more). As flexibility in functionality is of utmost importance to follow (or initiate) developments, it is usually a good idea to allocate

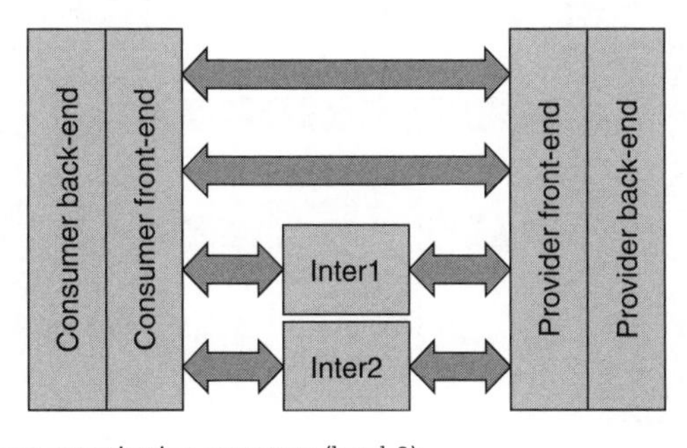

Figure 5.4 e-Business organization structure (level 3)

these distinct business functionalities to distinct organization building blocks – also referred to as *organizational units* or *organizational modules*. This is shown in an abstract way in Figure 5.5 as an elaboration of Figure 5.4, resulting in an organization structure at *level 4*. The *CFx* modules represent consumer front-end modules, the *PFx* modules provider front-end modules. The number of front-end modules depends on the e-business scenario at hand.

For illustration purposes, the abstract picture of Figure 5.5 is made more concrete in Figure 5.6 by filling in the front-end modules and intermediaries with an example selection. We will see more examples when discussing our two running cases at the end of this chapter.

Three things are noteworthy with respect to the above discussion of front-end modules:

- It is of course possible to also modularize the back-end functionality. We have not shown this here, as it is not specific for e-business in the O aspect of BOAT: traditional business requires a modular back-end organization as well. When we move to the BOAT architecture aspect in the next chapter, however, this issue becomes more interesting – but that is for later.

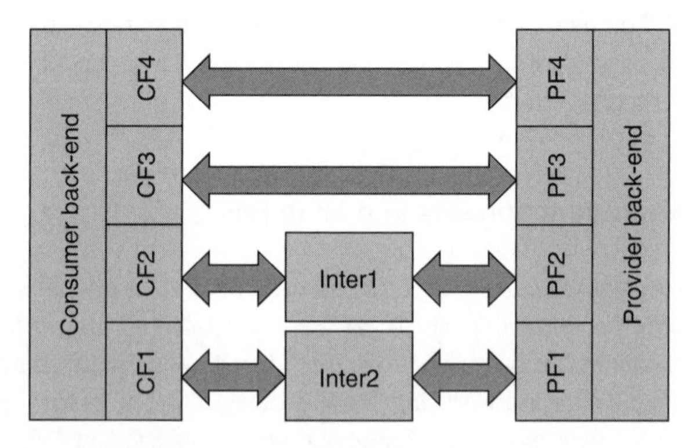

Figure 5.5 Abstract e-business organization structure (level 4)

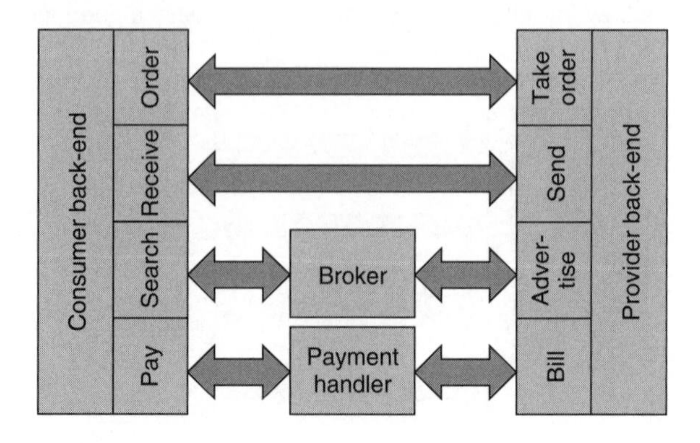

Figure 5.6 Concrete e-business organization structure (level 4)

- In case of B2C e-business, the C side usually has very limited business functionality. If so, the distinction between front-end and back-end functionality is not very helpful. A limited set of functional modules (e.g. only buying and paying, as shown in Figure 5.7 with the C side on the left) may be sufficient – or even a single module to represent all of the activities of the consumer.
- If an organization employs multiple channels for the same business function (multi-channeling, as discussed before), it may be wise to have one organizational module for each channel. This further increases the level of flexibility of an organization (obviously at the expense of a larger number of modules and hence possibly more complexity). If the provider organization of Figure 5.6 takes orders via the Web (W) and via email (E), its organization structure may reflect this, as shown in Figure 5.8.

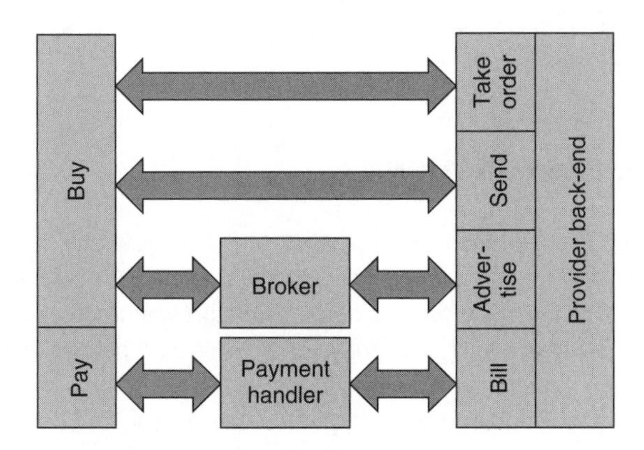

Figure 5.7 Concrete B2C e-business organization structure

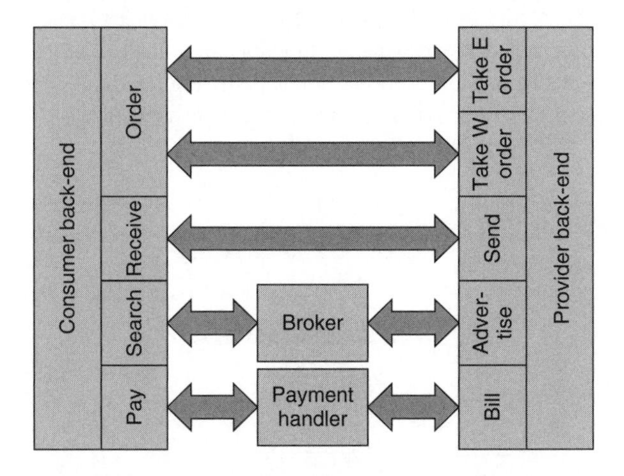

Figure 5.8 Concrete e-business organization structure with multi-channeling

5.3.3 The concept of mid-office

In some organization approaches, front-end and back-end organization modules are coupled by a mid-office. This mid-office functions as an 'advanced switching board' between back-office organization modules and front-end modules, thus linking the business functions they perform. The purpose of the mid-office is to further enhance organizational flexibility. Its functionality includes for example flexible integration of basic products provided by the back-end organization (e.g., insurance or banking products) towards diverse channels in the front-end organization. The resulting organization structure is shown in Figure 5.9 (based on that in Figure 5.5). We have detailed the back ends of the consumer and provider organizations to better show the integrative function of the mid-office.

For reasons of clarity and brevity, we will not use the mid-office concept in the rest of this book. If required, however, the discussions can be easily extended to include this concept.

5.4 E-BUSINESS FUNCTIONS

In the previous section, we have discussed how organizational modules (units) implement business functions in e-business organizations. We have not discussed, however, how to identify these functions in a systematic way. In other words: we have not discussed how to arrive at an orderly set of business functions that we can use in an organization structure. This we do in this section.

We first take a look at business function models as a basis and detail one specific model. Then, we analyze how the distinction between front-end and back-end functions can be placed in this model. Based on this, we extend the function taxonomy of this model towards a taxonomy fit for e-business scenarios. Doing so, we arrive at a set of back-end business functions and a set of front-end business functions. These sets can be used as templates (reference models) for the identification of business functions in a concrete e-business scenario.

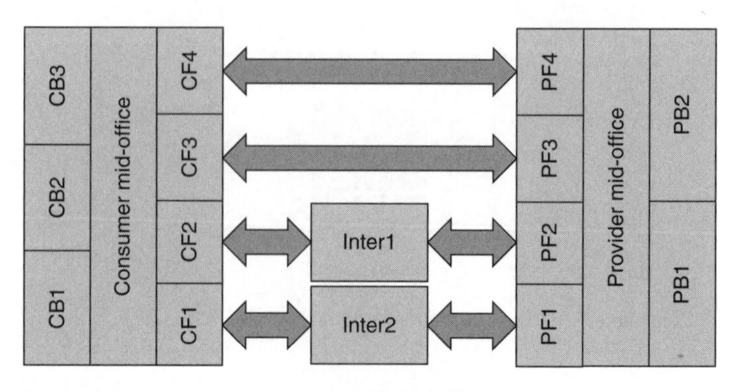

Figure 5.9 e-Business organization structure with mid-office

5.4.1 Business function model

Business models exist that provide a conceptual structure for the identification of general business functions. These models help in constructing complete and non-redundant sets of functions. Below, we start with discussing a very well-known example of these models: Porter's value chain model. Then, we 'overlay' this model with the distinction between front-end and back-end functions, as we have seen before in this chapter. Finally, we discuss how to adapt Porter's model to e-business. This discussion is the basis for the business functions identified in the sequel of this section.

Porter's value chain model

Porter's value chain model (1985) is a model of a business organization highlighting its main business functions. An adapted version of the model is shown in Figure 5.10.

The model distinguishes between two classes of business functions: primary functions and secondary functions. Primary functions are directly geared towards the main business goal of the organization: the production and delivery of goods. Secondary functions support the primary functions by providing a necessary context to execute the primary functions.

Primary functions are shown as vertical columns in the bottom half of Figure 5.10. The *inbound logistics* function enables the transport of materials used as input in production. The *operations* function performs the actual production of goods. The *outbound logistics* function enables the transport of produced goods to consumers of these goods. The *marketing and sales* function takes care of attracting these customers and arranging the actual sales. Finally, the *services* function is responsible for post-sales service to customers.

Secondary functions are shown as horizontal layers in the top half of Figure 5.10. The *procurement* function takes care of ordering the goods and services required in the other functions (most importantly the *operations* function). As its name suggests,

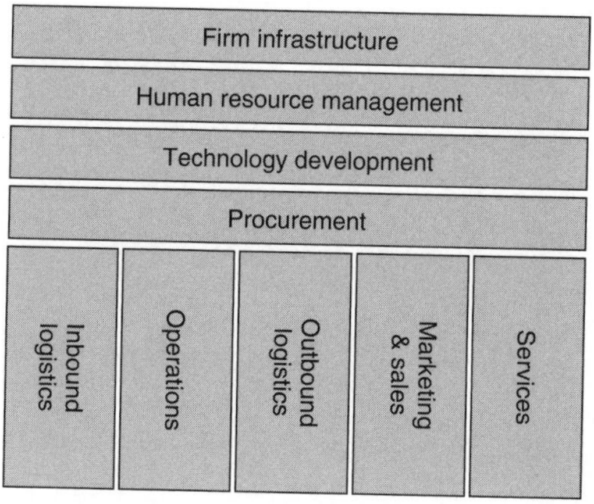

Firm infrastructure
Human resource management
Technology development
Procurement
Inbound logistics
Operations
Outbound logistics
Marketing & sales
Services

Figure 5.10 Functions in Porter's value chain model

the *technology development* function concentrates on the development of new technologies used in the *operations* function or in the produced goods. The *human resource management* function manages the personnel of the organization. Finally, the *firm infrastructure* function is responsible for providing the general infrastructure of the organization, such as the (financial) administration.

Front-end and back-end functions

In the previous section, we have seen that in e-business, it is important to distinguish between front-end and back-end functions in primary business functions. The front-end functions implement the collaboration in an e-business scenario, hence they most determine the e-business character of an organization.

Which business functions are important in the front end of an organization depends on the role that the organization plays in the scenario, whether a provider with a sell-side perspective or consumer with a buy-side perspective.

When we map Porter's model to the provider front-end perspective in this context, we obtain the selection highlighted in Figure 5.11: the most important functions are *outbound logistics, marketing and sales* and *service.* Obviously most organizations require all the other functions too, but they are not part of the provider front-end perspective.

If we do the same for the consumer perspective, we get the function selection shown in Figure 5.12. Here, the focus is on *procurement* and *inbound logistics.* As with the provider perspective, the other functions will be present in most organizations as well, but they are not part of the consumer front-end perspective.

Adapting Porter's model to e-business

Porter's model was designed for 'traditional' organizations where physical production and transportation are of major importance. Therefore, we cannot effectively apply

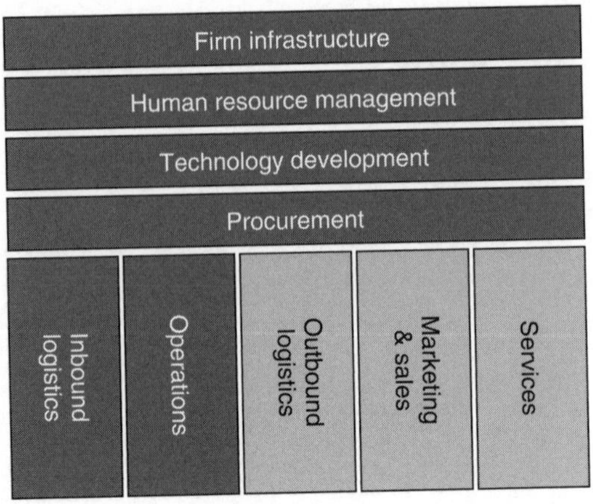

Figure 5.11 Provider (sell-side) front-end business functions

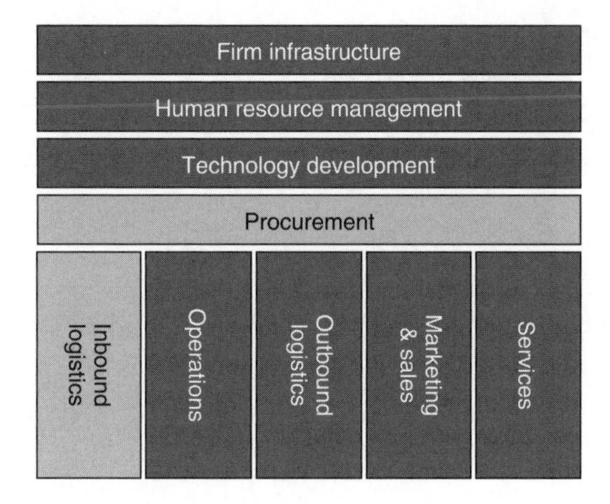

Figure 5.12 Consumer (buy-side) front-end business functions

the model directly to an e-business context. As it is a commonly accepted model, though, we use it as a basis for the identification of e-business functions. Hence, we need to extend and detail Porter's model. We do this in the next two subsections for front- and back-end e-business functions respectively.

5.4.2 Front-end functions

We take the front-end functions from Porter's model (as identified in the previous section) as the basis for the structured identification of e-business front-end functions. By doing so, we arrive at the basic set shown in Table 5.1. While the table is certainly not the 'ultimate set' of business functions, it is however a structured starting point for e-business design and analysis. It also shows how a set of functions can be derived in a structured way starting from a well-accepted business framework like Porter's model.

5.4.3 Back-end functions

We can perform the exercise we did for front-end functions in a similar way for back-end functions. As back-end functions are not as specific for e-business as front-end functions, we perform this exercise briefly. The result is shown in Table 5.2. We do not distinguish between consumer side and provider side in the table, as the characteristics of these sides are mainly relevant for front-end functions.

Note that we have included *procurement* in Table 5.2 (it is also listed as a front-end function in Table 5.1). As a back-end function, it is now seen without the typical e-business perspective: an organization that sells products in an e-business scenario may have to buy products in a traditional scenario. Therefore, we don't detail this function here.

Table 5.1 Front-end e-business functions

Porter function	*e-Business function*	*Comment*
Provider side		
Marketing and sales	advertising	usually via intermediary
	negotiating	
	contracting	possibly via intermediary
	selling	
	billing	
Outbound logistics	sending goods	possibly via intermediary
	status information provisioning	
Service	goods information provisioning	
	update provisioning	in case of digital goods
	value added service provisioning	
Consumer side		
Procurement	searching	usually via intermediary
	negotiating	
	contracting	possibly via intermediary
	buying	
	paying	usually via intermediary
Inbound logistics	receiving goods	possibly via intermediary

Table 5.2 Back-end e-business functions

Porter function	*e-Business function*	*Comment*
Operations	production	may be digital objects
	stock keeping	n.a. if digital objects
Procurement	procurement	
Technology development	product configuration	
	catalog management	
Human resources management	knowledge innovation	
Firm infrastructure	financial administration	linked with e-payments
	IS management	

5.5 E-BUSINESS PROCESSES

e-Business organization structures (as discussed in Section 5.3) describe the organization of business functions (as discussed in the previous section) of participating organizations in an e-business scenario. They do not, however, describe how the various business functions are activated during the execution of an e-business collaboration. To capture this, we need to introduce the notion of e-business processes and their models.

In this section, we first discuss the essence of the business process concept. Then we show how to specify business processes – we introduce a simple graphical notation for this purpose. As e-business concerns the collaboration between multiple organizations, e-business processes span multiple organizations. We discuss this aspect in Section 5.5.3. After that, we are ready to treat e-business processes. We end this section by discussing the differences between static and dynamic processes – the latter concept allows processes to be woven between organizations that set up collaborations on-the-fly while doing business.

5.5.1 The essence of business processes

A business process is a set of business activities that are performed in a specific order to achieve a specific business goal (see the introduction of the previous chapter). A business process can be geared towards primary business goals, like selling a product. It can also be geared towards secondary business goals, like making a monthly financial overview of a company.

The activities of a process implement the necessary business steps to reach the business goal. These steps are performed by *actors* (also called *agents*) in an organization which are located in organizational units as discussed in Section 5.3. The steps are part of business functions as discussed in Section 5.4. The actors that perform steps are often human beings, but can also be machines. In an e-business context, the latter are typically automated information systems (think for example of the *completely automated business* direction discussed in Section 4.4.5).

A business process is specified in a *business process model*. Such a model specifies the order of the steps. In the next subsection, we will see how to actually specify business process models. Steps in a business process model can be elementary business activities or *subprocesses*. Subprocesses are processes at a lower level of aggregation, used to break up the complexity of business process models or to reuse parts of business process models for different business goals.

The ordering of steps in a business process model can be simple – for example a linear sequence – or can be complex, containing alternative paths and parallel paths. The ordering of steps in time is referred to as the *control flow* of a business process model. When discussing processes, the focus is on this control flow, and not so much on the internal details of the individual steps in the process.

A business process model specifies the structure of a *type* of business process, i.e., all possible executions of that process. For example, a model of a sales process specifies how all sales are to be performed. A single execution of a business process according to a business process model is called an *instance* of that model or a *business process case*. Performing one specific sale is thus an instance of a sales process.

5.5.2 Specifying business process models

In the previous subsection, we discussed the essence of business processes, treating the most important concepts of business process models. In this subsection, we turn to the specification of business process models, i.e., to the way to represent them in documentation.

Figure 5.13 shows an example B2C e-business process model. We use a simple, informal graphical process specification notation[3] consisting of process activities and arrows which connect these activities. The arrows denote temporal sequence. Thus, an arrow from activity A to activity B denotes that the execution of A precedes the execution of B. The meaning of the process element types we use is shown in the legend in Table 5.3.

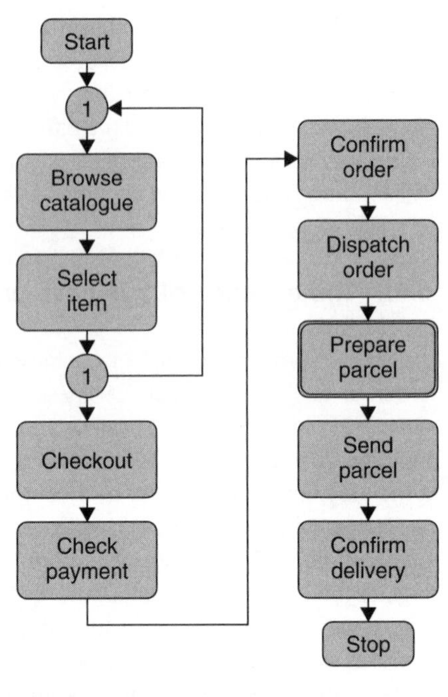

Figure 5.13 Example e-retail business process

The example in Figure 5.13 is a simplified e-retailing process. The process starts with a Web shop customer browsing a catalog and selecting an item to buy (typically placing it in an electronic shopping cart). These two activities can be repeated multiple times. After finishing the selection of items to buy, the customer proceeds to the checkout. The payment is next checked. Then, the e-retailer confirms the order (typically by email) and dispatches the order to its delivery department. The parcel is prepared and sent to the customer (usually through a logistics partner – an intermediary). Finally, a delivery notice is sent to the customer (typically, by email).

Table 5.3 Legend of process specification element types

Symbol	Meaning	Symbol	Meaning
Start	Start of process. Can occur only once in a diagram	1	Alternative split. The process continues with only one of the outgoing paths
Stop	End of a process. Can occur more than once in a diagram	1	Alternative join. The process continues when one of the incoming paths is completed
Activity	Process activity. Denotes an elemental business function	A	Parallel split. The process continues with all outgoing paths in parallel
Sub-process	Subprocess. Placeholder for a refinement in another diagram	A	Parallel join. The process continues when all the incoming paths are completed

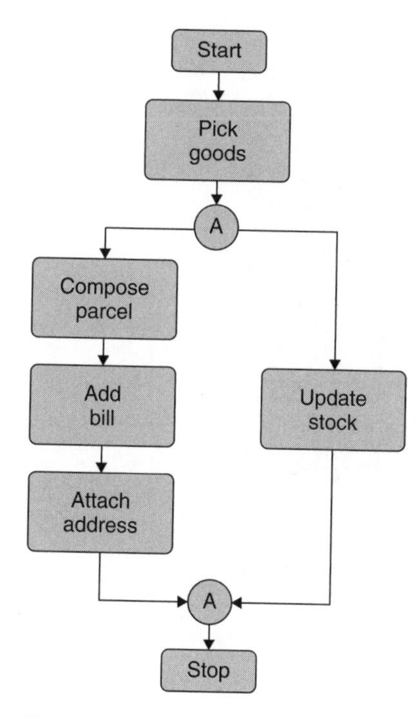

Figure 5.14 Refinement of subprocess of Figure 5.13

The *prepare parcel* step is a subprocess as it contains more detailed activities. Its elaboration (refinement) is shown in Figure 5.14.

In Figure 5.14, we see that preparing a parcel starts with choosing the goods to be delivered. Then, two paths are followed in parallel. In one path, the parcel is composed and the bill and address sticker are added to it. In the other path, the stock administration is updated to reflect that items have been removed from stock.

The process specification in Figure 5.13 is simplified, as it does not show that the process can be aborted at various points. For instance, the customer can decide not to buy anything, may not proceed during check-out, the payment may not be authorized, etc. This means that in the full process specification, there are many more alternative paths leading to the end of the process. Also, the process specification is based on the fact that only goods are sold that are actually in stock. Including activities to put a sales order in a waiting state and trigger an order for new stock further complicates the process.

5.5.3 From intra- to inter-organizational business processes

Intra-organizational business processes are completely executed (also termed *enacted*) within the boundaries of a single organization. As such, focusing on intra-organizational processes is not very interesting for the scope of this book (as we are interested in inter-organizational e-business scenarios – see Section 1.2). Therefore, we focus on inter-organizational business processes below. We first discuss the nature of these processes. Then, we pay attention to control flow types which classify the distribution of the responsibility of process execution over the parties in an e-business scenario.

Inter-organizational business processes

Inter-organizational business processes are executed by two or more collaborating parties – and hence are interesting from an e-business perspective. They are used to actually implement collaboration in business models as discussed in the previous

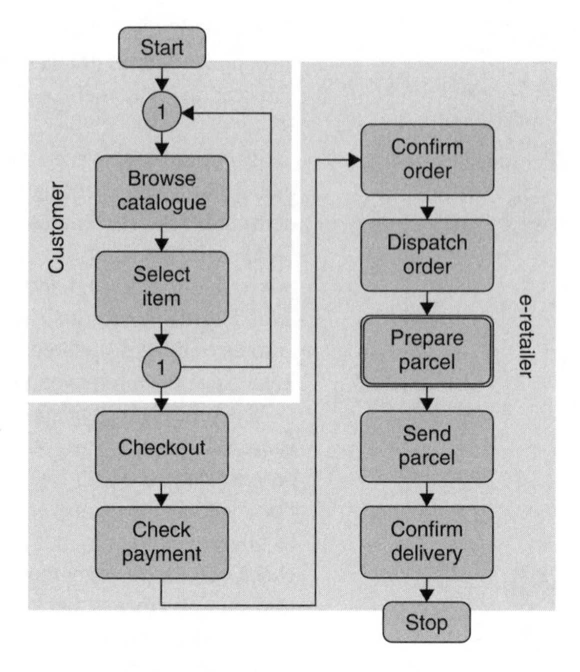

Figure 5.15 Example e-retail business process with organizations

chapter. We make a business process explicitly inter-organizational by allocating the steps in the process to specific parties in an e-business scenario – or put very simply: we indicate who does what.

Figure 5.15 shows the business process of Figure 5.13 as an explicit inter-organizational business process. The inter-organizational character of the process is specified by indicating which part of the process is executed by which involved party.

In the example of Figure 5.15, the situation is simple: the first two activities of the process are executed by the customer, the other by the e-retailer. The control flow distribution between the two parties is simple too: the control of the process execution is passed from customer to retailer at one single point. Below, we discuss the issue of control flow distribution further.

Inter-organizational flow control types

Inter-organizational business processes exist in three kinds where it comes to the distribution of the flow control[4] of the business process, i.e., the allocation of the responsibility to make the process flow.

The simplest is that of *unilateral flow control.* In this type, one party completely controls the flow of the entire process. This means that this party takes all the routing and scheduling decisions in the process. The other collaborating party (or parties) participates in the process only by executing individual tasks upon request of the controlling party. These individual tasks can be executed, for example, by using web-based interfaces to the systems of the controlling party – we discuss the technology for this in Section 7.4.2.

More complicated is the case of *bilateral flow control*. In this type, two parties collaboratively control the flow of the business process. The business process is divided into two parts and each party is responsible for one part. This means that the two parties have to synchronize the states of their parts of the process and exchange process data to keep the entire thing running smoothly. This can be very simple where one organization 'kicks off' the other (as for example in Figure 5.15) or more complicated in the case of multiple synchronization points.

The case of *multilateral flow control* is a generalization of the bilateral flow control case. Here the situation is similar, but there are more than two parties involved in process control to cater for flow control distribution over more than two parties. This flow control type can occur in virtual enterprise scenarios, where multiple organizations collaboratively execute a complex business process (Grefen *et al.* 2009, Mehandjiev and Grefen 2010).

An abstract example of a multilateral control flow is shown in Figure 5.16. Here, five organizations (indicated by the ellipses) together execute an inter-organizational business process, which starts at the top-left organization and ends at the bottom-right organization. The process contains both intra-organizational control flow links (the solid arrows within the ellipses) and inter-organizational control flow links (the dashed arrows between the ellipses). The five organizations together are responsible for the flow control of the entire process, i.e., the flow control is distributed over them.

Multilateral flow control makes synchronization more complex, especially so if the collaboration topology contains cycles (i.e., if organizations are 'connected' via more than one path). In this latter case, parties might even do inconsistent things if the processes are not very well designed.

In the bilateral and multilateral flow control classes, participating organizations need to expose details of their business processes to the other organizations in order to synchronize their processes. They do not need to expose all details of their internal processes, however. The internal processes may contain details that are confidential

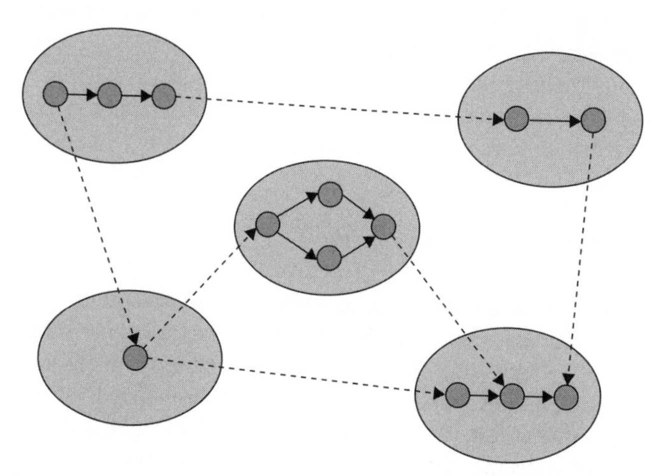

Figure 5.16 Multilateral control flow

(for reasons of competition) or simply irrelevant for other parties. Consequently, organizations expose abstractions of their *internal processes* as *external processes* at the inter-organizational level (Grefen *et al.* 2003). Such an abstraction is also referred to as *business process view* or *workflow view* (Chiu *et al.* 2001).

5.5.4 Business processes in e-business

With the ingredients of the preceding subsections, we can turn to the discussion of business processes in e-business. Obviously, e-business processes are business processes – but they are business processes of a special kind. First, they are inter-organizational by nature. Therefore, it is important to map process steps to the right parties, and within the parties to the right organizational modules. Second, they are typically complex, involving a number of e-business functions performed by two or more parties. Therefore, it is important to map process functions to an e-business function taxonomy. We discuss both aspects below.

Process steps and organizational modules

An aspect that is more important in e-business settings than in traditional settings is the allocation of activities (steps) in a process model to the parties in the e-business setting. This is so important, because the process is performed by multiple parties that are usually autonomous with respect to each other. In other words, the allocation of activities to partners determines the feasibility of the implementation of a process model to a large extent.

We can go one step further and allocate the process steps to functional organization modules of involved parties (as discussed in Section 5.3) and allocate inter-organizational connections between activities to channels between partners. As an example, we can map a simple e-buying business process to the organization structure of Figure 5.6. By doing so, we get a hybrid organization/process diagram like the one in Figure 5.17. Note that we have chosen a simplified process notation for reasons of simplicity here – circles denote process steps, splits and joins have been omitted. This diagram gives a high-level overview of how an e-business process progresses through the business functionalities of involved organizations.

Process steps and e-business functions

In Figure 5.15, we have shown a simple e-retailing business process. The steps in this process specification are of an ad-hoc nature, i.e., they have been selected without using an underlying framework. To check the completeness and consistency of the process specification, these steps in this figure can be mapped to the e-business function taxonomy that we have identified in Section 5.4. As the process involves both supplier and consumer sides, we need functions from both perspectives. Thus, we can identify the following mappings (referring to Table 5.1):

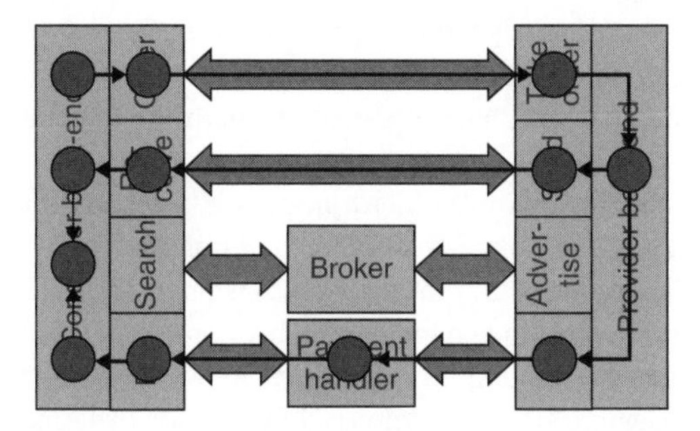

Figure 5.17 Inter-organizational e-business process

- the *browse catalog* and *select item* steps belong to the function *buying* (consumer side);
- the *checkout* step belongs to the function *selling* (provider side);
- the *check payment* step belongs to the function *billing* (provider side);
- the *confirm order* and *confirm delivery* steps belong to the function *status information provisioning* (provider side);
- the *dispatch order, prepare parcel* and *send parcel* steps belong to the function *sending goods* (provider side).

As can be seen, not all functions from Table 5.1 are included in the process specification. The reason for this is that this is a pure e-retailing process with a supplier emphasis. Functions *advertising, searching, receiving goods* and all *service* functions are hence out of the scope of this process specification. Note that the *advertising* function cannot even be part of the same process model as *buying*, as an advertisement has a different life cycle than a purchase order. The functions *negotiating* and *contracting* are typically not applicable to standard e-retailing scenarios.

5.5.5 Static versus dynamic processes

There is one aspect of e-business processes that remains to be discussed here: the difference between *static* and *dynamic processes.*

We call an e-business process *static* if its specification is completely predefined without taking specific, individual e-business orders into account. The parties involved in the execution of a static process instance can be chosen during execution (e.g. a consumer may decide which provider to use in a buying process), but the control flow and steps of the process are not changed during the process. Selecting involved parties is *role resolution* within a scenario: specific organizations are assigned to roles like provider, consumer or intermediary, based on pre-specified roles.

We call an e-business process *dynamic* if its complete specification is determined right before execution of a process instance on the basis of one individual e-business order – or even during the execution of the process instance. The latter approach means that the execution of a process starts with an 'incomplete' specification, which is 'filled in' when all parties are selected. This implies that role resolution is coupled to process specification. The dynamic approach to e-business process management allows high levels of flexibility in collaboration, but does also imply high levels of complexity (both in the organizational aspect and in the architecture and technology aspects).

An example of a dynamic e-business process is a process the specification of which contains 'blanks', i.e., placeholders for parts of the process that are not yet specified. Depending on the nature of a process instance, these 'blanks' can be filled in differently. In case the instance handles a high-volume transaction, the blanks may be filled in with more details than in the case of a low-volume transaction.

In e-business research, advanced approaches towards dynamic business process support have been used for example for dynamic outsourcing scenarios (Grefen *et al.* 2000) and dynamic business network formation (Grefen *et al.* 2009). In dynamic service outsourcing, the 'blanks' approach as discussed above can be used to have these 'blanks' filled in by selecting specific processes of external parties.

5.6 OPERATIONS AND CHANGE MANAGEMENT

In operating an e-business organization (as in any other business organization), two aspects are of importance: keeping the existing situation operating smoothly, and preparing for changing the existing situation. The former is called *operations management*. The latter, called *change management*, is extremely important in e-business – remember that change is the only constant in e-business. We discuss both types of management below.

5.6.1 Operations management

Clearly, operations management includes managing the internals of organizations involved in e-business – but that is not the focus of this book. We focus here on aspects that are specific to e-business: managing inter-organizational relations and managing IT resources.

Managing inter-organizational relations

Managing inter-organizational relations at the operational level between organizations is obviously very important in e-business. In this context, operations management has three important elements:

- *Synchronizing business states* between partners involved in an e-business relationship. This may involve managing relations defined in electronic contracts (Angelov 2006), making sure that all rights and obligations specified in these contracts are handled in the appropriate way. Maintaining required levels of trust between business partners is a major issue here (Keen *et al.* 2000). Trust management between organizations in e-business typically has to be performed more explicitly than in traditional business, because business relations are often not based on long-standing collaborations with personal contacts.

- *Synchronizing process states* of processes that are executed across multiple organizations in an e-business relation (as illustrated in Figure 5.17). Synchronization is required to make sure all collaborating parties have the same view on the progress of e-business processes, both for monitoring and controlling purposes. Synchronizing process states includes the handling of exceptional situations, which may require advanced automated decision making mechanisms or escalation to human decision makers.
- *Synchronizing data states*, i.e., making sure that the correct data is passed at the right moments during the execution of e-business processes. Synchronization is required to ensure that all collaborating parties have the same view on the 'contents' of e-business processes, again both for monitoring and controlling purposes. Often, data synchronization relies on message passing between collaborating parties. In this case, strict communication protocols must be enforced.

We summarize the above elements of inter-organizational relation management in Figure 5.18. Note that the three elements are in general not independent. A change in process state, for example, may imply a change in data state.

Managing IT resources

Resource management is an important element in operations management in any organization – so too in an e-business organization. Information technology (IT) resources form one class of resources to be managed. IT resources include both software (such as e-business systems) and hardware (such as server machines and

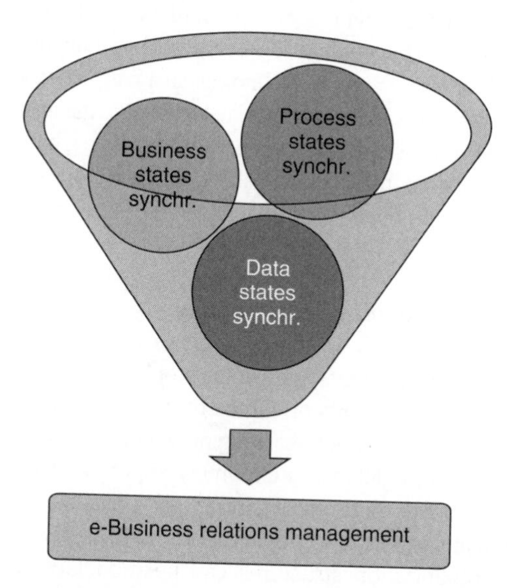

Figure 5.18 Ingredients of e-business relations management

physical networks). In an e-business organization, IT resources are even more of a key resource than in other organizations, as they are the main infrastructure for the execution of primary business processes. Failure of the IT infrastructure often means a direct loss for business. Therefore, IT resource management requires a good deal of attention in e-business organizations.

Important elements of IT resource management are:

- *managing IT infrastructure capacity* and planning future capacity, taking into account variations in system load;
- *keeping back-up infrastructure stand-by* for immediate transfer of activities when the primary infrastructure fails;
- *taking care of security of e-business systems* to avoid unauthorized use of these systems. Security covers both the functionality of systems and the information they exchange. Note that e-business systems are by definition open to the outside world, so can be vulnerable in this respect if not configured the right way;
- *making sure that system maintenance staff is available* to guarantee 24/7 operation of the organization. Even relatively short system down-times may imply a substantial loss of business, both in actual transactions and in customer confidence.

The first three elements may be coupled to the use of specific technology, some of which we discuss in Chapter 7.

5.6.2 Change management

Change management is essential in an e-business organization to ensure that the organization is prepared to change and to actually implement changes. As we have seen in Chapter 1, changes can be triggered by changing market situations (requirements pull) or by changing technological possibilities (technology push). Rapid developments in the e-business arena make change management an even more pressing issue in e-business than in 'traditional' business. Change management is related to strategic alignment as discussed in Section 3.4, as changes in various aspects of an organization need to be aligned (see Figure 3.4).

Enabling changes in organization structures

An important aspect of change management is preparing for new organization structures and realizing these, i.e., reorganizing the business functionality of an organization. To be able to do so without rearranging everything from scratch over and over again, organization modularity is extremely important: by organizing business functionality in appropriate modules (organizational clusters), many changes can be realized by manipulating individual organization modules. We have seen earlier in this chapter how organization structures can be modularized to accommodate change.

Clearly, when organization structures are changed, process and data structures defined in the context of these organization structures may need to be changed as well. But even without changing organizations structures, process and data structures may be subject to change.

Preparing organization staffing for changes

In obtaining effective and efficient change management within an organization, the role of human resource management (HRM) is essential. To enable changes, the organization must make sure that well-qualified people are in pivotal places in the organization. Apart from that, people must be in such positions that they can indeed keep track of changes in the context of the organization. This makes continuous knowledge acquisition or *life-long learning* a sine qua non in an e-business organization.

Predicting the unpredictable

As we have remarked repeatedly, changes in the e-business arena are frequent and often quite abrupt. Developments have taken place that may appear logical in hindsight, but that were hard (if at all possible) to predict beforehand.[5] This is partly caused by the technology-push forces in e-business, and partly by the open character of Internet-based business, which allows drastic ideas to be implemented.

Consequently, it is hard to anticipate future changes when operating in e-business, certainly if these changes are further away than the near future. Only considering predictable, nearby changes, however, implies a great risk of soon lagging behind.

One way to explore 'the unpredictable' is *extreme thinking*. In this approach, future scenarios are sketched by taking one or two primary variables in a business model and assigning them extreme values – even if these values will never occur in reality. The scenarios are taken to be in the long-term future in e-business terms, say five to ten years away. These extreme scenarios are next used to discuss the future (for instance, in BOAT terms). The extreme character of the scenarios forces people out of their 'comfort zone', i.e., forces them to think creatively. After the extreme future has been explored, the mid-term future is discussed by interpolating between the current situation and the extreme scenarios in the long term future. The mid-term future scenarios combined with the current situation are a basis for change management. These steps are illustrated in Figure 5.19.

After this discussion of e-business operations management and change management, we turn our attention again to the BOAT framework to explore the relationship of the element in this chapter (the O aspect elements) to those in the previous chapter (the B aspect elements).

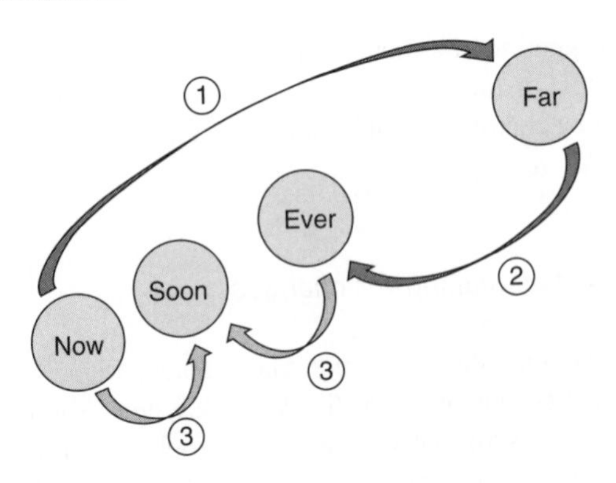

Figure 5.19 Extreme thinking steps

5.7 MAPPING B ELEMENTS TO O ELEMENTS

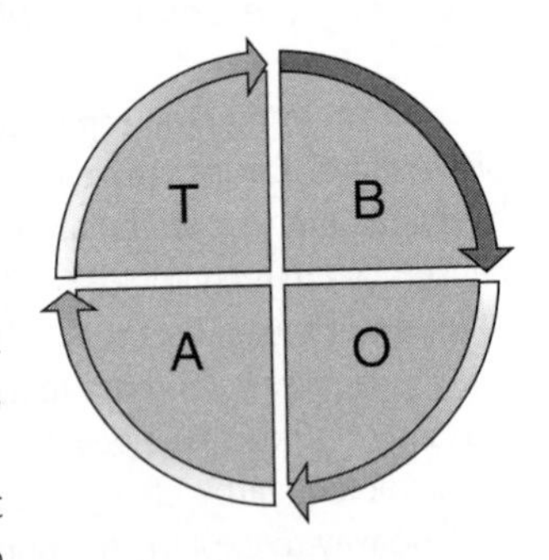

In Chapter 4, we discussed the business (B) aspect of e-business, looking at the classes of ingredients that contribute to business models. As we have seen in this chapter, the organization (O) aspect is an operationalization of the B aspect. As such, we should be able to identify a clear mapping from B aspect elements to O aspect elements in a specific e-business scenario.

Below, we discuss the mapping of B aspect elements to O aspect elements – but without the intention to be complete, as a complete mapping between B and O aspect is complex and highly dependent on the e-business scenario at hand. We first focus on operationalizing business drivers and business chain operations, as discussed in Chapter 4. Then, we present the operationalization of one business structure (dynamic service outsourcing) as an example for the classes of business directions and business structures – the other elements in these classes are left to the reader.

5.7.1 Operationalizing business drivers

In Section 4.2, we have seen the concepts of *reach* and *richness* as very basic ingredients to e-business models: they are the basic business drivers for e-business.

The concept of *reach* is clearly related to communication between organizations. Hence, we can operationalize it in terms of the channels between collaborating parties (as introduced in Figure 5.3). Geographical reach, for example, can only be increased if channels with the right characteristics[6] are placed between organizations, i.e., channels that help in bridging distance. Increased modal reach can be obtained by the use of multi-channeling, as discussed before in this chapter.

The level of *richness* that can be offered by an organization is heavily related to the functionality of the front-office organization building blocks we find in the organization structure (see Figure 5.5): the front-end building blocks 'implement' the interaction with partners. To offer increased richness, the functionality of these building blocks has to be expanded, or new blocks have to be introduced into the organizational structure. For example, in the O aspect, a new interactive advertising functional block may be added to obtain increased richness in the B aspect.

We summarize the above observations in Figure 5.20.

5.7.2 Operationalizing business chain operations

In Section 4.3, we have seen how business chains can be modified by the introduction of e-business. The main concepts here are *disintermediation* and *reintermediation*. These concepts can be easily operationalized in terms of the organization structures presented in this chapter.

If disintermediation or reintermediation pertains to an intermediary organization, this means respectively removing or inserting an intermediary between two collaborating e-business partners. This can easily be illustrated in a structure based on the notation as shown in Figure 5.5.

If disintermediation or reintermediation does not pertain to an intermediary organization, but to a main e-business party, we get a different situation. In this case, we remove or add a party that is in between two other parties in the roles of consumer or provider respectively. Consequently, disintermediation means deleting this party from the chain and connecting the front ends of the other parties. Likewise, reintermediation means inserting this party in the chain by reconnecting the front ends to this new party.

An example of the operationalization of disintermediation of a main party is shown in Figure 5.21. The top of the figure shows a simple business chain from which

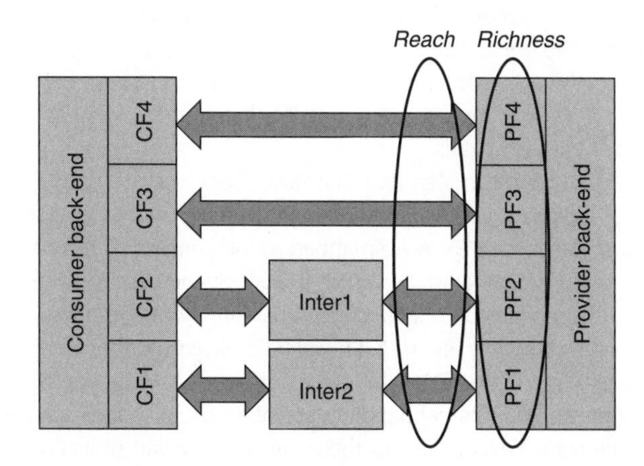

Figure 5.20 Reach and richness in organization structure

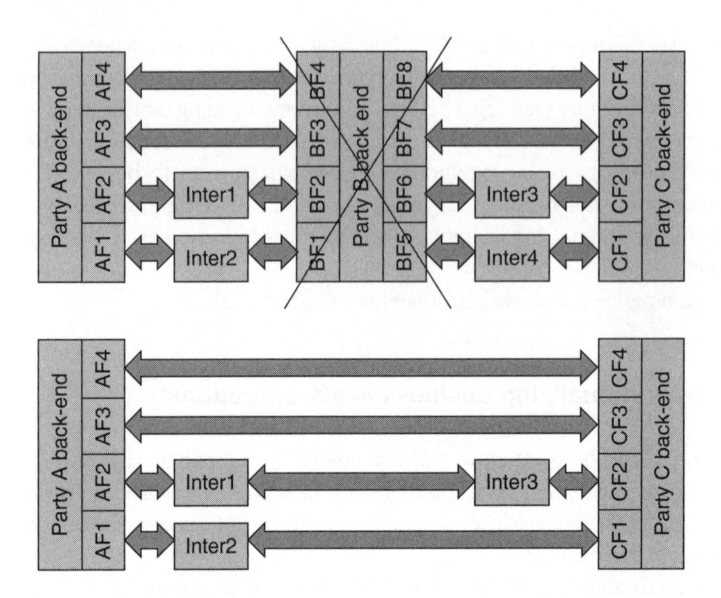

Figure 5.21 Operationalized disintermediation example

a party is disintermediated. The bottom of the figure shows the result. Note that some intermediary organizations take the role of two intermediaries in the old scenario, but that there might also be two intermediary organizations connected 'in sequence' between the two main parties. The latter may occur, for example, if both organizations wish to keep using their preferred (and different) payment intermediaries; consequently, payments are handled by transactions between the two intermediaries.

5.7.3 Operationalizing dynamic service outsourcing

As we have seen in Section 4.5.4, dynamic service outsourcing is an e-business structure in which an organization has one or more of its non-core business activities performed by external parties, for whom these activities are core competences. An external party is selected dynamically (possibly just-in-time), depending on market and client order characteristics.

In this chapter, we have seen how business processes are used for the operationalization of business models and their ingredients. Dynamic service outsourcing as a business structure can easily be mapped to the concept of business processes: outsourcing means 'transplanting' part of a business process to an external party that performs this process on behalf of the outsourcing organization.

An example is shown in Figure 5.22, which is based on the example e-retailing business process in Figure 5.15. In the example, the e-retailer has chosen to dynamically outsource its parcel handling activities, because logistics is not among its core competences. This means that the corresponding part of its business process (the activities *prepare parcel* and *send parcel*) is performed by external parties, which

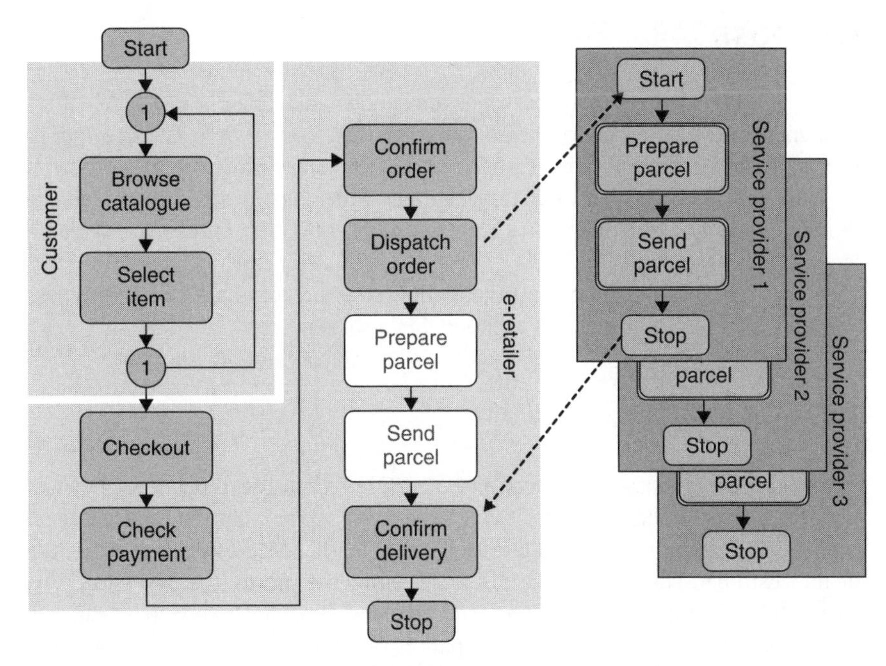

Figure 5.22 An example of operationalized dynamic service outsourcing

act as business process service providers to the e-retailer. In the example, the e-retailer dynamically chooses between three service providers, depending on the client order at hand. Outsourcing results in additional inter-organizational control flow (see Section 5.5.3), as indicated by the dashed arrows in the figure.

Note that the *send parcel* activity is a regular activity in the original process of the e-retailer, but a subprocess in the processes of the service providers (like the *prepare parcel* activity). As logistics is their core business, they have a more detailed specification of this activity. The contents of this refinement are of no concern of the retailer, though. This enables each service provider to implement their two externally visible activities differently within their organization, while keeping the process interface to their customer the same. This is an application of *business process abstraction* from internal to external business process specification, as discussed in Section 5.5.3.

5.8 RUNNING CASES

Below, we turn our attention again to our running cases POSH and TTU and apply the concepts of this chapter to them. For reasons of brevity, we do not apply all concepts to both cases, but have made a selection of interesting combinations of concepts and case characteristics.

5.8.1 POSH

POSH sells two kinds of products, which are handled in a different way. Small office equipment and supplies are delivered from their own stock by a logistics partner to clients. Large furniture is delivered from (and if necessary produced to order by) a furniture manufacturer that POSH collaborates with. This means that we can see the POSH scenario as a three-party scenario: supplier (POSH), customer and manufacturer.

Below, we first elaborate the organization structure of the POSH e-business scenario, then turn our attention to the POSH e-sales process.

Organization structure

The e-business organization structure of the POSH e-business scenario is shown in Figure 5.23. As remarked above, it is a three-party scenario. In the top right-hand corner we see the structure of POSH itself. At the left-hand side, we see the structure of the customer. The case with a business customer is shown (the B2B case). The case with a consumer customer (the B2C case) is a simplification of this case, as a consumer typically does not have separate organizational modules: the entire organization consists of one module. At the bottom, we see the organization of the furniture manufacturer, as far as is relevant for the POSH e-business scenario

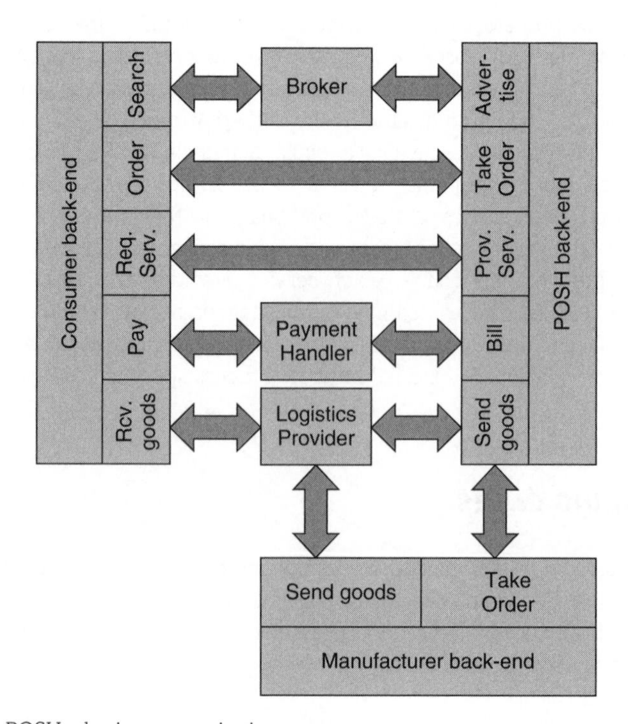

Figure 5.23 POSH e-business organization structure

(obviously, this party has a more complex organization structure). There are three intermediary parties in the scenario: a broker through which POSH advertises, a payment handler that handles billing and payment for POSH, and a logistics service provider that takes care of delivery of goods – the same service provider handles small and large goods.

Note that it is a design choice to model the furniture manufacturer as a third party. An alternative would be to consider it as an additional intermediary. The choice made is based on the observation that the manufacturer produces traded objects (as discussed in Section 2.4) and consequently takes a main role in the value chain of the e-business scenario. As such, it is not just an 'additional' service provider that has a minor role in the value chain.

Business functions and business process

In their e-sales business process, POSH makes a distinction between consumer (C) and business (B) customers. Business customers get their catalog earlier for their order entry than consumer customers, have a checkout procedure with more delivery options, and are billed offline for later payment where consumers pay directly (e.g. using their credit card).

POSH decides to have their e-sales process cover the *marketing and sales* and *outbound logistics* function classes of Table 5.1. As each instance (case) of the e-sales process coincides with one sales transaction, the *advertising* function is not included. The *negotiating* and *contracting* functions are not considered applicable for the business domain – although POSH is considering the inclusion of contracting at a later stage to cover large B2B orders, as these orders can incur large financial risks.

The high-level specification of the process is shown in Figure 5.24. Customers are required to make a choice when contacting POSH. Based on the choice, a split is made in the process between consumer and business customers.[7] Business customers have to log-in to a pre-existing account to identify themselves. Both order entry steps are subprocesses, which have elaborations comparable to the *customer* part in Figure 5.15. The *handle order* step is a subprocess with considerable complexity – within this step, the distinction is made between small goods delivered from POSH stock and large goods delivered from the furniture manufacturer.

5.8.2 TTU

TTU provides two very different kinds of services (as e-business objects, see Section 2.4): document translation services and real-time interpretation services. In document translation, they provide offline translation of physical documents and online translation of digital documents. In interpretation, they offer interpreter services in telephone conferences and interpreter services in video-conferences.

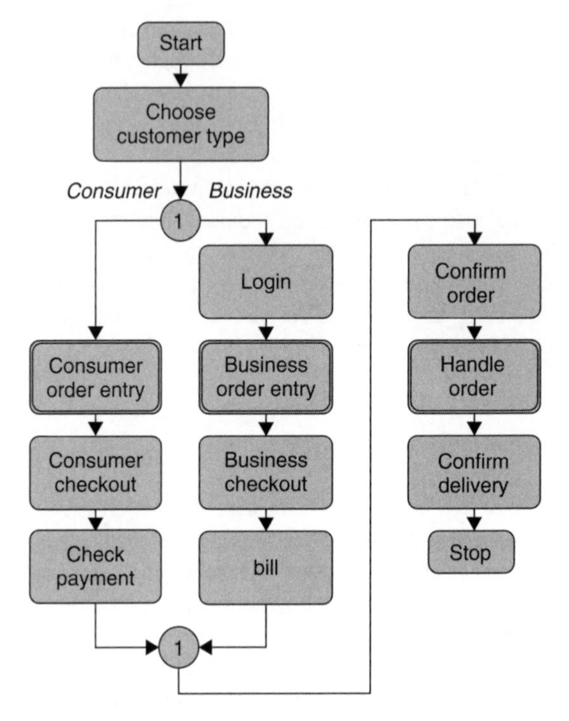

Figure 5.24 POSH e-sales business process

Business functions and business process

To cater for the differences in the services, TTU has a product-oriented e-sales process structure (as opposed to POSH, which has a client-type-oriented process structure).

The TTU e-sales process is shown in Figure 5.25. As TTU only works for registered customers (typically business customers), they have to log-in first, then choose the product they wish to order. The process continues based on this choice.

In contrast to the POSH e-sales process, e-business object delivery, billing and payment handling are not part of the TTU process. This is a process design choice. The reason TTU makes this choice is the fact that they prefer to bill after service delivery (as the amount depends on the delivered effort) and do not consider delivery part of sales.

Change management

TTU recognizes that innovation is of paramount importance for their existence. TTU does not employ translators or interpreters – they use freelancers who are hired in a just-in-time fashion. This means that TTU itself only offers digital services (the coupling of organizations requiring language services and individuals who can

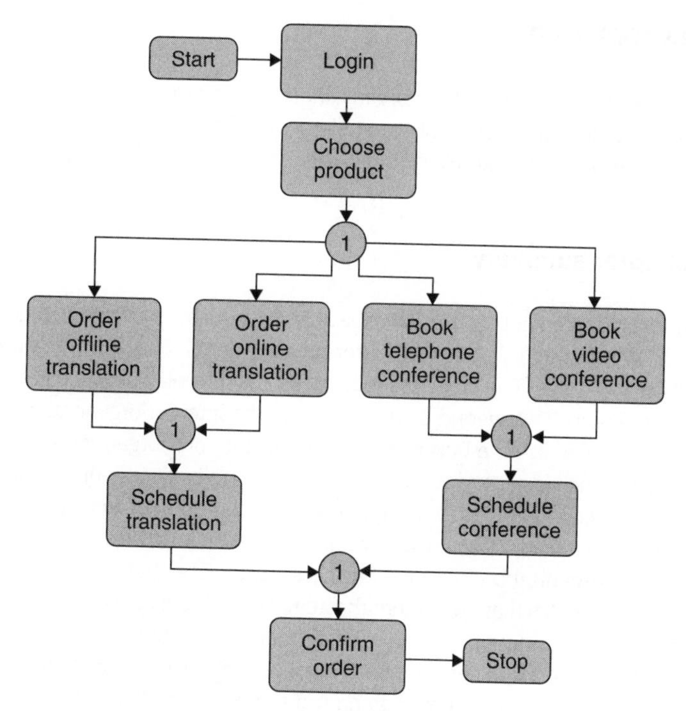

Figure 5.25 TTU e-sales process

provide them) – hence their business can easily be copied by competitors if it remains too static.

The facilitator for innovation within TTU is its R&D department. TTU is keen to keep this department aligned with their business operations. For this reason, TTU has decided to have an innovation and change management (ICM) team consisting of key members from the organization, from the management, R&D and operations departments. The ICM team has regular meetings to discuss possible new developments in an open atmosphere. Three points are always on the agenda:

1 New requirements to TTU services indicated by existing customers.
2 New technological developments in document translation, audio and video conferencing.
3 New business opportunities, i.e., possible new services and possible new customer groups.

Developments in automatic translation and telepresence technology (Wikipedia 2009e) make point 2 a very important issue for TTU. For point 3, TTU uses the extreme thinking approach (see Figure 5.19).

5.9 CHAPTER END

In this chapter, we have treated the organization aspect of the BOAT framework. In this section, we first summarize the main elements of this O aspect, then provide a number of questions and exercises to allow the reader to apply the theory.

5.9.1 Chapter summary

The first main ingredient of the O aspect is formed by e-business organization structures. We distinguish between inter-organizational and intra-organizational organization structures. The first class focuses on the interplay between parties in an e-business scenario. The second class focuses on the internal organization structure of individual parties in an e-business scenario. In the inter-organizational class, we identify main parties (e.g. providers and consumers of e-business objects) on the one hand and intermediary parties (that support the collaboration of main parties) on the other. In the intra-organizational class, we make a distinction between the back-end and front-end organization of an e-business party. The front end contains the organizational modules that implement the actual e-business collaboration. The back end contains core business functions with an internal orientation.

The second main ingredient of the O aspect is e-business functions. Again we make a distinction between back end and front end to classify functions. Functions can be derived from standard business frameworks (like Porter's value chain model) – however, extension and specialization towards e-business specifics of such models is necessary.

The third main ingredient of the O aspect is formed by e-business processes. e-Business processes specify the order in which e-business functions are executed to achieve business goals. Main e-business processes are inter-organizational processes that cover the activities of multiple partners involved in an e-business scenario.

Next to the core of three main ingredients (structures, functions and processes), operations management and change management are important aspects of the O aspect. Operations management is concerned with organizing e-business operations (i.e., the execution of e-business processes and functions) in an effective and efficient manner. Change management is concerned with keeping the organization prepared and agile for the adoption of new changes. The ever-changing world of e-business causes changes to be frequent, triggered either by the business context or the technological context. The O aspect ingredients are summarized in Figure 5.26. A clear mapping of B aspect elements to O aspect elements is required to enable well-structured change management.

5.9.2 Questions and exercises

1 The business process in Figure 5.17 contains an implicit split and an implicit join. Is this pair of split/join of the alternative type or of the parallel type (see Table 5.3)?

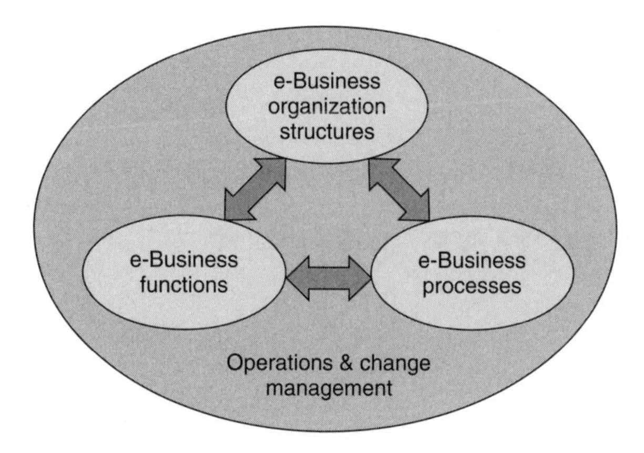

Figure 5.26 O aspect ingredients

2 How much down-time (time in which no business activities can be performed) a year is acceptable for an e-business organization? How much of this can be planned and unplanned? Take a well-known existing e-business scenario (such as Amazon.com) and try to make an estimate.
3 Change the organization diagram of Figure 5.23 to the situation where the manufacturer is considered an intermediary (as discussed in the text). In other words: convert the three-party scenario to a two-party scenario.
4 Try and find an existing e-business scenario with more than three parties. Specify the organization structure of this scenario in an e-business organization diagram. Explain whether the scenario does indeed need this many parties by considering whether the parties are not really intermediaries, or whether the scenario cannot be decomposed into two independent e-business scenarios.
5 As discussed in the accompanying text, the process specification in Figure 5.13 is simplified. Extend this specification to the full specification. Note that this involves adding a number of alternative paths, using alternative splits and joins.
6 Design an elaboration of the *handle order* subprocess of the POSH sales process as shown in Figure 5.24. Allocate steps in the process to the involved parties. Note the different procedures for small goods (delivered from POSH stock) and large goods (delivered from manufacturer). Make further assumptions where necessary and document these.
7 Change the specification of the TTU sales process (see Figure 5.25) such that the *translation* and *interpretation* parts of the process are handled in subprocesses. In other words: transform the single-level process specification into a two-level specification.

6

Architecture aspect

Learning goals

By the end of the chapter you should:

- Understand the concept of e-business architectures and their organization in aggregation and abstraction dimensions;
- Understand the structure of hierarchically organized e-business architectures;
- Understand the role of reference and standard architectures in an e-business context;
- Understand the mapping of organization aspect elements (as discussed in Chapter 5) to architecture elements.

6.1 INTRODUCTION

Having discussed the business and organization aspects of e-business in the two preceding chapters, we now focus our attention on the architecture aspect. Architectures are blueprints for e-business information systems, i.e., for the automated systems that support the business interactions as discussed in the preceding chapter. In other words, architectures are designs of the structures of e-business systems – not so different from architectures in the building world where they are designs of the structure of houses or office buildings. In e-business, architectures form the interface between the non-IT aspects (the B and O aspects of the BOAT framework as discussed in the previous chapters) and the IT-aspects of e-business (the T aspect of BOAT, which we discuss in the next chapter).

Given the scope of this book, we focus on e-business-specific architecture elements in this chapter. This means that we do not discuss architecture in the broader context of general software engineering. Other good books are available that do treat software system architecture in general, e.g. Bass *et al.* 2003.

In the first section below, we will see that architectures of e-business systems are necessary to provide structure in a rapidly changing context. After the need for architectures has been established, we move to the contents of architectures. We discuss the nature of information system architectures, of which e-business architectures form a subclass. In the next three sections, we discuss e-business architectures at three aggregation levels. As usual in this book, we end the chapter with our running cases, exercises and a chapter summary.

6.2 THE NEED FOR ARCHITECTURE

On the business side of e-business, we see a swift increase in required functionality of automated support for e-business operations. e-Business systems become more and more complex as they cover a broader spectrum of business interactions. As we have seen in Section 4.4.5, this may even lead to e-business systems covering (almost) all operational processes in an automated way. At the same time, an increasing level of quality is required of e-business systems, as e-business operations are mission-critical for organizations engaging heavily into e-business. e-Business systems should not make errors, should have short response times, should be flexible, should always be available, and so on. Clearly, these two developments create an area of tension.

On the technology side of e-business, we see something similar developing. A quickly increasing spectrum of diverse technologies becomes available, catering for all kinds of e-business functionalities. We will see a selection of these technologies in the next chapter. The complexity that the deployment of a combination of all these technologies creates, however, requires an increasing level of e-business system structure to keep technology 'under control'. Without proper structure, e-business systems end up being a heap of 'spaghetti' of interrelated technologies. Again, the abundance of technologies and the required structure create an area of tension.

As we have seen already in Section 1.5, technology push and requirements pull (demand pull) forces reinforce each other. This increases the speed of developments in the e-business area in a cyclical way. This increasing speed of change further stresses the two mentioned areas of tension. All these forces are illustrated in Figure 6.1.

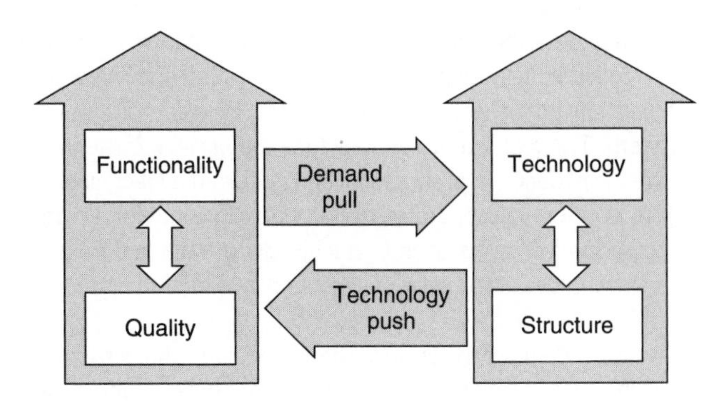

Figure 6.1 Tension fields in e-business development

To keep the relation between the business and technology sides manageable, clear structures must be designed that describe the mapping of both sides to each other. These structures must be of an abstract nature, such that they are independent of specific, concrete choices made at either the business or the technology side. This independence of specific choices ensures that the structures become stable in time.

In terms of the BOAT framework, these structures must form an 'interface' between the B and O aspects on the one hand and the T aspect on the other hand. This is exactly what the *architecture* aspect of the BOAT framework is about: it has a pivotal function between the other aspects, as shown in Figure 6.2. This pivotal role is closely related to business-IT alignment as discussed in Section 3.4.

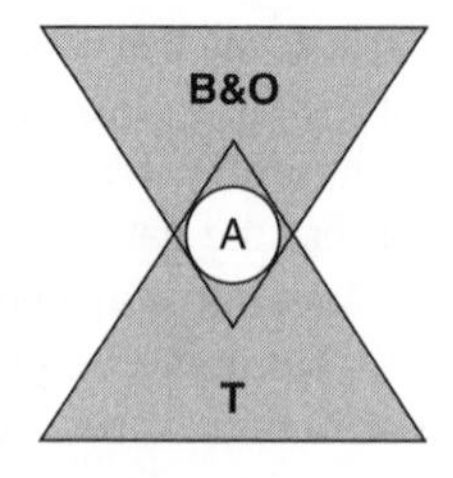

Figure 6.2
Architecture as a pivot in the BOAT framework

6.3 A BASIS FOR E-BUSINESS ARCHITECTURE

As stated in the introduction of this chapter, architectures are blueprints for e-business information systems. We have seen above how they form the pivot between business-oriented aspects and technology-oriented aspects. Before we embark on the discussion of the structure of e-business architectures, we need a better understanding of what architectures exactly are. Providing this basic understanding is the goal of this section. We first discuss the concept of *e-business architecture*. Next we discuss two dimensions along which we can position architecture descriptions. Last, we discuss several classes of architecture descriptions.

6.3.1 The concept of e-business architecture

Information systems have become more and more complex – we have discussed this for e-business systems in the previous section, but this holds too for other types of information systems. To deal with this complexity, the concept of *architecture* has emerged in the information system field. The architecture of an information system can be seen as a high-level blueprint of that system that allows us to understand its internal structure to aid in its design, redesign, configuration and maintenance. This is not so much different from the (technical) architecture of a complex building, a bridge or a subway system. The fact that an architecture is a *high-level* blueprint means that the focus is on the main, conceptual structures and not on small technical details. Again, this is comparable to other types of architectures: the architecture of a complex building or bridge is not specified in terms of individual bricks or nuts and bolts.

We use the following basic definition of a general information system architecture:[1]

> The architecture of an information system specifies the structure of that system in terms of functional software components supporting specific functions and interfaces supporting the interactions among those components.

The fact that an information system architecture describes software and interfaces means that hardware components (such as server machines) and physical connections (such as glass fiber links) between these are not part of the architecture. Hardware architectures exist too, but they are not in the scope of this book.

As the definition states, an architecture describes a *structure* of a system. This means that we should use a clear way to represent that structure. Therefore, architectures are preferably described by means of diagrams (as opposed to a natural language textual description). There are specific diagram techniques for information system architectures, allowing specifying various kinds of characteristics. In this book, however, we use a simple notation. Later in this chapter, we will see examples of architectures.

The concept of *e-business information system architecture* is a specialization of the general information system case discussed above. Obviously, the interfaces supporting interactions are of utmost importance in the e-business case, as e-business is about interactions between business parties enabled by automated systems (recall our definition of e-business from Section 1.2). In the rest of this book, we will use the term *e-business architecture* as an abbreviation of *e-business information system architecture* – just to be brief.

6.3.2 Aggregation and abstraction levels

We can describe e-business architectures at various levels. To be sure of what we describe, we need to understand these levels. Below, we explain two important dimensions along which we can describe architectures: the aggregation dimension and the abstraction dimension.

The aggregation dimension

Architectures can be specified for large information systems, but also for parts of these large information systems, for parts of these parts, and so on. In other words, architectures can be specified at multiple levels of detail or *aggregation*. The aggregation levels are positioned along the aggregation dimension for architectures. When we move down this dimension, we zoom in on architectures, analyzing smaller structures with a higher level of detail. When we move up this dimension, we zoom out, analyzing larger structures with a lower level of detail.

What holds for information system architectures in general also holds for e-business system architectures: these can also be described at multiple aggregation levels. In this chapter, we discuss e-business architectures at three aggregation levels:

1 *Market-level architectures* describe the structure of e-business systems at the level where multiple parties engage into business within a market. Market-level architectures are inter-organizational architectures, as they focus on the relationships between systems of the parties in a market. This implies that they describe systems of multiple parties.

2 *Party-level architectures* describe the structure of e-business systems at the level of individual organizations, i.e., individual e-business parties. As we discuss e-business systems, the interfaces to the outside world are important, but the outside world itself is not covered. Hence, party-level architectures are intra-organizational architectures.
3 *System-level architectures* describe the structure of individual systems of an individual e-business party. An individual system is typically a functional component in a party-level system that supports a specific business function (as identified in the O aspect of the BOAT framework).

Market-level architectures can be refined[2] into party-level architectures, which can be refined into system-level architectures. The other way around, system-level architectures can be aggregated into party-level architectures, which can be aggregated into market-level architectures. We show both relations in Figure 6.3. The number of party-level architectures related to one market-level architecture depends on the number of parties in an e-business scenario (we show two in the figure for reasons of simplicity). The number of system-level architectures related to one party-level architecture depends on the number of e-business systems used by the corresponding party (we again show two in the figure for reasons of simplicity). The number of systems depends on the complexity of the functionality supported by the party and the functionality offered by the systems: the more complex the functionality supported by a party, the more systems, the greater the functionality of the systems implies fewer of them.

The abstraction dimension

Information system architectures (and hence e-business architectures) can be described at various levels of *abstraction*: we can describe an architecture in very abstract terms, but also in very concrete terms – and in between. The various abstraction levels are positioned along the abstraction dimension.

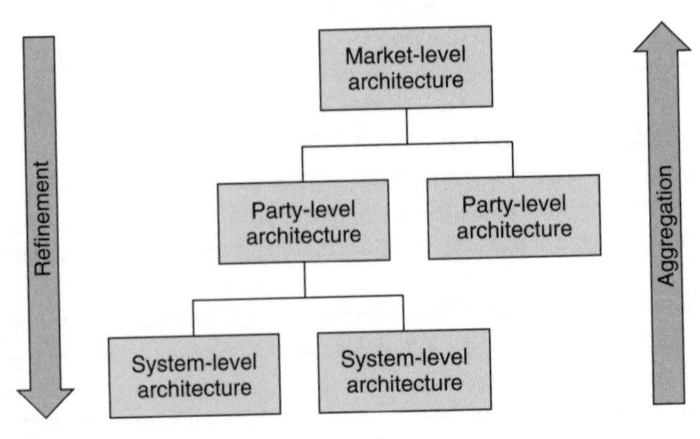

Figure 6.3 e-Business architecture aggregation levels

If an architecture is described in abstract terms, the components in the architecture are specified very generally, typically by only labeling their functionality (or class of functionality). A label may be for example *e-payment system* or *enterprise resource planning system*. If an architecture is described in very concrete terms, the components are described very precisely, typically by labeling the functionality plus the exact type of the component in terms of software vendor and software version. A concrete label is for example *XPay E-Payment Server Version 3.14a*.

In the rest of this chapter, we will see that we use abstract architectures to show general structuring principles for e-business systems, i.e., principles that are applicable in various scenarios. Here we find for example principles regarding the structure of systems relating to the inter-organizational nature of e-business or the fact that e-business systems must be flexible in their functionality. We use concrete architectures to show the structures of e-business systems in specific e-business scenarios. We discuss concrete architectures for example in the context of our two running cases POSH and TTU.

Aggregation versus abstraction

Where the aggregation level of an architecture is about the number of components in the system described (the 'size' or scope of the system), the abstraction level is about the number of attributes of the components (the concreteness of description) in the architecture. In principle, the abstraction level and aggregation level can be chosen independently for an architecture description.

6.3.3 Reference, standard and instance architectures

When talking about information system architectures – and hence about e-business architectures – it is good to distinguish between various kinds of architecture, depending on their origin and goal. There are three kinds of information system architecture in this respect that one can distinguish:

1 An *instance architecture* is the architecture of one specific information system in one specific context, in other words a specific instance of a type of system. An example is the architecture of the e-business system of one specific organization. An instance architecture is not explicitly designed to contain structures that can be reused in multiple contexts.
2 A *standard architecture* is an architecture that is defined as a standard for a class of information systems within a specific organization context. This specific context is typically a large company or a consortium of companies. A standard architecture may be defined for instance for all procurement systems within a holding of companies. As such, a standard architecture can be used as the basis for the definition of an instance architecture of a specific system within its class and within the organization context of the standard architecture.

3 A *reference architecture* is an architecture that is defined as a standard for a class of systems across organizations, i.e., without having an organizational context. An example is a reference architecture for business process management systems in general (we discuss an example in Section 7.4.2). A reference architecture is often defined by an independent party, such as a standardization body or a government organization. A reference architecture can be used as a basis to define a standard architecture, or to directly define an instance architecture. A reference architecture can also be the basis for other reference architectures (where the other reference architectures are typically more elaborated).

The three architecture kinds and their relationships are shown in Figure 6.4. The arrows indicate the 'can be based on' relationship between architectures.

A reference architecture is more abstract than a standard architecture, as a standard architecture contains organization-specific choices. A standard architecture is more abstract than an instance architecture, as an instance architecture contains specific choices for the one situation it is designed for. Hence, the three architecture kinds can be positioned along the abstraction dimension that we have discussed earlier in this section.

As interoperability between systems plays a very important role in e-business, reference and standard architectures are of great importance in this domain. The use of standardized architecture structures is a basis for ensuring that systems based on these architectures will 'fit together', i.e., that they will be able to communicate and collaborate in automated processes.

Now we have completed our discussion of the basics of architecture in this section, it is time to move on to actual e-business architectures in the next section.

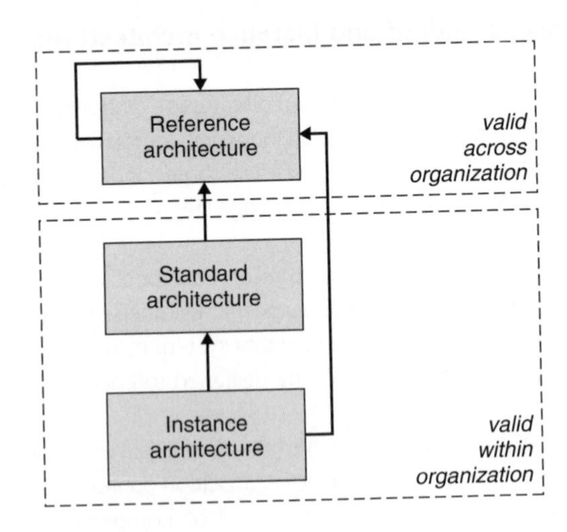

Figure 6.4 Reference, standard and instance architecture

6.4 MARKET-LEVEL ARCHITECTURES

In this section, we discuss the highest aggregation level of e-business system architectures: market-level architectures. We first discuss the concept of market-level architecture. Next, we explain the structure of such an architecture. Then, we pay attention to the role of reference and standard architectures at the market level.

6.4.1 The concept of market-level architecture

A market-level architecture describes how the main software systems of the participating organizations interact in an e-business scenario. We use the following definition (a specialization of the general definition of information system architecture discussed in the previous section):

> The market-level architecture of an e-business system defines the structure of that system at the inter-organizational level in terms of functional software components supporting specific functions of all involved business parties and high-level interfaces supporting the interactions among those components.

There are several words in this definition that deserve some further explanation. A market-level architecture has an *inter-organizational* character. This means that a market-level architecture describes the information systems of all partners participating in an e-business scenario, not of a single partner. As we have seen in the previous chapter about the O aspect of BOAT, often this means two main parties are complemented with a number of intermediary parties. But of course, multi-party scenarios are possible too. In a market-level architecture, the emphasis is on support for collaboration between the parties. A market-level architecture contains *functional software components*, i.e., software systems that support specific business functions. It also contains *high-level interfaces*, i.e., the links between these software modules. The emphasis is on interfaces between software components belonging to different parties, as these implement the collaboration between the parties (i.e., the market-level interactions).

6.4.2 The structure of market-level architectures

After having discussed the concept of a market-level architecture, it is time to turn to its structure. As a market-level architecture describes the interactions between the systems of all parties involved in an e-business scenario, its overall structure is determined by the topology of these parties (the business network) collaborating in the e-business scenario. Typically, there is a strong congruence (structural similarity) between high-level models in the O aspect of BOAT and market-level architectures in the A aspect, as both contain interactions between the same business networks of organizations: the O aspect contains interactions between organizations, the A aspect interactions between systems of those organizations.

Figure 6.5 shows an example market-level architecture. Here, the abstract system architecture has been elaborated, of an e-business scenario consisting of two collaborating parties (party A to the left and party B to the right) and one intermediary party (party I in the bottom of the figure). The shaded areas in the figure indicate the party boundaries. We will show more concrete architectures at the end of this chapter when discussing our running case studies.

Obviously, the party topology depends on the business scenario: there may be more than two collaborating parties, no intermediary at all, or multiple intermediaries. A market-level architecture with many parties can get quite complex. Note that we typically model *party types*: if there are many similar parties in a scenario, we show them as one type in an architecture. In a retailing scenario, for example, there is typically one provider (the selling party) and a large number of consumers (the buying parties). The party type is instantiated multiple times when realizing a market-level e-business system conforming to the architecture.

A market-level architecture focuses on the relations *between* the involved parties, showing the systems and interfaces between the parties implementing these relations. In the figure, the systems are the boxes, the interfaces the arrows between the parties.

The interfaces are labeled with the types of messages they are meant to exchange (labeled *m1* to *m6* in the figure), for example *purchase order, reservation confirmation* or *payment*. We will see more elaborated examples when we get to our running cases at the end of this chapter. Note that an interface often exchanges more than one message type (for a bidirectional interface usually at least two). Therefore, each

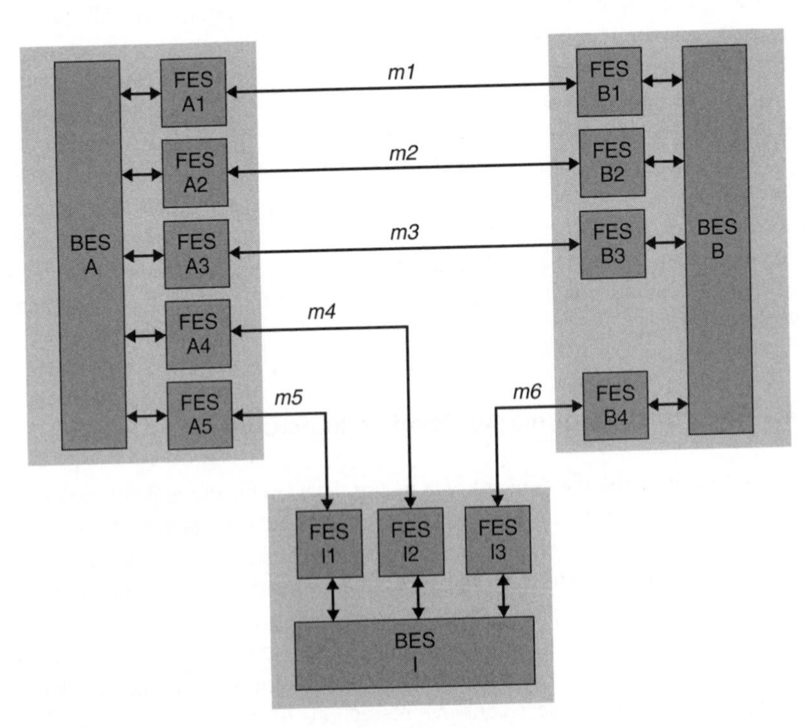

Figure 6.5 An example abstract market-level architecture

message label represents a set of message types. The interfaces to the back end systems are elaborated in the party-level architectures, as discussed in the next section.

With respect to the systems in the example architecture, we clearly see the separation between front-end systems (labeled *FES* in the figure) and back-end systems (labeled *BES* in the figure) at all three parties. This separation is analogous to the separation between front-end and back-end functions in the O aspect (as discussed in Section 5.3.1).

The front-end systems support front-end business functions, like purchasing, reserving or paying. As the interaction between systems of collaborating parties is modeled in a market-level architecture, the front-end systems are individually identified. Note that there is not necessarily a one-to-one mapping between front-end business functions in the O aspect and front-end systems in the A aspect: one system may support multiple functions, or one function may require multiple systems. Note also that multi-channeling between two parties may have an impact on the architecture: each channel may result in a pair of front-end systems with an interface.

Back-end systems are shown as black boxes (without internal details), as their internal structure is not relevant for system interfaces at the market level. The back-end systems are elaborated in party-level architectures.

Note that it is possible to abstract a market-level architecture by aggregating all systems of a party into one composed system. If we do this for the example in Figure 6.5, we get the architecture shown in Figure 6.6. This aggregated architecture corresponds in level of aggregation with the level 2 organization architecture as shown in Figure 5.3. The architecture showing the individual front end systems of the parties is, however, much more informative about the interfaces between systems – which is the basis for support for e-business interaction. Hence, we skip the aggregated market-level architecture in our approach.

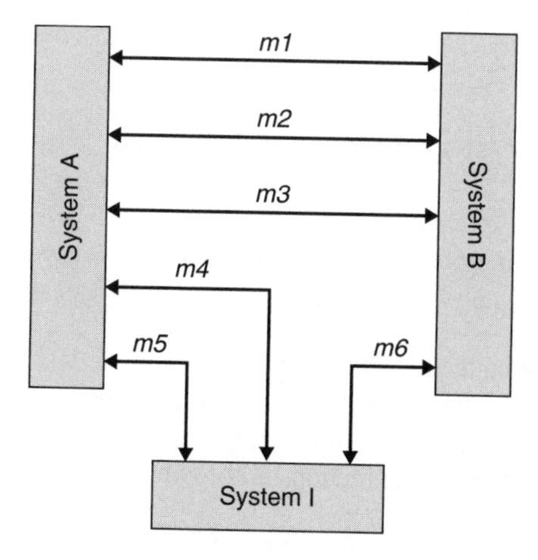

Figure 6.6 Example aggregated abstract market-level architecture

6.4.3 Market-level reference and standard architectures

In market-level architectures, the interoperability of e-business systems of multiple autonomous parties is a major issue – if not *the* major issue. Hence, standardization of the functionality of components in an architecture is very important: this way, other parties know 'what to expect' when contacting an e-business system of another party. Obviously, standardization of the interfaces is equally important, as they actually implement this contacting. Reference architectures (and standard architectures in smaller scopes) can be used to obtain standardization across parties.

As e-business scenarios can be classified, it can be expected that there will be similarity in architectures for scenarios within the same class. Classification can for instance be performed on the basis of the business model of the scenario (as defined in the B aspect of the BOAT framework – see Chapter 4). For example, party-level architectures for e-retailing will all have similarities as they require support for a number of standard business functions (as identified in the O aspect of BOAT – see Chapter 5).

In the architecture aspect of BOAT, reference architectures should be technology-independent: one should first focus on *what* functionality must be included, and only later on how this functionality is actually realized in specific technology.

Many 'reference architectures' that currently exist for e-business interaction, however, are technology-specific. In other words: they do not focus on the general, conceptual interaction of e-business systems in terms of abstract functionality, but focus on describing the structure of a specific technological solution to e-business interaction. Therefore, this kind of architecture belongs in the technology (T) aspect of the BOAT framework. In Chapter 7 we will see examples from this class: ebXML and RosettaNet.

6.5 PARTY-LEVEL ARCHITECTURES

In the previous section, we discussed market-level architectures. In this section, we take one step down the aggregation hierarchy and discuss party-level architectures.

6.5.1 The concept of party-level architecture

A party-level architecture describes the system structure of one single party (possibly an intermediary) in an e-business scenario. We use the following definition (again a specialization of the general definition of architecture discussed in Section 6.3.1):

> The party-level architecture of an e-business system defines the structure of that system at the intra-organizational level in terms of functional software components supporting specific functions of one business party and high-level interfaces supporting the interactions among these components.

Where a market-level architecture is inter-organizational, a party-level architecture is intra-organizational. As such, a party-level architecture is a refinement of a part of a market-level architecture: the part that coincides with one party. This implies that a complete elaboration of a market-level architecture leads to more than one party-level architecture, i.e., one per party involved in the e-business scenario (as shown in Figure 6.3). All party-level architectures together form a partitioning of the refinement of a market-level architecture.

In a party-level architecture, we provide more details than in a market-level architecture:

- we detail the back-end systems (which are black boxes in the market-level architecture);
- we show interfaces between back-end systems;
- we detail the interfaces between front-end systems and back-end systems;
- we show main platform systems that are shared between systems, such as database management systems (including the main shared databases), workflow management systems, or middleware.

6.5.2 The structure of party-level architectures

In Figure 6.7, we see an example of an abstract party-level architecture (we will see a concrete example when we get to our running cases at the end of this chapter). This architecture is the refinement for party A of the market-level architecture shown in Figure 6.5. In the figure, the boundary of party A is indicated by the shaded area.

In the party-level architecture, we show the same front-end systems as in the corresponding market-level architecture for the party at hand (*FES A1* to *FES A5* in the example). We show the other parties of the market-level architecture as *external entities*, depicted by rounded rectangles and dashed interfaces, corresponding to the market-level architecture. Note that the message labels are consistent with the market-level architecture. The rest of the party-level architecture is an elaboration of the black-box back-end system in the market-level architecture of the party at hand.

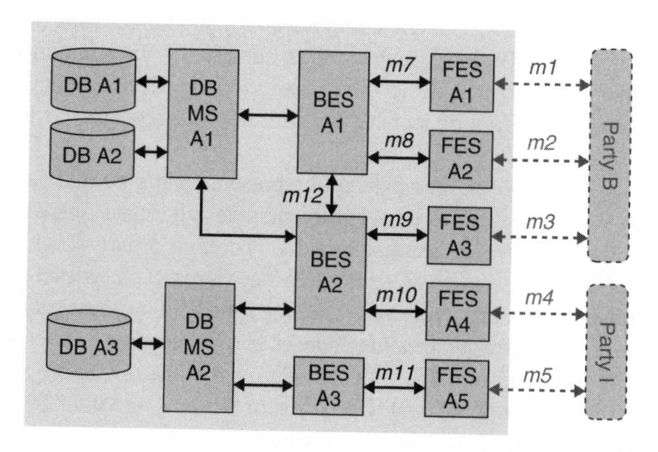

Figure 6.7 An example party-level architecture

In the example, we show three back-end systems (*BES A1* to *BES A3*) and two database management systems (*DBMS A1* and *DBMS A2)*. The back-end systems support the back-end business processes of the party, such as financial administration, product management and inventory management. The database management systems manage the data for the back-end systems (in databases *DB A1* to *DB A3*).

The interfaces between front-end systems and back-end systems on the one hand and between back-end systems on the other hand are labeled with the message types (which can be sets of message-types, as in the market-level architecture).

6.5.3 Party-level reference and standard architectures

As for market-level architectures, reference (and standard) architectures are also important for party-level architectures. At the party level, reference architectures provide standard solutions for the high-level organization of complex e-business systems within one party.

The use of standard solutions implies reusing existing knowledge to prevent reinventing the wheel over and over again. As such, the use of reference and standard architectures can decrease both the realization time of e-business systems and the costs of this realization. Also, the number of flaws in an architecture design is often reduced, as reference architectures present 'proven solutions'.

Another important advantage of the use of reference architectures is the easy adaptation of available standard software components. Obviously, when following standards, the likelihood of a 'match' is greater than when using complete greenfield designs.

6.5.4 Party-level architectures and enterprise architectures

An *enterprise architecture* (also called *corporate architecture*) is an overall blueprint of the structure of all main information systems in an organization. In other words, an enterprise architecture specifies the complete information processing infrastructure of an organization. e-Business architectures specify the information processing infrastructure related to a specific e-business scenario. Consequently, there is a relation between the corporate architecture and the e-business architecture(s) of an e-business organization.

Each party-level e-business architecture represents one e-business scenario. An organization may, however, be involved in multiple e-business scenarios (and in multiple traditional business scenarios as well). Therefore, a party-level architecture is a subset of an enterprise architecture. In other words: a party-level architecture is an enterprise architecture projected onto one specific e-business scenario.

Typically, if a business organization engages in multiple e-business scenarios, the different party-level architectures within overlap within the enterprise architecture, i.e., they share common functionality in terms of systems and interfaces identified in the architectures. This is illustrated in Figure 6.8 for an organization that engages in three e-business scenarios.

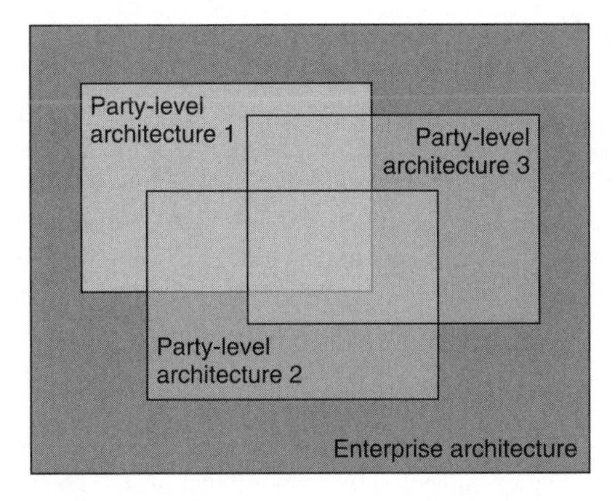

Figure 6.8 Party-level architectures in the context of an enterprise architecture

6.6 SYSTEM-LEVEL ARCHITECTURES

After the discussion of party-level architectures in the previous section, we now move one level further down the architecture aggregation dimension and arrive at system-level architectures. A *system-level architecture* is a refinement of one component in a party-level architecture as discussed in the previous section. Below, we discuss the concept and structure of system-level architectures. We end the section by also discussing the role of reference architectures and standard architectures at this architecture aggregation level.

6.6.1 The concept of system-level architecture

A system-level architecture describes the system structure of one specific e-business information system of one party (possibly an intermediary) in an e-business scenario. We use the following definition (like the previous definitions, a specialization of the general definition of information system architecture discussed in Section 6.3.1):

> The system-level architecture of an e-business system defines the structure of one specific information system in terms of functional software components supporting specific subfunctions of a business function of a business party and interfaces supporting the interactions among those components.

Obviously, a system-level architecture is intra-organizational, as it is a refinement of an intra-organizational architecture. A system-level architecture can be the specification of the structure of either a front-end system or a back-end system identified in a party-level architecture.

6.6.2 The structure of system-level architectures

The structure of a system-level architecture heavily depends on the nature of the system that is specified. Architectures of simple systems consist of a few components, those of complex systems may consist of many components.

Figure 6.9 shows an example of an abstract system-level architecture (we will see a concrete example when we get to the running cases at the end of the chapter). The architecture is the elaboration of system *BES A1* from the party-level architecture shown in Figure 6.7 (the boundaries of this system are shown by the shaded area in the figure). The system-level architecture shows that *BES A1* consists internally of four modules, labeled *BES A1.1* to *BES A1.4*.

As the figure shows, systems with which the system at hand communicates are shown as external entities, indicated by rounded rectangles. The interfaces to these systems must be consistent with those specified in the corresponding party-level architecture. Interfaces between the components of the system at hand are specified and labeled with message sets (*m13* to *m15* in the example).

6.6.3 System-level reference and standard architectures

At the system level of e-business architectures, reference and standard architectures play an important role as well, as they do at the party and market levels. At the system level, they define blueprints of structures of individual e-business systems.

Reference architectures define system structures that are generally applicable, i.e., the application of which is not confined to a single organization. Having standardized structures is of great importance to enable interoperability between systems, certainly where systems are located at different, autonomous parties. Reference architectures define standardized interfaces to standardized functional modules. Reference architectures exist for specific classes of systems, such as workflow management

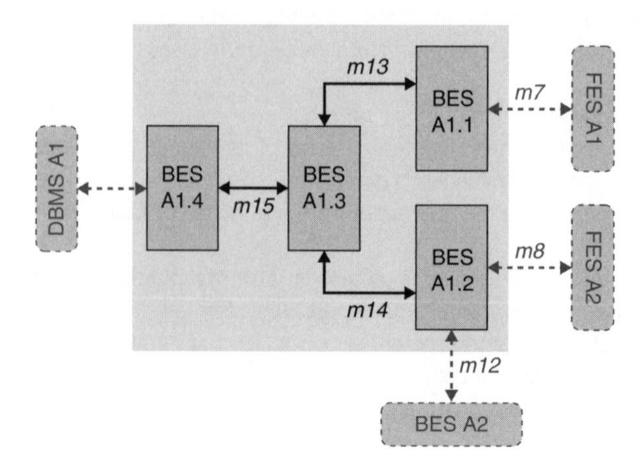

Figure 6.9 An example system-level architecture

systems (Workflow Management Coalition 1994) or electronic contracting systems (Angelov and Grefen 2008).

Standard architectures have a similar function within the scope of an organization. Consequently, they are less important for enabling inter-organizational interoperability. They are important, however, for standardizing structures in large organizations, which may have many instantiations of the same system type.

6.7 MAPPING O ELEMENTS TO A ELEMENTS

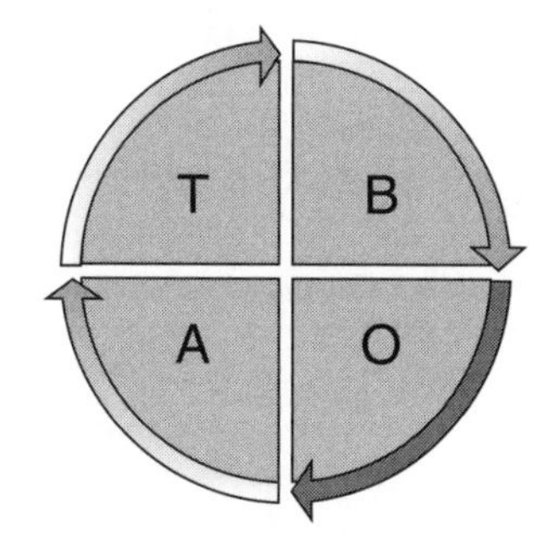

As we have seen in this chapter, high-level architectures in the BOAT A aspect have structural similarities with organization structures in the O aspect. Obviously, this is not a coincidence: there is a mapping between O aspect elements and A aspect elements. In this section, we discuss two principles that guide this mapping.

6.7.1 The form is function principle

For e-business, a close alignment of business requirements and information systems is essential. This close alignment can be obtained by striving for isomorphism between organization structures (as defined in the O aspect) and information system structures (as defined in the A aspect). This is expressed by the *form is function principle* (Grefen 2003): the structure of an architecture should follow the business functionality it is designed for. Important elements identified in the O aspect should also be visible in the A aspect, and the way they are organized with respect to each other in both aspects must have a clear mapping.

In the simplest case, there is a one-to-one mapping between high-level descriptions in O and A aspects: each module in the O level corresponds to a module in the A aspect. Often, however, reality is a bit more complex than this. Take for example the situation illustrated in Figure 6.10. At the left, we see the level 4 organization structure of an e-business party *A* (analogous to Figure 5.5; the other parties are omitted for reasons of clarity). At the right, we see part of a market-level architecture showing the same organization *A* (analogous to Figure 6.5; other parties again omitted). The number of front-end organization modules (four) is different from the number of front-end architecture modules (five), so obviously, there cannot be a one-to-one mapping.

Explicitly describing the mapping in a concrete situation is strongly advised, as this will make high-level dependencies explicit when changes occur. The description can have the format of a mapping matrix, an example of which is shown below for the mapping of Figure 6.10. The matrix specifies which O aspect module relies on which A aspect module for its automated support.

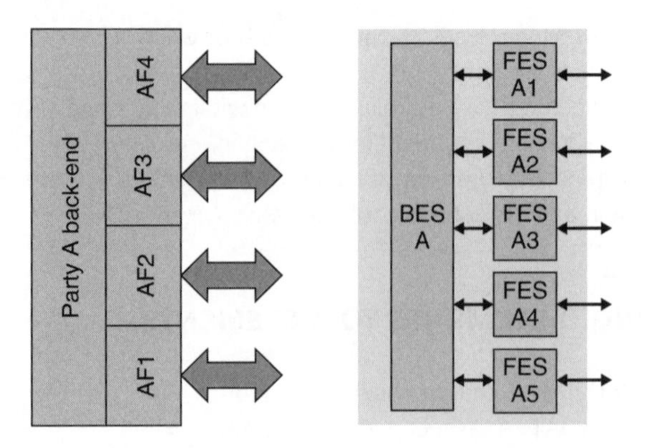

Figure 6.10 O aspect structure (left) versus A aspect structure (right)

Table 6.1 O to A aspect mapping matrix

		A aspect modules				
		FES A1	*FES A2*	*FES A3*	*FES A4*	*FES A5*
O aspect modules	*AF1*	X				
	AF2		X			X
	AF3			X		
	AF4				X	X

6.7.2 Modular design of information systems

In complex architectures (like those of most e-business systems), a strictly modular design greatly enhances the maintainability of the architecture. Modularity implies that an architecture is partitioned into functional modules, each of which plays a specific role in the architecture as a whole. This partitioning can be based on the partitioning of the organizational functions of an organization – following the *form is function principle* as discussed above. Note that functions in an organization are often relatively stable, whereas their interconnection changes more quickly as business models evolve. Maintainability relates to a number of issues that are of high importance for e-business systems.

First of all, e-business systems (and thus their architectures) are subject to frequent change as a consequence of the volatile market they have to operate in – remember that in e-business, change is the only constant factor. A modular architecture design means that it is possible to replace (or add or delete) specific modules in the architecture, while leaving other modules as they are. This greatly enhances the level to which a system is 'future-proof'.

Second, most e-business systems are of considerable complexity. This means that it is usually not feasible to build such a system from scratch. Where possible, one should rely on existing modules where they are available on the market (so-called *common off-the-shelf* (COTS) components) and only build new modules where functionality is so specific (or new), that ready-made solutions are not available. This is often referred to as the 'make-or-buy decision'. Nowadays, this question is more and more answered with 'buy', where bought modules are parameterized (tuned) for the context in which they have to operate. To be able to flexibly deal with the make-or-buy decision, a modular architecture is required, where modules are identified based on the high-level (O aspect) business functions they perform.

6.8 RUNNING CASES

In this section, we return again to our two running case studies and discuss their architecture aspect. For reasons of brevity, we do not elaborate the POSH and TTU architectures in full detail (that would require a substantial number of pages). Instead, we show a number of architectures at the three aggregation levels to illustrate the concepts discussed before in this chapter.

6.8.1 POSH

Below, we first discuss the market-level architecture of the POSH scenario. Then, we elaborate the party-level architecture of POSH – we omit the party-level architectures of the other parties. Of this party-level architecture, we further elaborate one module into a system-level architecture.

Market-level architecture

The market-level architecture of the POSH scenario is shown in Figure 6.11. We see again the three parties in the scenario, plus three intermediaries (organization boundaries are indicated by background boxes). We have shown the customer party at the left-hand side of the figure and POSH at the right-hand side of the figure to be consistent with the organization structure diagram in Figure 5.23. We show the architecture of one customer. Obviously, not all customers have exactly the same information system configuration, but compatibility with the architecture is required to enable coupling of systems.

Because the architecture shows the structure of the information systems that support POSH's business organization, there is a structural similarity with the structure of the organization (as discussed in the previous chapter and shown in Figure 5.23). This is a consequence of following the *form is function* design principle that we discussed earlier in this chapter. We can see though that the mapping is not one-to-one: there are systems in the architecture that support multiple organizational modules, both at the POSH and the customer side. For example, the *order management* system at POSH supports both the *take order* and *bill* functions identified in the organization aspect.

The architecture in Figure 6.11 shows the message sets (labeled *m1* through *m10*) that the parties use to communicate. They can be specified in a table like the one below. Note again that a message set can contain more than one type of message

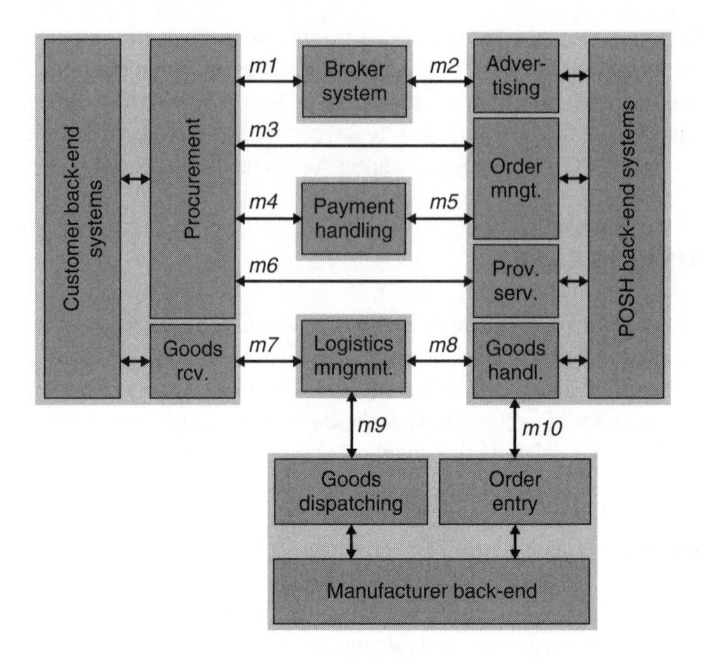

Figure 6.11 POSH scenario market-level architecture

Table 6.2 Message sets of POSH market architecture

Message set	*Contents exchanged*
m1	Provider search request, Provider search result
m2	Provider profile, Provider offer
m3	Order, Order confirmation
m4	Payment order
m5	Payment notification
m6	Service request, Service information
m7	Delivery notification, Delivery confirmation
m8	Shipment request, Shipment confirmation
m9	Shipment request, Shipment confirmation
m10	Production order, Production confirmation

(as shown in the table). Each message type can be annotated with originator and recipient for additional clarity (this explains in which direction a message type flows along an arrow in the architecture diagram) – we have omitted this here for reasons of simplicity.

Party-level architecture

The party-level architecture of POSH is shown in Figure 6.12. We see the same front-end modules and the same interfaces to external parties as in the market-level

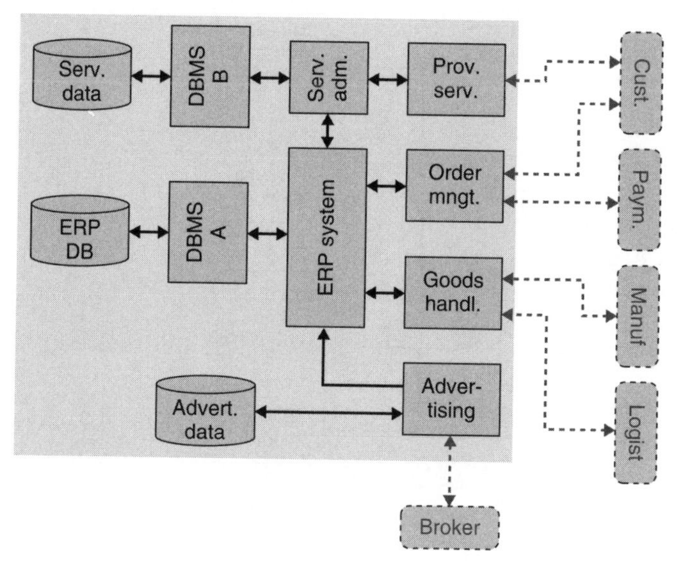

Figure 6.12 POSH party-level architecture

architecture (this should always be consistent). The modules are shown in a different layout order to make the resulting architecture diagram clearer. For reasons of brevity, we have omitted the specification of message sets in the architecture.

The back-end systems module of the market-level architecture has been elaborated to show its internal structure. We see that POSH uses an enterprise resource planning (ERP) system as the core of its back-end administration. The administration of providing furniture-related services is supported by a dedicated system. Both systems use a database management system (DBMS) for their data management. The *advertising* front-end module uses data it retrieves from the ERP system – apart from that it has a dedicated data set in a number of files (there is no DBMS employed here as the data set is relatively simple and small).

System-level architecture

In Figure 6.13, we show the system-level architecture of the *order management* front-end system of the POSH party-level architecture (see Figure 6.12). The shaded background denotes the system boundaries. As the *order management* system is a front-end system, there are interfaces to external parties and interfaces to other systems internal to POSH. These interfaces are consistent with those in the party-level architecture. We have again omitted the specification of message sets.

As we can see in the figure, the *order management* system consists of four modules: one that allows customers to use POSH's electronic catalog and select items to buy, one that manages electronic shopping carts in which customers collect selected goods, one that performs the actual order handling, and one that handles billing to

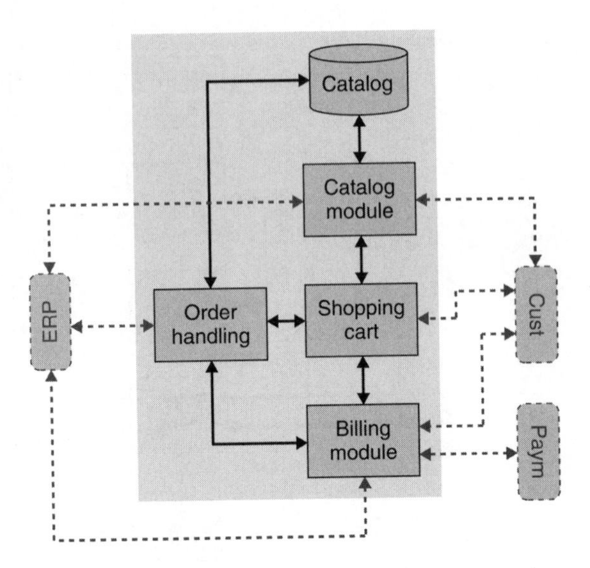

Figure 6.13 System-level architecture of POSH order management system

customers. Three modules interact with POSH's ERP system, in which stocks are registered and deliveries are planned.

6.8.2 TTU

Below, we discuss the market-level architecture of TTU. We leave party-level and system-level architectures to the reader. After the discussion of the architecture, we spend a few words on reference architectures in the TTU context.

Market-level architecture

Figure 6.14 shows the market-level architecture of the TTU scenario. We see two elaborated parties: TTU on the right-hand side and a customer on the left-hand side. The architectures of the four intermediaries in the scenario have not been elaborated for reasons of simplicity.

We can see that the architecture consists of two 'parts' (as indicated by the horizontal dotted line). The part shown at the top of the figure supports the administrative processes: marketing, sales and billing. The part shown at the bottom of the figure supports the actual primary services of TTU: translation and interpretation. We concentrate on the latter part in the explanation below – the former part is comparable to the POSH scenario.

The back-end systems of TTU include functionality to support the translation of documents. Documents (both electronic and physical) are passed between TTU and customer through the *document handling* front-end system at TTU and the *mail*

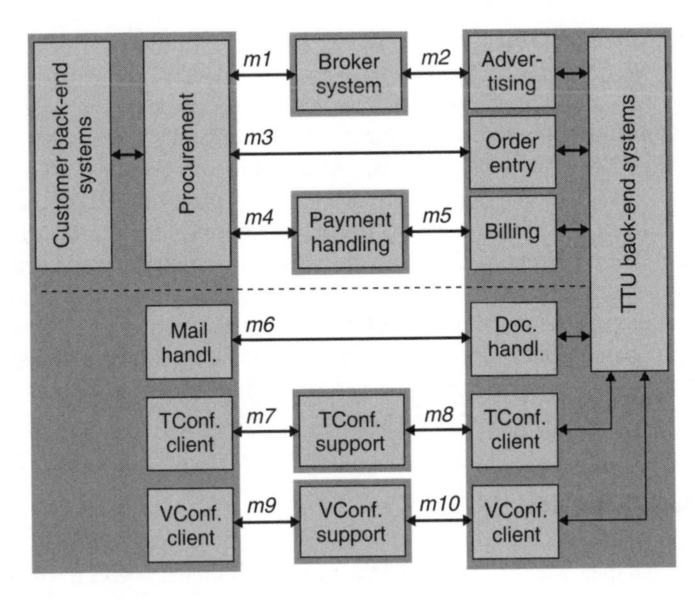

Figure 6.14 TTU scenario market-level architecture

handling front-end system at the customer. The *mail handling* system has a connection to the back-end systems at the customer to register the receipt of documents (just like the receipt of other ordered goods). Telephone (*TConf.*) and video (*VConf.*) conferences are supported by intermediaries. Both parties have clients to the server systems of these intermediaries. The clients at TTU are coupled to back-end systems to start and register conferences – as this is core business for TTU, they need a proper coupling to back-end systems. At the customer side, these clients are stand-alone systems – dealing with conferences is not core business here.

The architecture in Figure 6.14 shows the message sets (labeled *m1* through *m10*) that the parties use to communicate. They are specified in Table 6.3. Message flow directions have been omitted from the table for reasons of brevity.

Table 6.3 Message sets of TTU market architecture

Message set	*Contents exchanged*
m1	Provider search request, Provider search result
m2	Provider profile, Provider offer
m3	Order, Order confirmation
m4	Payment order
m5	Payment notification
m6	Document to translate, Translated document
m7	Teleconference details, Teleconference contents
m8	Teleconference details, Teleconference contents
m9	Videoconference details, Videoconference contents
m10	Videoconference details, Videoconference contents

Reference architectures

TTU supports audio and video conferences across a spectrum of platforms, ranging from traditional telephone conferencing systems via broadly used communication platforms like Skype[3] to advanced telepresence platforms and dedicated meeting support systems. Currently, the interfaces to these platforms are not very well standardized. For TTU, it is important to couple these platforms to their back-end systems, so that conferences can be set up or joined automatically and activities in conferences can be registered automatically (for billing afterwards). Also, cross-platform interoperability is important to be able to link heterogeneous servers and clients into one conference, or even to couple multiple conferences. Development of reference architectures in this field is hence of prime interest to TTU to avoid an 'explosion' of different software structures and interfaces.

6.9 CHAPTER END

We end the chapter with a summary of the most important concepts of this chapter and a set of questions and exercises.

6.9.1 Chapter summary

Architectures of e-business systems are required to manage the complexity and efficient developments of these systems. Architecture has a pivotal function between business and organization aspects on the one hand and technology aspects on the other hand.

Architectures can be positioned along the aggregation and the abstraction dimensions. The position along the aggregation dimension determines the 'granularity' of the architecture (the size or scope of its components). The position along the abstraction dimension determines the concreteness with which components in the architecture are specified.

The architecture of an e-business information system defines the structure of that system in terms of functional software components supporting specific functions and interfaces supporting the interactions among those components. We identify three aggregation levels for e-business architectures:

1 *market-level architectures* describe the structure of e-business systems at the level of collaboration between multiple parties in an e-business scenario;
2 *party-level architectures* describe the structure of e-business systems within the boundaries of a single party;
3 *system-level architectures* describe the internal structure of individual e-business systems.

Party-level architectures are projections of enterprise architectures, as they describe the structure of the information systems supporting a single e-business scenario in which an organization (enterprise) participates.

Reference architectures describe proven system structures that can be reused across organizations. Standard architectures describe system structures that are reused within a single organization. Instance architectures describe structures of concrete systems. Instance architectures can be based on standard or reference architectures. Standard architectures can be based on reference architectures.

6.9.2 Questions and exercises

1 Specify the message sets for the party-level and system-level architectures of the POSH scenario (as shown in Figure 6.12 and Figure 6.13). Use the format shown in Table 6.2.
2 The market-level architecture of the TTU e-business scenario is shown in Figure 6.14. Design a party-level architecture for TTU based on this market-level architecture. Discuss your major design choices.
3 Design a system-level architecture for the TTU *order entry* system. Use the TTU e-sales process shown in Figure 5.25 as input for your design, as this process is supported by the *order entry* system.
4 Select a real-world B2C e-business scenario and try to describe its market-level architecture. Make assumptions (educated guesses) where you cannot trace required details.
5 Select a real-world B2B e-business scenario and try to describe its market-level architecture. Make assumptions (educated guesses) where you cannot trace required details.
6 Does a system-level reference architecture for database management systems exist? Use the Internet to try and find one.

7

Technology aspect

Learning goals

By the end of the chapter you should:

- Know the various classes of information technology used in e-business systems and understand their relationships to each other;
- Understand basic Internet and Web technologies, as well as important advanced platform technologies for e-business;
- Understand the main classes of aspect-oriented technology for e-business;
- Understand the main classes of function-oriented technology for e-business;
- Be able to map architecture aspect elements (as discussed in Chapter 6) and business aspect elements (as discussed in Chapter 4) to technology aspect elements.

7.1 INTRODUCTION

In this chapter, we discuss the fourth aspect of the BOAT framework: the technology (T) aspect. In the technology aspect, we discuss how specific information technologies are used to implement the information systems specified in the architecture (A) aspect (as discussed in the previous chapter).

In this chapter, we start with the 'bare basics' of e-business technology: Internet and Web technology. After having covered that, we distinguish between three classes of advanced technology. First, we discuss *advanced infrastructure technology*, i.e., information technology used to create a general, high-level basis (also called *platform*) for entire e-business information systems. Apart from infrastructure technology, there is more specific information technology. This technology can be subdivided into two classes. First, we have technology related to specific aspects of all (or most) business functions – we call this class *aspect-oriented technology*. Second, we have technology related to all (or most) aspects of specific business functions – we call this class *function-oriented technology*. The three technology classes are shown with their relations in Table 7.1.

Table 7.1 e-Business technology classes

		Functions	
		All	Specific
Aspects	All	*infrastructure technology*	*function-oriented technology*
	Specific	*aspect-oriented technology*	*not covered*

We discuss the three technology classes in Sections 7.3 to 7.5. In the two sections that follow, we pay attention to mapping issues between BOAT aspects: first to mapping from the A to the T aspect, then to mapping from the T to the B aspect.[1] The chapter is – as usual in this book – concluded with a summary and exercise questions.

Note that this chapter focuses on technology that is of special relevance for e-business information systems. Clearly, most technology for information systems in general is also applicable to e-business systems. We do not discuss general software engineering technology in this chapter, such as object-oriented technology (including CORBA, Java Beans, and so on). Many technologies come (and sometimes go) – see for example Gartner's hype cycle report (Fenn and Linden 2005). It is not the purpose of this chapter to be complete, but rather to discuss the role of major technology classes in e-business. Other books are available that provide a more complete or more detailed description of e-business technologies (e.g. Whyte 2001, Nelson and Nelson 2002, Van Slyke and Bélanger 2003).

Note also that, although this chapter presents technology in various classes, one of the main challenges in the B aspect is the integration of multiple technology classes to arrive at 'seamless' e-business systems. A well-designed architecture (as discussed in the previous chapter) is an essential starting point to arrive at this integration.

7.2 THE BARE BASICS: INTERNET AND WEB TECHNOLOGY

Obviously, the communication infrastructure on which most modern e-business systems are based is the Internet and the Web as a layer on top of the Internet. As we have seen in Chapter 1, the history of e-business is even heavily related to the history of the Internet and the Web. Therefore, the Internet and Web form the technological 'bare basics' for modern e-business. Below, we briefly discuss the most important of Internet and Web technology to provide a basic understanding of this infrastructure.

7.2.1 The Internet

The Internet is the global network that forms the communication platform for most modern e-business scenarios. We have already seen a few words about its history in Section 1.3. The Internet consists of a connected network of networks – which explains its name – to which Internet hosts are connected. The operation of the Internet relies on a stack of protocols that specify how computers communicate using the Internet. The protocols are organized into four layers which make up the Internet Protocol Suite (see Figure 7.1): *Link Layer*, *Internet Layer*, *Transport Layer* and *Application Layer*. Below, we briefly discuss these four layers and the protocol suite. More details can be found in dedicated publications on Internetworking (for example, Stevens 1994, Comer 2005).

Link Layer protocols

The basic network structure underlying the Internet is defined using so-called *Link Layer protocols*. These protocols are defined for the operation of network links, i.e., network connections at a low-level, technical level.

Link Layer protocols support low-level communication functionalities. An important functionality is physically finding hosts on the Internet. This can be performed by means of the *Address Resolution Protocol* (ARP). Another important functionality is managing specific hardware networks. This is performed by means of protocols for specific network types, such as *Ethernet*.

Internet Layer protocols

The basis for Internet communication between Internet hosts is formed by the *Internet Protocol* (IP). The Internet Protocol is defined on top of the Link Layer protocols. IP sends data packets from one Internet host to another without the requirement of setting up a connection first between the hosts. Therefore, IP is a connection-less protocol to operate a packet-switching (inter)network.

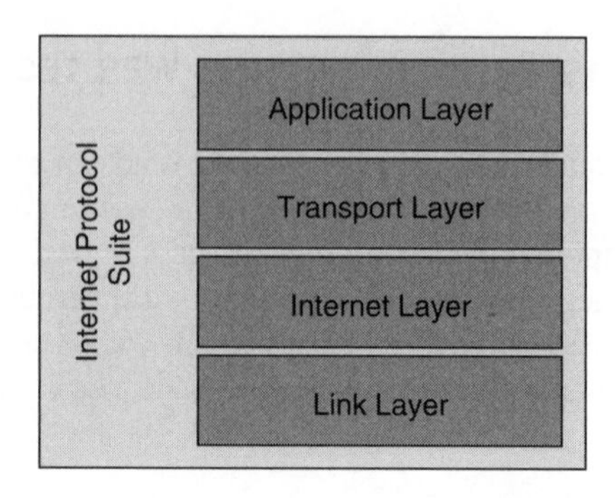

Figure 7.1 Internet Protocol Suite

The Internet Protocol uses the *Internet address* or *IP address* to identify a host. In IP Version 4 (IPv4), the IP address is a 32-bit number, typically shown as four numbers in the range 0 to 255 (called *octets* because they each consist of eight bits) with dots in between, for example 121.122.123.124. As the range of IPv4 addresses is getting too small to accommodate the growth of the Internet, IP Version 6 (IPv6) uses a 128-bit address (consisting of 16 octets).

Transport Layer protocols

On top of the Internet Protocol, the *Transmission Control Protocol* (TCP) is defined, forming the basis of the *Transport Layer* of the Internet. TCP provides reliable, ordered delivery of a stream of bytes from a program on one Internet host to another program on another Internet host. TCP controls a number of traffic-related issues, such as message size, message exchange rate and network congestion resolution.

The combination of TCP and IP is often referred to as TCP/IP, pronounced as 'TCP over IP' (Stevens 1994, Comer 2005). TCP/IP defines the basic communication mechanism for the Internet.

Application Layer protocols

More functionally specific protocols are defined on top of TCP/IP as *Application Layer protocols*. These protocols support specific classes of Internet applications.

Well-known examples of Application Layer protocols are the protocols for transmission of email messages, the most common of which are the *Simple Mail Transfer Protocol* (SMTP), the *Post Office Protocol* (POP) and the *Internet Message Access Protocol* (IMAP).

Protocols for getting the Web running (such as HTTP) are also Application Layer protocols based on TCP/IP, as we will see in the next subsection.

The Internet Protocol Suite

Together, the Link Layer protocols, Internet protocols, Transport protocols and Application protocols form the *Internet Protocol Suite* (as illustrated in Figure 7.1 and summarized in Table 7.2). Given this protocol suite, the Internet has a four-layer structure, which is also referred to as the *Internet Architecture*.

Table 7.2 Internet Protocol Suite structure

Protocol Suite Layer	*Function*	*Example protocols*
Application Layer	Internet applications	POP, MIME, HTTP
Transport Layer	Internet transport	TCP
Internet Layer	Internet packet switching	IPv4, IPv6
Link Layer	Network operation	ARP, Ethernet

7.2.2 The (World Wide) Web

The World Wide Web (WWW), or Web for short, is a communication infrastructure using the Internet as its underlying platform and *hypertext documents* as its basic information structuring paradigm. A hypertext document is basically a document containing local content (like text and figures) and *links* to other hypertext documents. The documents are commonly referred to as *Web pages*. The Web is navigated (or 'surfed') by following the links from Web page to Web page. Below, we first discuss *Web protocols*, which define communication in the Web. Next, we discuss the structure of *Web addresses* (URLs) that are used by the protocols. Then, we pay attention to *Web languages* that are used to specify the 'contents' of the Web. We end this subsection with a few words on the *Web 2.0* concept.

Web protocols

The *HyperText Transmission Protocol* (HTTP) is the basic protocol on which the Web is built. HTTP supports the transmission of hypertext documents over the Internet. HTTP is a request/response protocol, in which a *client* (for example a Web browser) requests the transmission of a Web page from a *server* (a Web server), which sends it as a response to the request. HTTP is defined as an application protocol on top of TCP/IP (see also Table 7.2).

The *HyperText Transmission Protocol Secure* (HTTPS) is a combination of HTTP with the SSL/TLS protocol to provide message encryption and secure identification of Web servers. HTTPS is commonly used for supporting transactions that require transfer of sensitive data, such as payment transactions.

Web addresses

Hypertext documents residing in the Web are uniquely identified by a *Uniform Resource Locator* (URL). A URL consists of an abstract domain address and an (optional) document address within a domain.

The domain address of a URL has a hierarchic structure showing the hierarchy of Web domains. Top-level domains are the last part of a domain address – they indicate countries (like *.nl* for the Netherlands) or global topical domains (like *.com* for commercial organizations or *.org* for noncommercial organizations). Topical domains can also be organized by country, in which case one finds a combination in the URL (like *.co.uk* for commercial organizations in the UK). Typically, organization names precede the top-level domain name in a URL. Before that, departments within organizations may be indicated, possibly with more than one level. A complete URL may thus look for example like one of these:

http://department.organization.country
http://subdepartment.department.organization.topicaldomain

A document address of a URL identifies a specific Web page within the context of a Web domain. It is specified after the domain address and can have a folder-like structure. As an example, the URL of the current home page of the author of this book is:

http://is.ieis.tue.nl/staff/pgrefen

The domain address of this URL follows the structure as explained above. The document address indicates that there is a Web page with the name *pgrefen* within a folder structure named *staff*. When Web pages are generated automatically, the document address may be a rather incomprehensible string to the casual observer. We see this for example with Web pages displaying search results of search engines or product catalogs.

The *http://* prefix is often omitted when mentioning URLs. When a URL starts with *https://*, the HTTPS protocol is used to access the Web page indicated by the address. The structure of a URL is summarized in Figure 7.2.

Web languages

Hypertext documents are mainly specified using the *HyperText Markup Language* (HTML). HTML is a tagged language for specifying the structure of pages of human-readable information. A tagged language is a language that uses tags (specific labels) to identify characteristics in a text – in HTML for example the start and end of headings. HTML is mainly used to specify the structure and links between Web pages. Using style sheets, the structure of a Web page can be mapped to a specific layout.

Following the idea of a tagged language, the *eXtensible Markup Language* (XML) is a general-purpose tagged language that can be used to define specific tagged languages for specific purposes. As such, an XML-based language can be designed, for example, to specify financial transactions or to specify purchase orders between e-business parties. HTML can be defined using XML as well. XML allows the definition of the grammar of specific tagged languages.

Semantic Web

The Web protocols, addresses and languages as discussed above are mainly concerned with the structure of the Web. Languages like HTML describe the

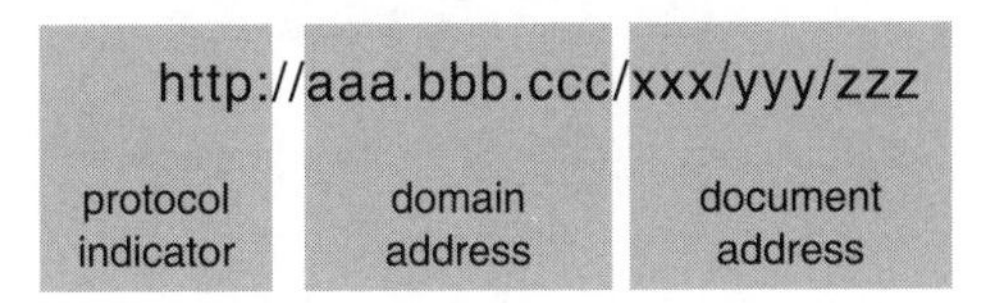

Figure 7.2 URL structure

structure of Web documents, i.e., the *syntax* of these documents. A development in Web technology is to also try describe the meaning of the contents of Web elements such as documents and messages, i.e., the semantics of Web elements. This development results in a so-called *semantic Web.*

Semantics are usually based on the use of ontologies. An ontology is a conceptual structure in which the meaning of concepts and the relations between concepts are specified, typically within a certain domain (for example, a business domain like banking or car manufacturing). Put very simply, an ontology is used as an 'extended dictionary' on the basis of which automated systems can interpret and reason about semantic messages. To achieve this, messages are 'annotated' with an identification of the ontology by means of which their contents can be interpreted. As an example, we have taken the market level architecture of Figure 6.5 and annotated the messages with ontologies. The figure shows that messages *M1*, *M2* and *M3* have to be interpreted with ontology *O1* and messages *M4*, *M5* and *M6* with ontology *O2.*

Languages have been developed for the specification of ontologies in the Web context, the best-known of which is the Web Ontology Language (OWL) (Wikipedia 2009f).

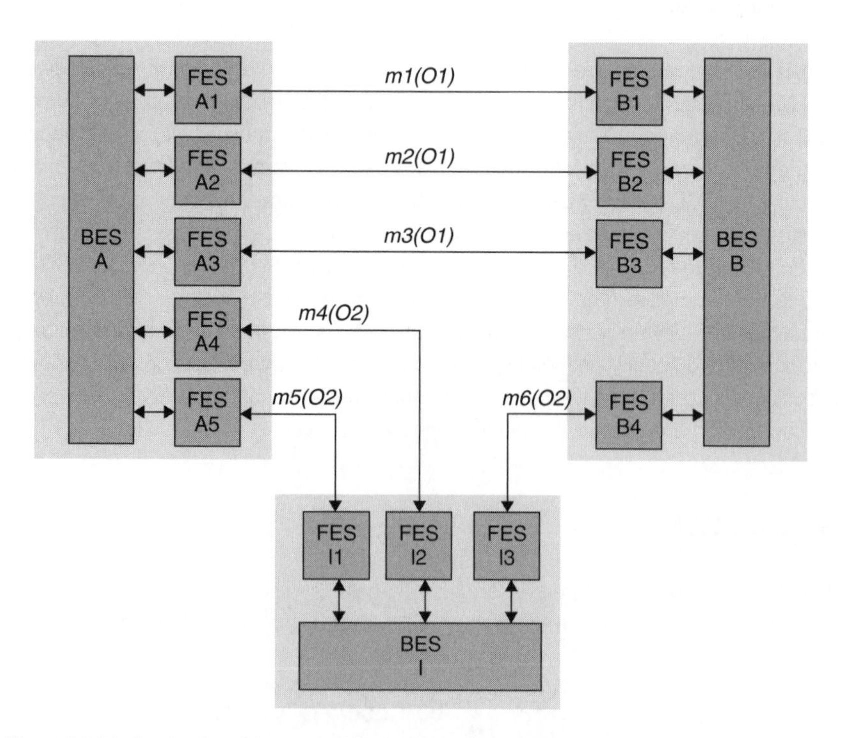

Figure 7.3 Market-level architecture with ontologically annotated messages

Web 2.0

A term that started to appear at the beginning of the twenty-first century is *Web 2.0* (Wikipedia 2009g). The term refers to 'the second generation of the Web'. Generally, this 'generation shift' is meant to indicate a change from the Web as a set of static interlinked Web pages to the Web as an integrated application platform for business and personal use, facilitated by a number of technological developments such as:

- application logic that is built into Web sites (instead of into programs that reside on local computers);
- advanced levels of interactivity of Web sites and Web-based applications, going beyond simple Web surfing (see for example Web-based communication applications);
- functional integration of Web sites and other information systems, making the Web more than merely interlinked local sites (for example enabled by Web Services, which we discuss in Section 7.3.3);
- advanced use of multi-media characteristics, going beyond the text-and-simple-graphics approach that the Web originally used to be; we find this for example in applications like YouTube[2] and Flickr[3] (shown in Figure 7.4).

Not everybody is convinced about the Web 2.0 concept, though. This is not because the developments mentioned by Web 2.0 enthusiasts are not considered important (there is little doubt about that), but because these developments can also

Figure 7.4 An example Web 2.0 application

be seen as a continuous evolution – so that there are no 'two versions' of the Web, but rather a continuum in time of new possibilities.

7.2.3 Some brief remarks

Two rather trivial but important remarks need to be made here to avoid confusion that is often encountered 'in practice':

- First, the Internet and the Web are not the same thing (although many use the terms in an interchangeable fashion). The Web is a hypertext-based information structure using the Internet as underlying communication technology. So, technically speaking, one cannot 'surf the Internet' like one 'surfs the Web'.
- Second, protocols and languages (for Internet or Web) are different things, although they are often intermixed. Protocols are used to specify *how* communication takes place, languages to specify *what* is communicated. In other words, put very simply: protocols are about transport, languages about content.

Now we have discussed the Internet and Web as the 'bare basic' technologies for e-business, we move on to more advanced technologies, starting with advanced infrastructure technology in the next section.

7.3 ADVANCED INFRASTRUCTURE TECHNOLOGY

e-Business infrastructure technology provides a broad, general-purpose software platform for the implementation of e-business systems. It usually provides two main elements:

- a technological context in which functional modules (as identified in the architecture aspect) can be implemented; this context is a software engineering context that provides predefined primitives that cater for basic e-business operations (at some abstraction level, depending on the kind of technology);
- a technological context facilitating the interoperability between functional modules; this context provides languages, protocols and mechanisms for exchanging information between software modules (where the abstraction level is again dependent on the specific kind of technology).

As infrastructural technology needs to provide quite a bit of functionality, it is of a medium to high level of complexity. To structure its functionality, the technology usually comes with a software architecture describing its structure. Note that an architecture of this kind may be easily mapped to an architecture in the A aspect of the BOAT framework if the infrastructure technology is structured at a high level of abstraction (i.e., close to business terms). The mapping may be harder in the case of lower-level infrastructure technology.

Below, we discuss four classes of well-known infrastructural technology: ebXML, RosettaNet, Web Services and multi-agent systems. For more detailed descriptions, the reader is referred to the material indicated in the reference list. Then we take a short look at hybrid platforms, which employ more than one class of infrastructural technology. Note that many infrastructural technologies at this level assume an 'underlying layer' (actually an infrastructure or platform too) of Internet technology.

7.3.1 ebXML

The ebXML standard provides a framework for the implementation of software that supports e-business processes over the Internet (OASIS 2006). As the name suggests, ebXML standards are based on XML. The ebXML development was initiated in 1999 by the standardization organization OASIS[4] and the United Nations/ECE agency CEFACT.

In the ebXML framework, parties that want to do business transactions with each other find each other through an ebXML registry (see Figure 7.5). This registry is an advanced form of electronic yellow pages server. As such, it supports an intermediary that provides for dynamism in e-business relations (this contributes to extending reach – see Section 4.2).

As shown on the left side of Figure 7.5, business following the ebXML framework follows a number of steps. First, a process and information model is entered into an ebXML registry – this happens in the context of a specific industry group (related to a specific market). Based on this, companies operating in the market can register

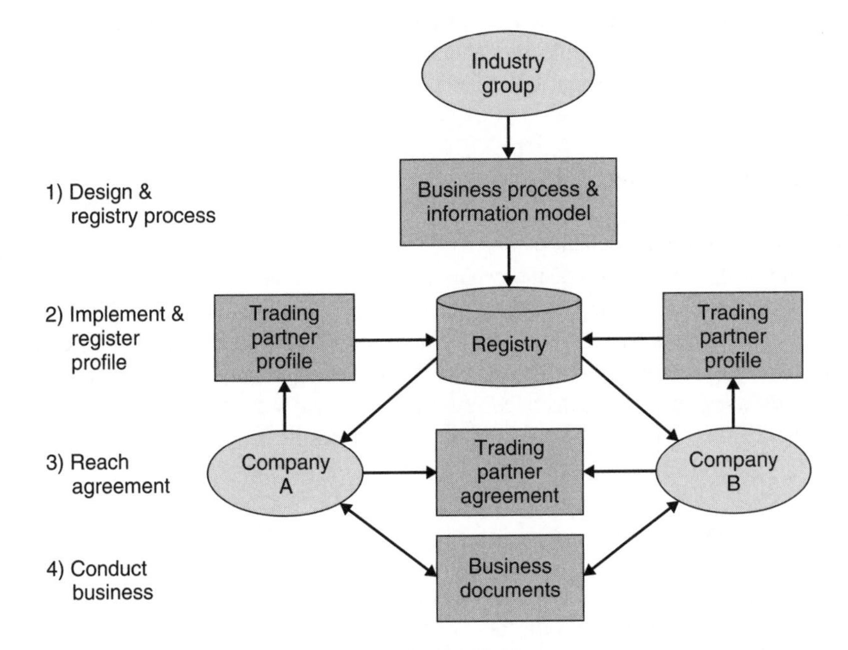

Figure 7.5 ebXML overview (adapted from OASIS 2006)

their trading partner profiles. Based on these profiles, companies can find interesting trading partners. Again based on their profiles, a trading partner agreement is specified, which defines the business relationship between the companies. The companies can next conduct actual business by exchanging business documents between their ebXML-compliant systems.

ebXML defines a high-level technological framework, in which business documents and interactions are standardized. To fully adapt to ebXML, organizations have to adopt this complete set of standard documents and interactions. This makes the investment to start using ebXML substantial – hence the high threshold for certain situations.

7.3.2 RosettaNet

RosettaNet[5] is a non-profit consortium of computer, electronics, telecommunications and logistics companies that has created a set of standards with the same name for the support of e-business processes.

RosettaNet standards define message guidelines, business process interfaces and system implementation frameworks that support business interactions between companies. RosettaNet standards are based on XML. As such, RosettaNet is comparable to the ebXML standard that we have discussed before.

In more detail, the aim of RosettaNet is to align the business processes of parties collaborating in supply chains (RosettaNet Program Office 2009). The alignment is implemented through the creation of so-called *Partner Interface Processes* (PIPs). PIPs define how two business processes that are each run by a different party are standardized and interfaced. A PIP includes all business logic, message flow, and message contents to enable the alignment of the two processes. The set in RosettaNet consists of about 100 PIPs.

7.3.3 Web Services

Web Services are the default platform of choice for new e-business applications at the end of the first decade of the twenty-first century. The Web Services framework specifies an Internet-based set of technology standards for loosely-coupled, distributed systems (Alonso et al. 2004, Papazoglou 2007). Below, we first introduce the Web Service concept. Next, we discuss the main standards making up the Web Services framework. Then, we place Web Services in the broader contexts of Service-Oriented Computing and Service-Oriented Architecture.

Web Service concept

The basic concept of the Web Services framework is a *Web Service*, which is an encapsulated piece of software functionality that can be invoked through a well-defined Web interface. It is encapsulated because only the interface is shown to the outside world – the implementation of the functionality shown in the interface remains invisible to the outside world. A service can itself invoke other services, so that complex services can be composed from simple services.

The main idea behind the Web Services approach is that of building complex functionality by composing modular functionalities in a loosely-coupled way using a ubiquitous communication infrastructure. A composition of Web Services is loosely coupled because these services can be dynamically linked to each other at run-time – this in contrast to 'traditional software' in which connections between modules are defined statically at build-time. The ubiquitous communication infrastructure is the Web. This enables coupling services within the boundaries of organizations, but also across these boundaries – obviously, the latter is of great importance for e-business.

In an e-business context, a Web Service typically implements a well-defined piece of business functionality. A Web Service may for instance implement an information service, an ordering functionality, or a payment service. By composing a number of these services, e-business systems can be constructed. In doing so, we are using a *Service-Oriented Architecture* way of structuring a system – we get back to this later.

Web Service standards

A number of standards exist that define the technical Web Services environment. We find standards for Web Service languages, Web Service protocols, and Web Service software functionality.

The basic language for the Web Services environment is XML, as discussed before as part of the Web basics (see Section 7.2.2). All other Web Service languages are defined in XML. The basic communication protocol is the *Simple Object Access Protocol* (SOAP), a protocol defined on top of HTTP that allows basic object access via the Web. Below, we give an overview of the most important standards defined on top of XML and SOAP.

There are two important languages in the Web Services environment. The central Web Service specification language is the *Web Service Description Language* (WSDL), which allows the specification of service interfaces. The *Business Process Execution Language* (BPEL or WS-BPEL) allows the specification of processes inside Web Services (we will revisit this language in Section 7.4.2).

A number of protocols exist in the Web Services environment that provide specifications for the interaction between Web Services to obtain specific characteristics of their overall behavior. The *Web Services Coordination* (WS-Coordination) specification provides an extensible framework for defining protocols that coordinate the actions of distributed service applications. Such coordination protocols are used for example to reach consistent agreement on the outcome of activities that are distributed over multiple services. The Web Services transaction protocols are built on top of WS-Coordination to provide transactional behavior to sets of Web Services. Two specific transaction protocols have been defined: *WS-AtomicTransaction* (WSAT) and *WS-BusinessActivity* (WSBA). WSAT provides a mechanism to implement atomic behavior over a set of services, i.e., to make sure that either all services in effect successfully complete or all services fail. WSBA provides a mechanism to compensate (in effect undo) parts of a business process implemented in services. *Web Services Agreement* (WS-Agreement) (OGF 2007) is a Web Services protocol for establishing agreement between two parties that want to engage in business. *Web Services Security* (WS-Security or WSS) is a protocol to apply security in a Web Services environment.

A standard for brokering is defined as *Universal Description, Discovery and Integration* (UDDI) (OASIS 2004), an XML-based standard for registries in which organizations can advertise their services or search services provided by other organizations. A UDDI registry can be accessed through SOAP and contains WSDL specifications of services offered.

An overview of the discussed standards is given in Figure 7.6. In the figure, we see the languages hierarchy in the left-hand column, the protocols hierarchy in the middle column and UDDI as a software specification in the right-hand column. The vertical dimension in this figure is an abstraction dimension. The standards at the bottom are lower-level and technology-oriented; those at the top are of a more abstract, application-oriented nature, using the standards below.

Service-Oriented Computing and Service-Oriented Architecture

The Web Service framework is the main basis for the *Service-Oriented Computing* (SOC) paradigm, which (as the name suggests) has its roots more in software engineering than business frameworks. Although the SOC paradigm is not per se coupled to the Web Services technology (services can be implemented in more traditional software technology), the combination is often made.

The fact that the Web Services stack is a rather open framework makes it easy to start using it for service-oriented computing: one does not need to adopt the entire framework for simple applications. In principle, the bottom two layers of Figure 7.6 suffice for very simple service-oriented applications. The implementation of full-blown e-business systems may, however, require the application of quite a number of standards from the framework – hence causing considerable complexity.

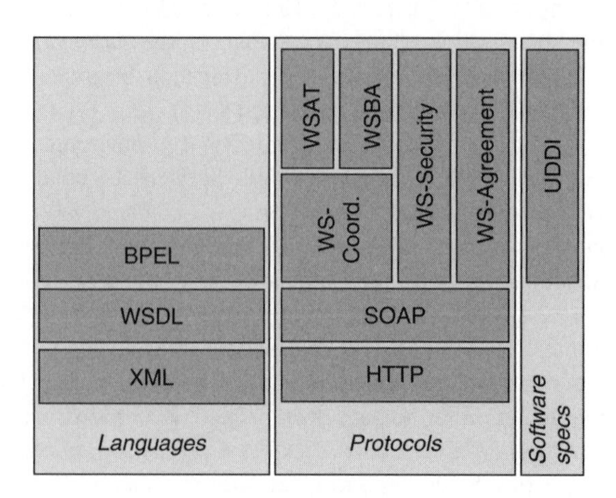

Figure 7.6 Overview of important Web Service standards

When we use the SOC paradigm as a basis for the architectural design of information systems, we speak of *Service-Oriented Architecture* (SOA). The SOC paradigm has been further elaborated into the *Grid Computing* paradigm. This paradigm uses services to implement networks of computing resources called *grids* to support large-scale distributed applications.

7.3.4 Multi-agent systems

A technology class that is currently mostly used for e-business in a research setting is the technology of multi-agent systems (MAS). In a multi-agent system, autonomous software modules (called *agents*) reason autonomously and communicate with their peers to achieve goals that have been given to them. In doing so, they do not merely react to commands given to them, but act on their own initiative to achieve their goals. As such, agents are autonomous, goal-oriented, pro-active software components.

The goal-oriented character of individual agents and the ability to communicate in agent communities makes them suitable for application in an e-business context (see e.g. Fasli 2007), for example to support automated negotiation (Fasli and Shehory 2007). In such a context, agents can represent parties that either collaborate or compete in specific markets to achieve the business goals of the parties they represent.

A popular application field for agents is that of electronic auctions (see for example Vetsikas and Jennings 2008, Dobriceanu *et al.* 2009). In these auctions, agents place bids following specific strategies. Agents have also been used for other purposes where goal-orientation and negotiation are important, such as the creation of virtual enterprises (Norman *et al.* 2004, Mehandjiev and Grefen 2010).

7.3.5 Hybrid platforms

In complex settings, the use of one infrastructure technology class may be too limited to build a complete e-business system. The use of multiple classes may be necessary for several reasons. One reason is that multiple computing paradigms are required in different parts of a system because these parts have different basic functionality requirements. Another reason is that various pre-existing (standard) modules are used as components in an e-business system and these modules require different platforms.

Below, we discuss an example hybrid platform that has been developed in the CrossWork research project.

The CrossWork hybrid platform

Figure 7.7 shows an example hybrid platform that has been used in the CrossWork project (Grefen *et al.* 2009, Mehandjiev and Grefen 2010) to support complex business processes in so-called *instant virtual enterprises* (IVEs). IVEs are highly dynamic virtual

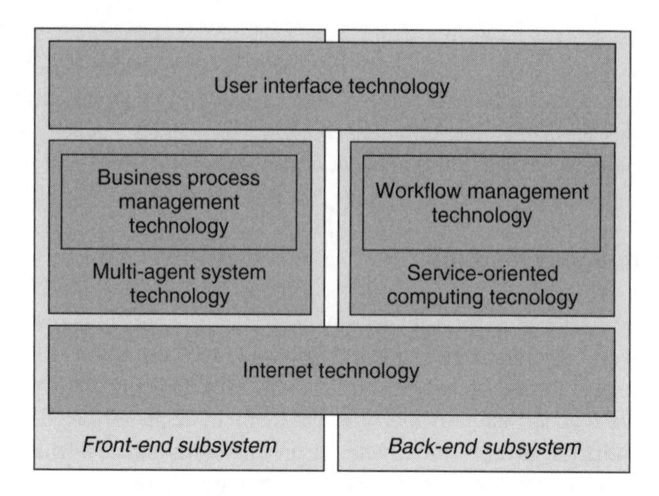

Figure 7.7 CrossWork hybrid platform

enterprises (see Section 4.6.3) in which organizations cooperate in a peer-to-peer fashion. In CrossWork, the IVE concept has been applied in the automotive industry to form business networks for the production of cars and trucks.

In the figure, we see at the bottom a basic Internet technology layer – as can be expected. On top of that, we see both a MAS and a SOC platform as advanced infrastructure layers. As shown in the figure, within the MAS and SOC platforms respectively, more specialized technology is embedded. Business process management (BPM) technology is embedded in the MAS platform to handle business process specifications. Workflow management (WFM) technology[6] is embedded in the SOC platform to execute business processes. To enable communication to human decision makers, a user interface (UI) platform has been added on top of the other technologies.

In the CrossWork project, the choice for a hybrid platform was made because one half of the system (the IVE construction part) requires goal-oriented reasoning technology, whereas the other half (the IVE execution part) requires technology that facilitates interoperability to COTS modules in a distributed topology.

7.4 ASPECT-ORIENTED TECHNOLOGY

As discussed in the introduction of this chapter, aspect-oriented information technology supports specific aspects of a range of business functions. Mostly, these aspects belong in the non-functional category: they do not relate to *what* functions do, but *how* they do it. Typical aspects are security, transactionality (Wang *et al.* 2008), performance and availability. As such, aspect-oriented technology can be related to a range of modules in the organization (O) and architecture (A) aspects – this in the sense that the technology supports specific characteristics defined for these modules.

In this section, we discuss the following classes of aspect-oriented technology (noting that this is not an exhaustive list):

- data management technology;
- process management technology;
- human communication technology;
- security technology;
- performance technology;
- mobility technology.

7.4.1 Data management technology

Clearly, data management is an important issue in electronic business systems – as in every business information system. Data management is usually supported by database management systems. In business applications, we typically find the type of *relational database management system* (RDBMS). This is no different for e-business applications. There are some points, however, where e-business applications differ from 'regular business' applications where it comes to data management: multi-media data plays an important role (for example in catalogs) and distributed transactions should be supported by database systems. We discuss these points below. To start with, we briefly discuss database management systems in general as a basis.

Database management systems

Most corporate database management systems are of the client/server kind.[7] This means that they consist of a *database server* and a number of *database clients* (as shown in Figure 7.8). The database server provides data management services to the clients: it holds the actual data and performs operations on the data, such as

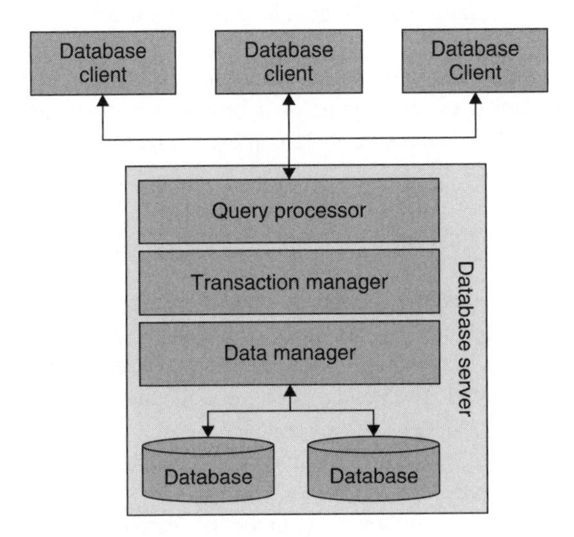

Figure 7.8 Simplified client/server DBMS architecture

queries and update transactions. It is designed to serve many clients simultaneously – in large organizations, this number can be in the range of thousands. Clients can be interactive interfaces for human users or information systems that require data management functionality.

The database server consists of three main software modules (we have simplified things here a bit for reasons of clarity):

1 The *query processor* takes commands (queries and updates) from the clients and transforms them into a format that can be easily processed by the other modules. Processing typically includes *query translation* and *query optimization*. Translation is required to transform a query in an external language to the language used internally in the database server – in this way, multiple external languages can be used. Query optimization is required to transform queries from a specification that is client-friendly to a specification that is execution-efficient – in this way, clients do not have to be aware of the efficiency of data management mechanisms in the server.
2 The *transaction manager* is responsible for the enforcement of correct transaction semantics. Among other things, this means that the *atomicity* and *isolation* of transactions must be managed. Atomicity means that a transaction consisting of multiple commands must be executed as a whole – we discuss this further below. Isolation means that each transaction should be executed without interference by other transactions. This is necessary because in a client/server environment, many concurrent transactions may be accessing and modifying the same data.
3 The *data manager* performs the actual operations on the databases, such as the retrieval of query results, the insertion of new data, and the modification or deletion of existing data. The data manager can manage one or more databases – in the figure, we show two databases as an example. In performing database operations, the data manager uses auxiliary data structures called *indexes*, which enable efficient access to specific data in large databases.

As stated above, e-business systems use database management systems to a large extent in a way similar to other types of information systems. Some aspects do require special attention in the e-business context though – we discuss these below.

Multi-media data

As e-business applications often contain extensive electronic catalogs, there can be demand for the management of large sets of multi-media data (like photographs, audio files, video files). This requires data management technology that is suited for this purpose. This technology should meet several requirements:

1 a large storage space for the data – in terms of the architecture in Figure 7.8, this means large databases;
2 the ability to find data fast based on a number of search criteria – this means that the data manager module requires indexes that can deal with multi-media data;

3 the ability to output large volumes of data fast – this means that the data manager must be high-performing, but also that there must be a fast client/server connection.

Requirement 3 is important to handle peak loads, which may appear frequent in e-business scenarios. A typical example is an online music store that sells music in MP3 format. The release of a new song (or album) of a popular artist will create a very high peak load. For this purpose, Internet data caching schemes exist, as well as organizations that exploit these on a commercial basis for third parties (we discuss an example when we get to performance technology in Section 7.4.5).

Distributed transactions

In e-business, business transactions are conducted over the Internet. These transactions are distributed, as they involve multiple autonomous parties. Although they are distributed, they should be reliable in their effects. For example, when it comes to transferring money, it should be guaranteed that both a debit action for one party at one system and a credit action for the other party at another system are successfully completed – or neither of them. In this case, *atomicity* of the transaction is required to make sure that no money evaporates (debit action succeeds but credit action fails) or appears out of the blue (debit action fails but credit action succeeds). To support this, we require distributed transaction processing (DTP) on top of data management. This means that the transaction manager of one database server must be able to synchronize with the transaction manager of another server.

We have already seen that the Web Services context provides transaction protocols (WSAT and WSBA, see Section 7.3.2) that cater for distributed transactions. Database management systems used in Web Services should offer primitives supporting these transactions. An example standard for this purpose is the *X/Open XA protocol* (Wikipedia 2009h) for distributed transaction processing.

7.4.2 Process management technology

In Chapter 5, we have seen that business processes are a key element in the operationalization of e-business models. To obtain required levels of efficiency, the execution of these processes must be supported by automated systems. Business process management systems or workflow management systems are specifically designed to support business processes (Leymann and Roller 1999).

Business process management systems

In Figure 7.9, we see a high-level architecture of a business process (workflow) management system (Workflow Management Coalition 1994). This is the reference architecture designed by the Workflow Management Coalition, a standardization body in the field of business process management. The core of the architecture is a *workflow enactment service*, consisting of a set of *workflow engines*. The workflow engines interpret workflow specifications (elaborated business process models as discussed in Chapter 5) and activate agents according to these models. Agents can be human users or automated applications. The workflow enactment service communicates with its environment using a *workflow application programming interface* and a set of *interchange formats*. There are five interfaces defined to the workflow enactment service:

- *Interface 1* is the interface to *process definition tools*. These tools are usually graphical editors used to specify a business process. After their definition, the process specifications are fed to the workflow enactment service to be enacted (executed).
- *Interface 2* is used to invoke *workflow client applications*. Workflow client applications are used by human users in an organization to access the tasks that the workflow enactment service has assigned to them and to perform these tasks. These applications resemble email clients, however, the user does not receive email to read but tasks to perform.
- *Interface 3* is used to invoke automated *applications* that perform tasks in a business process. These applications may run completely automatically, or may be interactive and have interfaces to human users.
- *Interface 4* is the interface to *other workflow enactment services*. These services may be employed by the same organization or by a different organization. Using IF4, a process enacted by one enactment service can invoke a process enacted by another service.
- *Interface 5* is the interface to *administration and management tools*. These tools are used by a workflow administrator (WFA) to keep the workflow enactment services running smoothly and dependable.

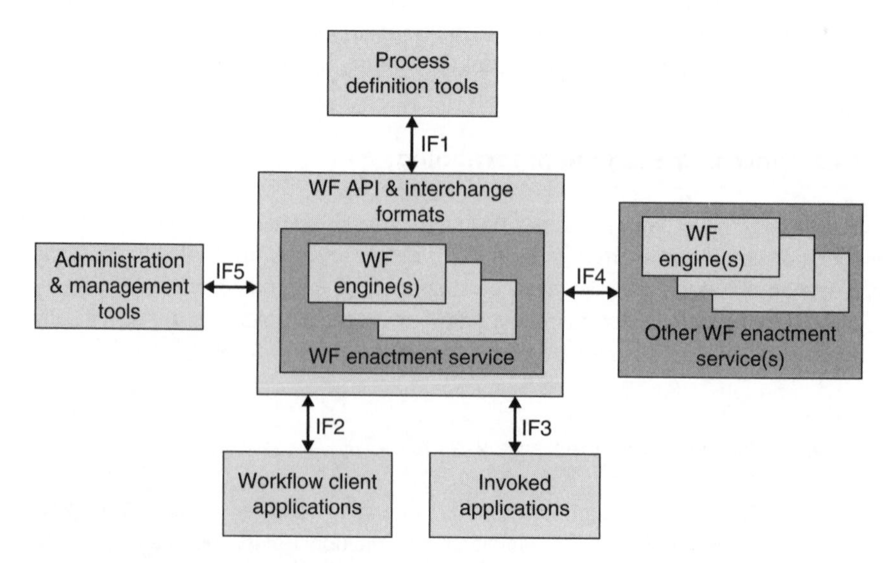

Figure 7.9 WfMC reference architecture (Workflow Management Coalition 1994)

Inter-organizational business process management

In Section 5.5.3, we discussed the difference between unilateral, bilateral and multilateral process flow control. For unilateral flow control, the execution of a business process uses IF2 and IF3. In case of an inter-organizational business process, the workflow clients or invoked applications may reside in another organization. A workflow client may be completely Web-based, such that only basic Web technology (see Section 7.2.2) is required at a collaborating party: the workflow client is completely represented as dynamically generated Web pages. This is certainly essential in highly dynamic e-business scenarios or B2C scenarios – it makes sense in neither case to install dedicated workflow clients for collaboration. For bilateral and multilateral flow control, IF4 is used. In this case, workflow enactment services of two or more organizations need to synchronize to enact an inter-organizational business process.

Advanced forms of inter-organizational business process management have been studied in research (but not yet widely applied in practice). Examples are the WISE, CrossFlow and CrossWork projects. The WISE project aimed at providing a software platform for process-based business-to-business electronic commerce in networks of small and medium enterprises (Alonso *et al.* 1999, Lazcano *et al.* 2001). The CrossFlow project (Grefen *et al.* 2000, Hoffner *et al.* 2001) has developed prototype support for the business process management in dynamic service outsourcing business scenarios (see Section 4.5.4) to form dynamic virtual enterprises (see Section 4.6.3). The CrossWork project (Grefen *et al.* 2009, Mehandjiev and Grefen 2010) has developed support for dynamic partnering scenarios (see Section 4.5.2) for dynamic virtual enterprises.

Business process management and Web technology

We have mentioned above how Web technology can be used for the realization of workflow clients. Currently, we see that business process management technology is further converging with Web technology. Web Service technology plays an important role in this convergence. A major element in this development is the emergence of business process engines that enact business processes specified in BPEL (as discussed with Web Services in Section 7.3.3). In process management, these engines take the role of the workflow engine in Figure 7.9.

As an example, the CrossWork project mentioned before has used BPEL as the basis for the enactment of inter-organizational business processes. This is the main reason for having service-oriented computing technology as a platform in the CrossWork back-end subsystem (see Figure 7.7): this platform supports a BPEL engine that is used to execute inter-organizational business processes in a virtual enterprise. An inter-organizational business process consists of interlinked intra-organizational business processes which are supported by 'traditional' workflow management technology.

7.4.3 Human communication technology

Although many e-business scenarios rely on high levels of automation (with the completely automated business as an extreme – see Section 4.4.5), human communication may be required structurally or as a means to handle exceptional situations. For this purpose, digital communication technology can be integrated into e-business systems to allow human communication over digital channels (usually, the Internet).

We can distinguish the following main types of communication technology, based on the media supported:

- *Offline text communication technology* provides the means to send text messages (often with file attachments containing other media) from one person to another in an offline fashion, i.e., without the necessity of sender and recipient being online at the same moment in time. Email is the most prominent example in this class. Technology that interfaces to cell phone texting also belongs in this class.
- *Online text communication technology* allows two (or more) individuals to exchange text messages in an interactive, session-based way (often augmented with the possibility of exchanging files containing other media in the same session). Chat technology such as provided by various messenger services is the most prominent example in this class.
- *Audio communication technology* provides the facilities to have a direct audio connection between two persons over the Internet – very much like a traditional phone call. A well-known provider of this technology is Skype.[9]
- *Video communication technology* is like audio communication technology, but also provides a bidirectional video link. Obviously, communication bandwidth is an important factor in the realization of video links. Simple forms of this technology are based on Web cams, more advanced forms on video conferencing systems.
- *Telepresence technology* is a technology that provides communicating parties the experience of 'being present' at the same location (Wikipedia 2009e). This technology relies on high-end audio and video technology – typically using advanced set-ups of multiple video cameras, screens, microphones and speakers installed in dedicated telepresence locations. As such, telepresence is the 'next step' after video conferencing. The current costs of telepresence equipment are such that it is typically applicable to high-end B2B communication only.

Much of the above technology is Internet-based nowadays (in the past, communication infrastructures like ISDN were used for audio and video communication). We can observe a shift to Web-based applications, thus removing the need for dedicated communication software at local sites (see also the discussion of Web 2.0 in Section 7.2.2).

7.4.4 Security technology

Security is a major issue in e-business for more than one reason. Obviously, one important reason is the fact that financial transactions are conducted in e-business.

A second important reason is the fact that in e-business, an organization's information systems are opened to the outside world (the front-end systems, as discussed in Chapter 6). A third important reason is the fact that sensitive information is exchanged in e-business, which may be information with privacy concerns or information with a competitive value.

We discuss two kinds of technology here. First, *user identification technology* is used to identify persons (or automated systems) in order to give them access to specific systems or specific functions of systems. Using such technology, registered customers can for instance be identified in e-retailing scenarios. Second, *cryptography* technology (Katz and Lindell 2007) is used to provide certain security aspects in transmitting electronic information (documents) between collaborating business parties.

User identification technology

In all business information systems, user identification is an important aspect to make sure that only the right people get access to systems and that the right people have the right access to specific functions or data. In e-business settings, access to systems is per definition important, as e-business systems are open to the outside world (remember our definition of e-business) and to a group of users that changes over time (both human users and external information systems).

The traditional method for user identification is having the user enter his or her User Identification (UID) and password. This method relies on semi-static data only, i.e., the access codes remain the same for relative long periods of time (depending on the password renewal strategy of the user and the system). It is therefore only safe if the user manages to keep the password perfectly hidden and if the transferred UID and password cannot be intercepted by third parties. For the latter reason, they are typically transmitted in encrypted form (we will see below how this works).

Key cards are a hardware means for user identification. A key card can have an embedded chip or magnetic strip containing the user data. If a key card is used without further identification, the loss of a card poses great security risks. Therefore, the use of the card can be coupled to a Personal Identification Number (PIN) that the user has to enter when using the card.

Hardware password generators are used for example in e-banking. These systems typically have a slot for a banking card containing a chip with user data and dynamically generate a password on the basis of a PIN and an input code supplied by the e-banking system. The fact that passwords are generated dynamically makes them usable once only – therefore, eavesdropping to obtain passwords is useless.

Biometric user identification is a relatively new technology where it comes to widespread practical application. It relies on detecting specific body characteristics of a user, typically by means of a fingerprint scan or an iris scan. It is not yet commonly used in e-business though.

Secure message exchange and cryptography

When exchanging messages in e-business, these messages should be exchanged in a secure way. Depending on the nature of a message, a number of security characteristics in exchanging electronic documents are important:

- *confidentiality* means that the message is only readable by the sender and the intended receiver;
- *integrity* means that the message cannot be changed during transport from sender to receiver by a third party without the intended receiver noticing;
- *authentication* means that the identity of the sender of a message is assured to the receiver by the message;
- *non-repudiation* means that the sending of a received message is 'undeniable' by the sender in case of a dispute between sender and receiver.

To obtain these characteristics, *cryptography* is typically used. Cryptography relies on the use of *keys* and *encryption* and *decryption algorithms*. Keys are (large) numbers that are used in mathematical algorithms to transform one piece of information into another. Two basic forms of cryptography can be distinguished: *symmetric cryptography* and *asymmetric cryptography*.

Symmetric cryptography

Symmetric cryptography relies on a single secret key that must be available to two business partners that wish to exchange messages in a secure way, as illustrated in Figure 7.10. The sending party uses the key to encrypt a message into an encoded message. The original message is readable and referred to as *cleartext* message. The encoded message is unreadable and referred to as *ciphertext* message. The receiving party uses the same key to decrypt the encoded message into the original message.

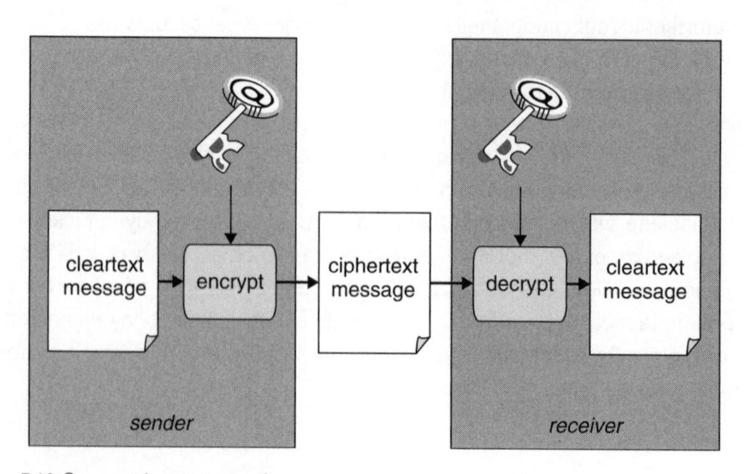

Figure 7.10 Symmetric cryptography

The encryption algorithm is such that it is virtually impossible to decrypt the message without knowing the key. In principle, one could try all possible keys, but by choosing keys that are large enough, the number of possible keys becomes so large that this is practically infeasible.

Symmetric cryptography ensures confidentiality and integrity of a message. Authentication is supported to a limited extent, as a ciphertext message can only be produced by a party that has access to the secret key (but by any party with access). Non-repudiation is not supported, as a receiver can construct a ciphertext message itself and claim that it was sent by a specific sender.

Although symmetric cryptography is safe, it has one great disadvantage: both parties need to have access to the same secret key. Obviously, it is not wise to exchange this key electronically in an unsecured message. It is not possible to exchange it in a secured message as there is no shared key available yet. Hence, keys are typically exchanged in a physical way for symmetric cryptography, for instance on a person-to-person basis. This may be acceptable for long-standing business relationships, but not for dynamic e-business relationships (compare the *time scopes* dimension discussed in Section 2.5). Asymmetric cryptography does not have this problem, at the expense of some additional complexity – we discuss this below.

Asymmetric cryptography

Asymmetric cryptography uses a combination of a public key that can be exchanged freely between business parties and a private (secret) key that remains with one party. The cryptographic algorithms are such that a message that is encrypted with one key can only be decrypted with the corresponding 'sister' key.

Figure 7.11 shows the usage of asymmetric cryptography. The sender retrieves the public key of the receiver (which is publicly available), uses it to encrypt the

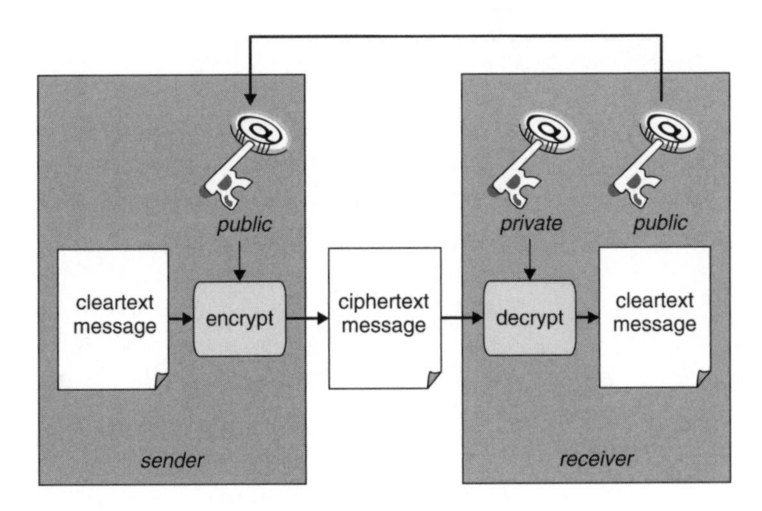

Figure 7.11 Asymmetric cryptography (protocol 1)

cleartext message and sends the obtained ciphertext message to the receiver. The receiver is the only party that has the private key that corresponds to its own public key, so it is the only party that can decrypt the ciphertext message.

The protocol of Figure 7.11 guarantees confidentiality and integrity of the sent message. Authentication and non-repudiation are not guaranteed, however, as anybody can retrieve the public key of the receiver and construct a ciphertext message. To guarantee these latter two characteristics, the keys are used in a 'reverse' protocol (as shown in Figure 7.12): the sender uses its private key to encrypt the message and the receiver retrieves the sender's public key to decrypt it. A message that can be decrypted with the sender's public key must have been encrypted with its private key, so it is guaranteed that the sender actually sent the message and the sender can never deny having sent it (as it is the only party who could have encrypted the message).

To ensure all four message security characteristics, a double encryption protocol is used that is the combination of those shown in Figure 7.11 and Figure 7.12.

Asymmetric cryptography technology is the basis for *public key infrastructure* (PKI) technology (National Institute of Standards and Technology 1997, Weise 2001, Vacca 2004), which underlies many security schemes in modern e-business systems. A PKI is a combination of software and policies to manage electronic keys and certificates in order to obtain trust in electronic business environments. PKI is in general a broad topic that has been evolving to meet the requirements of e-business (Weise 2001).

7.4.5 Performance technology

Obviously, proper performance of e-business systems is of utmost importance to keep an e-business organization running. Given the often volatile nature of e-business

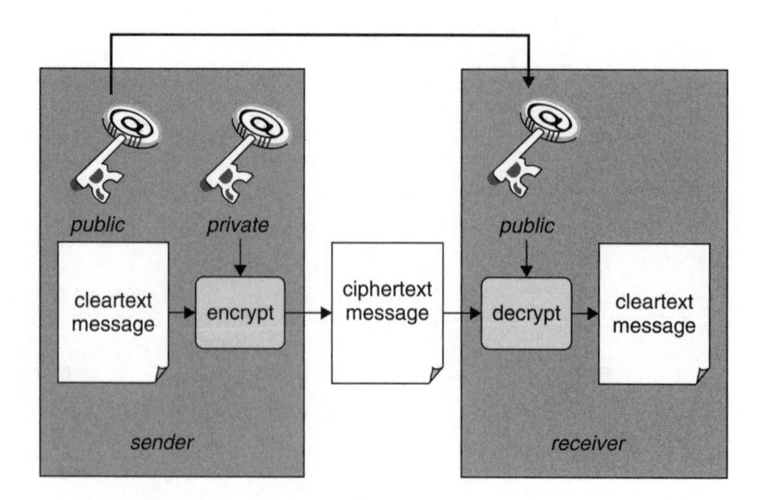

Figure 7.12 Asymmetric cryptography (protocol 2)

relations, poorly performing systems may cause collaboration parties (such as customers in e-retailing scenarios) to walk away quickly and look for a competitor that performs better. There are two aspects that we consider part of the performance aspect: *response time management* and *availability management.*

Response time management is concerned with guaranteeing that systems react quickly to user input. This is in general not an easy issue, as users expect almost instantaneous reaction and workload for e-business systems can fluctuate strongly. Various technologies are available for response time management, like technologies that cater for advanced load-balancing between e-business application servers, and technologies that perform distributed caching of digital objects such that extended geographical reach does not degrade performance.

Availability management is concerned with making sure that e-business systems are indeed available when they should. Given temporal reach considerations (see Section 4.2.1), this often means 24/7, i.e., the systems should always be available. For availability management, we find replication technologies that enable the deployment of multiple copies of specific functional modules (or databases), such that the failure of one copy will not cripple or even disable an entire e-business system.

Providing performance technology solution is actually a business on its own in the Internet world. Certainly when it comes to multi-media applications that are used by large numbers of users, explicit 'information logistics' is required to deliver a proper level of performance. There are companies that specialize in 'information logistics' in the Internet. A well-known example is Akamai[10] (see Figure 7.13).

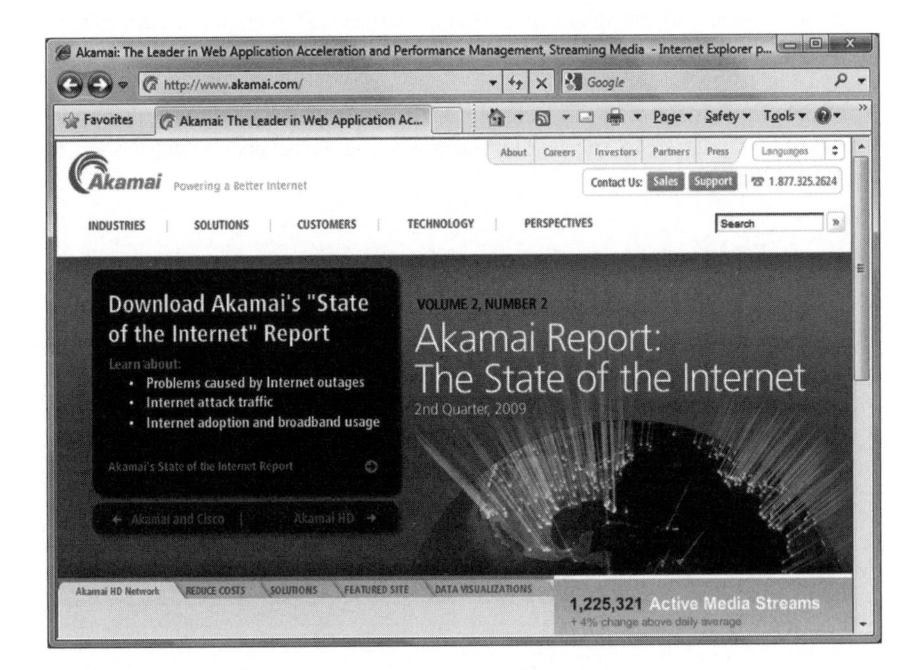

Figure 7.13 Example Internet 'information logistics' provider

7.4.6 Mobile technology

E-business performed 'on-the-go' from mobile platforms is becoming increasingly important – we have identified this as m-business (see Section 1.4). From a technology push perspective, this development is fueled by two developments:

- the availability of mobile Internet access to computing devices (typically laptop or notebook computers), such that users can perform 'regular e-business activities at irregular places';
- the growth of the technical possibilities of portable communication devices (primarily cell phones), making them fit for e-business use.

The support for both types of e-business access can be considered *e-business mobile technology*. Though we treat it as aspect-oriented technology (for the mobility aspect) here, it can also be considered platform technology (for mobile platforms) as discussed in the previous section.

Mobile technology includes a wide range of basic technologies, such as:

- small-footprint (light-weight) versions of e-business software to be used on light-weight platforms such as cell phones;
- context-awareness technology, such that the e-business options on a mobile device change per context, such as geographical location (e.g. using GPS technology);
- hardware and software technology that enables low power consumption of mobile devices (battery life being one of the major obstacles for high-performance, light-weight mobile devices).

Detailed treatment of these technologies is not within the scope of this book. The reader is referred to specialized books, such as Paavilainen's *Mobile Business Strategies* (2002).

7.5 FUNCTION-ORIENTED TECHNOLOGY

Function-oriented technology provides automated support for specific business functions. As such, it typically supports only a fragment of a complete e-business process. Function-oriented technology can often be related to specific modules as identified in the organization (O) and architecture (A) aspects.

There are many types of technology in this category. Making an interesting selection from the wide variety, we discuss the following types in this section:

- electronic catalog technology;
- electronic certificate technology;
- electronic payment technology;
- electronic contracting technology; and
- business intelligence technology.

As it is a selection, the above list is certainly not complete. Other types of function-oriented e-business technology are, for instance, electronic auction technology, collaborative authoring technology, and reputation management technology.

7.5.1 Electronic catalog technology

Electronic catalog systems are information systems that support the creation and the use of electronic catalogs. These are used for example in retail Web sites to support e-retailing business models (see Section 4.6.1).

To some extent, electronic catalogs are like traditional paper catalogs, as they present objects offered by a seller in an organized way to a potential buyer. But there are some important differences:

- Both paper and electronic catalogs support *browsing*, i.e., scanning a catalog following a predefined presentation order. In a paper catalog, this order is defined by the physical organization of the catalog. An electronic catalog can have multiple browsing orders, for example browsing by object category, browsing by price, or browsing by date of addition of objects.
- Both paper and electronic catalogs can support *searching*, i.e., finding a set of objects using specific criteria. A paper catalog typically only has at most one index for searching (often alphabetically). An electronic catalog can allow searching on the basis of many criteria – even on combinations of criteria.
- The *presentation* of objects in a paper catalog is limited by the paper nature – it typically consists of text and one or a few pictures per object. Electronic catalogs can offer more elaborate texts, user reports, many pictures, audio and video presentation, virtual use presentations and even interactive configuration and display of objects (the latter is often used in the car industry, for example, to allow potential car buyers to configure exactly 'their car'). Obviously, this requires proper multi-media data management (as discussed in Section 7.4.1).

7.5.2 Electronic certificate technology

Electronic certificates are used to prove specific characteristics of an e-business party to other parties. Certification is an important element in trust management. A certificate may prove for example that a party is a member of a trade organization, conforms to specific quality norms (such as ISO norms), or has a trustworthy banking representation. An electronic certificate is an electronic document that is secured by means of electronic signatures.

In electronic certification, we typically find four roles (as shown in Figure 7.14). The *certification authority* (CA) is a trusted third party (TTP) organization that assesses other organizations with the aim of issuing electronic certificates to them. The method of assessment depends on the type of certificate. Issued certificates are registered by the *registration authority* (RA). This is a TTP that keeps record of issued certificates. In practice, the CA and RA roles can be performed by the same TTP.

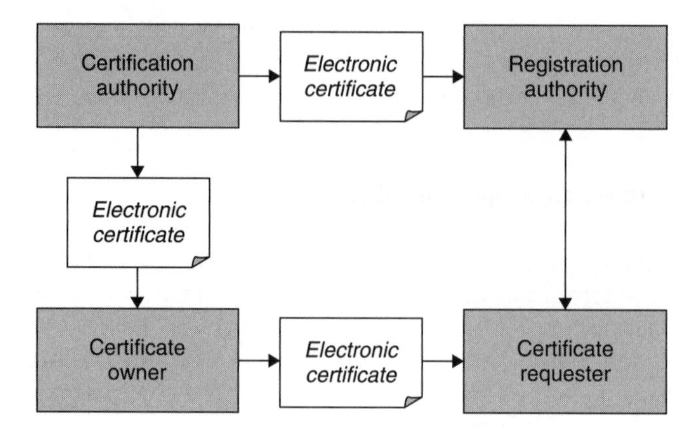

Figure 7.14 Parties in electronic certification

The *certificate owner* is the organization that requires an electronic certificate to prove specific qualities to parties it does business with. The *certificate requester* is the organization that wants to inspect a specific certificate before it enters into business with another party. It can receive the certificate from the certificate owner and check it with the RA.

In a dynamic supply chain scenario, for example, the certificate requester might be a supplier of goods that is going to ship the goods to a buyer that it has not yet done business with. Before shipping the goods, the supplier wants proof of the creditworthiness of the buyer by means of a banking certificate. In this case, the CA is the bank of the buyer. The RA may either be the same bank, or another TTP like a chamber of commerce.

A problem arises in electronic certification if the certificate requester does not trust the CA. In this case, an issued certificate does obviously not have much value. To make a CA trustworthy to a certificate requester, the CA itself needs to be certified, i.e., it must have a certificate of another, higher-level CA that is trusted in a broader context. If even this higher-level CA is not trusted by the requester, this CA again needs an even-higher-level certificate. For this reason, a CA hierarchy exists that has a so-called *root certification authority* at the top. Figure 7.15 shows an example CA hierarchy with three levels. The number of levels in a hierarchy depends on the type

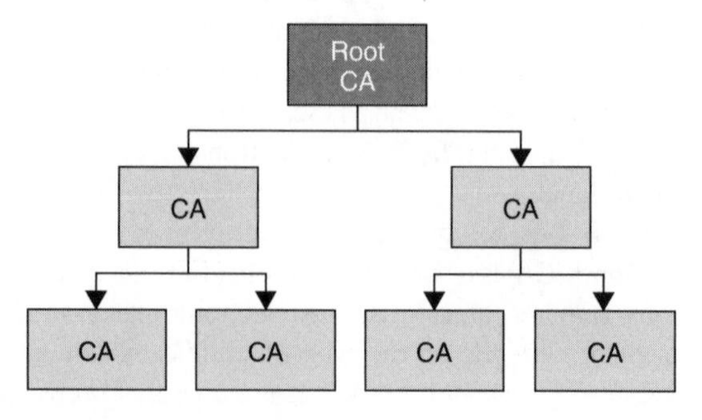

Figure 7.15 Certification authority hierarchy

of certificate and the geographic scope of the scenario. Three levels may for instance correspond with a regional, a national and an international scope.

7.5.3 Electronic payment technology

Electronic payment systems (O'Mahony *et al.* 2001, Párhonyi 2005) provide the functionality to perform financial transactions in an electronic way. Typically, they are a combination of information technology and payment procedures, so they are not solely technology.

Electronic payment systems can be divided into three main classes:

- gateways to traditional payment systems;
- facades to traditional payment systems;
- systems that manage 'digital cash'.

We discuss these three classes of systems below.

Gateways to traditional payment systems

Gateways to traditional payment systems allow parties to make direct use in e-business scenarios of payment systems that are also used in traditional (non-e-business) situations.

e-Business systems that include an interface to make credit card payments are widely used. When a customer buys one or more e-business objects, he enters his credit card details into the seller's system. Usually, the seller will verify these details and the client's credit status with the credit card company. Credit cards are, however, not generally used by the entire population in various countries.

A rather recent development is the coupling of e-retailing to regular e-banking systems. In this case, a buyer makes a payment to a seller directly from his regular e-banking account. A good example of this class of e-payment systems is the Ideal system developed by the Dutch banking community, which we briefly describe below.[11]

Using Ideal, a buyer is rerouted from an e-retailing system to the e-banking system of his own bank upon check-out. All banking account details are entered into the e-banking system of this own bank, much like regular e-banking transactions like funds transfers. The payment is confirmed using the bank's usual procedure (e.g. using a dynamically supplied transaction code). The retailer only knows which bank the customer uses, as the customer needs to be rerouted to this bank. Upon payment by the customer, the retailer is notified of this payment, so that the sales process can be completed. The process from the customer perspective is shown in Figure 7.16. The fact that the customer does not need to disclose any account details to the retailer solves many trust issues: the customer only needs to trust his own bank (which he hopefully does).

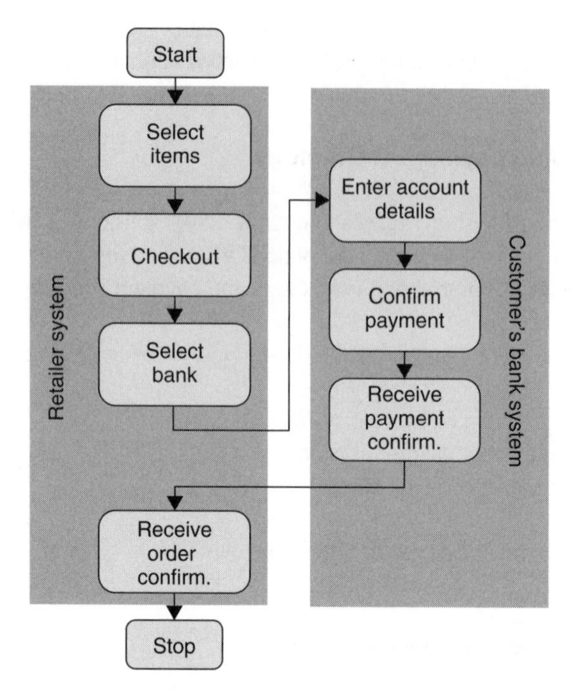

Figure 7.16 Ideal payment process from customer perspective

Facades to traditional payment systems

Facades to traditional payment systems provide an e-business front-end for payments that is linked to traditional payment systems, such as bank accounts or credit cards. It is a facade as it does not expose any banking details or credit card details of a party to another party. A well-known system in this category is PayPal.[12]

PayPal provides a mechanism to perform payments and money transfers through the Internet. It is an alternative to traditional, paper-based payment methods, such as checks and money orders. PayPal supports transferring money to practically anyone who has an email address.

Systems like PayPal typically have two characteristics that distinguish them from gateways to traditional payment systems:

1. They are suited for making small payments (also called *micro-payments*) because they have small overheads and therefore can operate without substantial transaction fees.
2. They can often be used (partly) anonymously, which makes them fit for conducting transactions without revealing one's identity or one's financial details.

We currently see a development towards integration of this class of payment technology into communication technology classes to allow easy (C2C) payments. An example is the integration of PayPal and Twitter into Twitpay.[13]

Digital cash management systems

Digital cash management systems are systems that manage 'virtual accounts' in which *digital cash* (or *electronic money*) can reside. These accounts are mostly owned by individuals. Therefore, digital cash management systems are mainly used in B2C and C2C e-commerce scenarios. Usually, funds are credited to these virtual accounts from traditional banking or credit cards accounts. Digital cash management systems are typically well-suited for making small, anonymous payments (as discussed for facade systems).

Digital cash typically resides in virtual accounts in the Internet, where it can be used to make payments. There are also systems in which the digital cash resides in physical devices. An example is the Dutch Chipknip, which is a smartcard that contains a virtual wallet. Systems based on physical devices do, however, require dedicated interfaces (like a smartcard reader), which makes them less usable for general e-business payments.

A special class of systems is formed by digital cash management systems in virtual worlds or virtual communities. These systems often use their own 'virtual currency'. A well-known example is Second Life, in which residents have accounts in the Linden Dollar (L$) currency, which has an exchange rate to the US$ currency (just like other non-virtual currencies). These accounts are used to make or receive payments in the virtual world or community. Though transactions are typically small, these worlds and communities can have substantial economic size.[14]

7.5.4 Electronic contracting technology

Contracts are the basis for establishing formal business relationships between autonomous organizations. Traditionally, contracts are physical paper documents. In the development of electronic means for communication and collaboration between organizations, electronic contracts have emerged as a digital alternative for physical documents. In this subsection, we first discuss two main forms of electronic contracting. Then, we focus on the structure of electronic contracts. Finally, we pay attention to electronic contracting systems.

Shallow and deep e-contracting

Electronic contracts are often used as a direct replacement for traditional paper contracts. Consequently, business processes in general and contracting processes in particular do not change much as a consequence of the use of electronic contracts – it is mainly the efficiency of the contracting process that is improved. As this form of e-contracting does not much affect the way of doing business, we call this *shallow e-contracting*. As discussed in this book, new business settings have emerged in recent years. These new business settings require new contracting paradigms in which the use of electronic contracts becomes an essential element to obtain a radical paradigm shift in contractual business relations. We call this *deep e-contracting*. Deep e-contracting allows new contractual paradigms like *micro-contracting* and *just-in-time contracting* (Grefen and Angelov 2002, Angelov 2006).

Micro-contracting is a form of contracting in which many small contracts are established instead of a few large contracts. Micro-contracts are typically small with respect to their time scope and the value of exchanged goods they describe: they specify small business transactions that are executed in a short period of time. Micro-contracting allows organizations to create maximum variability in the contents of contracts: each micro-contract can be tuned to a specific situation. In this way, business relations can be adapted very dynamically to current circumstances, following very dynamic e-business markets. An example domain where micro-contracting can be used is logistics (Grefen *et al.* 2000): instead of bulk contracts, contracts can be established for the handling of individual shipments. In this way, contract-based dynamic service outsourcing can be realized (see also Section 4.5.4). Obviously, micro-contracting processes need to be automated to a high degree to avoid enormous overheads of contracting in business processes.

Just-in-time contracting is a form of contracting in which contracts are established at the very latest possible moment, such that the conditions of that moment can be taken into account when specifying the exact contents of a contract. Conditions include specifics of customer orders, provider resources and market situations. To allow just-in-time contracting, electronic means are necessary to establish a contract in a very short time (in extreme cases in the order of a few seconds) – note that traditional 'pen and paper' contracting processes are not applicable here as they are simply too slow. Just-in-time electronic contracting can be used for example in dynamic advertising scenarios (Angelov and Grefen 2006), where advertising campaigns are adapted for example depending on current weather conditions or the outcomes of sports events.

Electronic contract structures

Electronic contracts are typically complex documents. As they are often used in scenarios with dynamic partnerships, they must often be fully self-contained. In other words: because there is no pre-existing business relationship in dynamic, contract-governed e-business, all agreements between parties must be specified in a contract.

Because of this complexity, clear contract structures are needed. A high-level contract content structure is provided in the *4W framework* (Angelov and Grefen 2003). This framework distinguishes four classes of contract content or four contract clause types (indicated by the four Ws):

1. The *Who* clause type contains descriptions of the parties that engage in a contractual relationship. Usually, there are two parties, but multi-party contracts are also possible (Xu 2004).
2. The *What* clause type contains descriptions of the exchanged objects (as discussed in Section 2.4). One object is often of a monetary type, but not necessarily so.
3. The *How* clause type contains a description of the process for the exchange of the objects described in the *What* clause type. It may also contain a description

of the process for the further use of the contract (such as complaint handling related to the contract).

4 The *Where* clause type contains a specification of the context in which the contract is to be interpreted. Most important is the legal context, often specified by the country of which the contract law is applicable.

The contract clauses together form the contract content or the *core contract*. To make an electronic contract valid, electronic signatures of the participating parties need to be added. Together, we get the contract structure shown in Figure 7.17.

A structure like the one in Figure 7.17 needs to be expressed in a specification language to obtain a transferrable document. For this purpose, electronic contracting languages are used that typically have an XML representation.

Electronic contracting systems

Electronic contracting systems (Angelov 2006) provide the functionality to establish and monitor contracts between business parties in an electronic way. A full-blown electronic contracting system supports all phases of a complete electronic contracting process:

- the *informational phase*, in which information is exchanged in a market between parties that explore possible collaboration;

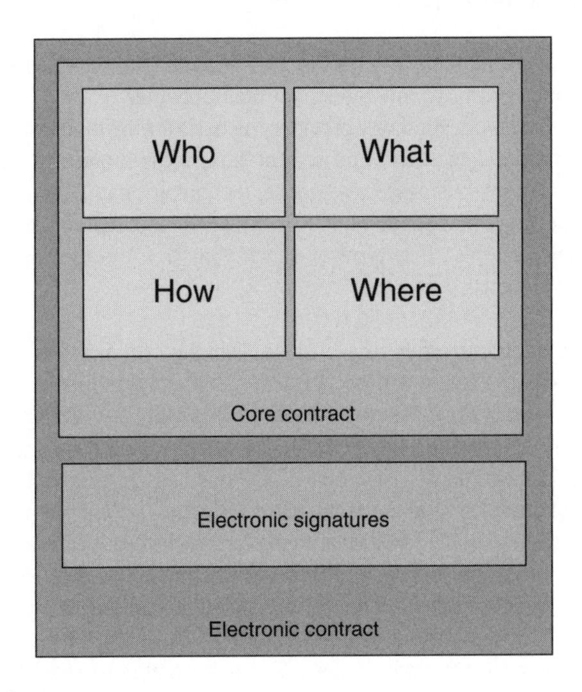

Figure 7.17 e-Contract structure

- the *pre-contracting phase* in which the details of a contractual relationship are negotiated and agreed upon in terms of a *contract offer*;
- the *contracting phase*, in which the contract is actually established by signing an agreed contract offer; here, electronic certificate technology is used as discussed in Section 7.5.2;
- the *enactment phase* in which the obligations specified in the contract are fulfilled by the respective parties in accordance with specified rights;
- the *evaluation phase*, in which the enactment is evaluated to confirm that all obligations have been fulfilled and all rights have been respected – if not, starting a settlement procedure to deal with contract violation.

Note that not all contracting necessarily includes all the above phases: in simple, clear markets, the informational phase may be superfluous; for simple, straightforward contracts, the evaluation phase may be superfluous.

An electronic contracting system enables the execution of all the above phases in an electronic way, i.e., without the use of any physical documents. Obviously, this makes contracting processes a great deal more efficient than the traditional pen-and-paper approach. As a consequence of this improved efficiency, contracts can be used for a greater range of business collaborations (such as the micro-contracting paradigm that we have discussed earlier in this section), hence guarding the rights of parties in e-business scenarios.

7.5.5 Business intelligence technology

e-Business can generate large volumes of business data, as activities are performed using automated systems, which can log all their activities.

Business intelligence technology provides the basis for the functionality to analyze large volumes of data, such as large sets of e-business browsing and transaction histories. Results from business intelligence technology can be used as input to customer relationship management (CRM) systems and to tactical and strategic decision making systems. This type of technology is important in an e-business context for two reasons:

1 To understand the customer: as e-business is highly 'anonymous' if compared to traditional business (there are no personal contacts, there are no nice physical locations), meeting customer demands is one of the key distinguishing factors between competitors (see also Section 4.4.2, where we discuss enriched customer relationship management).
2 To understand market developments: e-business markets are often highly volatile, much more so than many traditional markets; therefore, it is of major importance to closely and quickly follow market developments to be able to react or even pro-act (this issue is related to change management as discussed in Section 5.6.2).

Business intelligence technology is used to analyze data. To store this data, data warehousing systems (Inmon *et al.* 2001) are often used. These systems enable business intelligence to proceed freely without disturbing primary business that runs against operational databases.

7.6 MAPPING A ELEMENTS TO T ELEMENTS

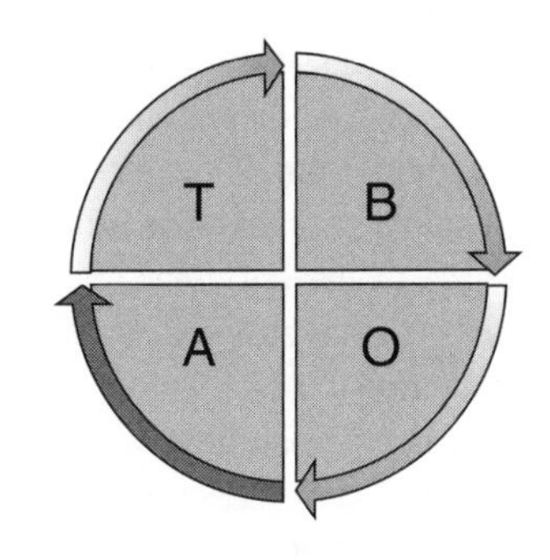

In the preceding sections of this chapter, we have seen a broad spectrum of technologies in the T aspect of the BOAT framework. These technologies are chosen to realize (or in another term 'embody') the architecture specified in the A aspect. Therefore, A aspect elements should be mapped to T aspect elements.

The nature of the mapping from A aspect elements to T aspect elements depends on the category of T elements:

- The basic Internet and Web technologies underlie almost any modern e-business application. As such, they can often be assumed to be present 'by default' and hence do not explicitly appear in mappings between A and T aspects.
- Advanced infrastructural technologies typically underlie a complete architecture (or a major part of it). As such, they typically are not related to specific modules specified in the A aspect, but form a 'basis below' the modules. Hence, they do not show up in A aspect diagrams as separate modules, but can influence the choice of modules.
- Aspect-oriented technologies are typically used in various modules of an e-business system. Security technology, for example, is important in all front-end modules as these have interfaces to the outside world. Aspect-oriented technology may in some cases be located in dedicated architecture modules showing up in detailed architecture diagrams (e.g., a database management system module, a business process management system module or a security management module).
- Function-oriented technologies typically support very specific functions and can hence be related explicitly to individual modules identified in the architecture in the A aspect. In other words, modules in the A aspect may be dedicated to contain specific function-oriented technology (like an electronic payment module or a contract management module). Typically, we find these modules in party-level architectures (see for example Figure 6.7) or system-level architectures.

Realizing an e-business system typically requires the use of a number of technology types. Integration of these types is a major issue, both to 'get the system running' and to ensure flexibility of the system towards the future. Good architectural design (in the A aspect) is a main key to proper integration.

7.7 MAPPING T ELEMENTS TO B ELEMENTS

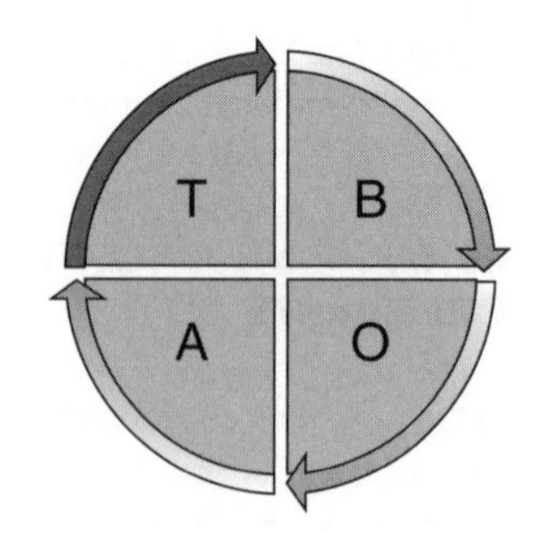

As we have seen in Section 3.3, the BOAT model is preferably used in the 'wheel mode' in an e-business context. This means that we have to consider the mapping from T aspect elements to B aspect elements to 'make the wheel go round'. In other words, we have to think about the technology push aspects of e-business developments (as discussed in Section 1.5).

It is not easy, however, to speak in general terms about relations from T aspect elements to B aspect elements, as they can have very different natures. We can give a few examples here to illustrate possible relations:

- Obviously, the use of communication technology elements can have an impact on the reach element in the B aspect (see Section 4.2): a more advanced communication platform can result in extended reach (typically modal reach, sometimes geographic reach). This holds both for system-to-system communication technology (such as Web Services) and human communication technology.
- Obviously, the use of multi-media technology can have an impact on the richness element in the B aspect: the use of a full spectrum of media can increase the richness of the communication to business partners. The same goes for technology supporting interactivity in the Internet context. As such, developments associated with the *Web 2.0* concept (see Section 7.2.2) can trigger new business opportunities.
- Specific technology classes can even directly foster the development of new business structures: the use of e-contracting technology opens new doors towards the formation of dynamic virtual enterprises (see Section 4.6.3), for example.

A general 'recipe' does not exist for mapping T to B aspect elements. This is the reason for the fact that 'discovering' new business models based on emerging technology is still an 'art' in itself. The structured discussion of B aspect elements in Chapter 4 may help to infuse some elements of business engineering into this art.

7.8 RUNNING CASES

In this section, we turn our attention again to our two running cases. We use these to discuss the application of some of the technologies discussed in this chapter. For reasons of brevity, we will not discuss all technologies.

7.8.1 POSH

POSH uses standard Internet and Web technologies as basic infrastructure technologies for their e-business systems. In order to support their B2B activities, they are studying the use of more advanced platforms, such as RosettaNet.

Their electronic catalog is essential to POSH – it shows all the products they sell. For small goods, simple descriptions and photographs suffice. For large goods (such as office furniture), a detailed description with a set of photographs and a measurement diagram is included in the catalog. POSH considers using videos for the presentation of furniture lines they sell to give the customer a more lively impression than photographs can (here, the introduction of technology will affect *richness* in the B aspect of BOAT). This will imply, however, that they will have to upgrade the service level agreement they have with the organization that hosts their Web site.

With respect to payment systems, POSH takes a traditional approach. For B2C orders, they request either payments per credit card or pre-payments to their bank account. For B2B orders, they bill the customer offline after delivery of an order. The latter is possible, as POSH has pre-existing relations with B2B customers (as reflected in their sales process – see Figure 5.24).

POSH considers using electronic contracting for large B2B orders. They see two advantages here:

1 A contract provides a basis for guarantees between the customer and POSH with respect to mutual obligations. Large B2B orders represent substantial financial transactions, so a contractual basis reduces risks.
2 A contract is a natural place to specify quality of service parameters, such as the delivery time of ordered goods, the mode of transportation and installation, and the after-service provided by POSH. Using per-order contracts allows differentiating on a per order basis, so that more flexibility is obtained.

7.8.2 TTU

As TTU is a young company, they are free to choose which technologies to use for their e-business system platforms, i.e., they do not have a technology legacy problem. They have chosen to use Web service technology as their main platform (on top of basic Internet and Web technologies). They specify all services they offer in WSDL.

Availability of their systems is essential to TTU, certainly when it comes to setting up online meetings with their clients: if important meetings need to be postponed because of unavailability of the systems of TTU, they could easily lose clients. Therefore, TTU has paid explicit attention to technology that allows functional back-up systems to seamlessly take over tasks in their primary systems.

Given the market they operate in, human communication technology is obviously very important to TTU, most specifically audio and video communication technology. They are currently investigating the use of telepresence technology, so that their interpreters can be included in teleconferences.

One especial point of interest to TTU is electronic certification. As they work with freelance translators and interpreters and want to guarantee high-quality service to their customers, some form of internal and external quality control is desirable. Having freelancers that are certified can help TTU's internal quality control system and provides opportunities to use explicit quality references in their marketing and sales processes. Electronic certification is, however, not yet available in the translation and interpretation market.

7.9 CHAPTER END

As usual in this book, we end this chapter with a summary and a set of questions and exercises.

7.9.1 Chapter summary

In this chapter, we have provided an overview of e-business technology. We have distinguished between four classes of technology that are used as the basis for e-business applications (as illustrated in Figure 7.18):

- *Internet and Web technology* are the bare basics for e-business systems, providing the basic communication and collaboration platform. This technology is based on a set of standard languages (such as HTML and XML) and protocols (such as HTTP).
- *Advanced platform technology* provides a layer on top of Internet or Web technology, offering more advanced collaboration primitives. The Web Services framework is currently a leading platform. It is based on the Web Services technology stack, consisting of a number of standard languages (such as WSDL and BPEL), protocols (such as WSAT and WSS) and software specifications (such as UDDI). ebXML, RosettaNet and multi-agent systems are well-known other platform types. In practice, hybrid platforms exist that combine multiple basic platforms.
- *Aspect-oriented technology* provides the support for specific aspects of e-business systems, such as security. Important aspects supported by this class of technology are data management, process management, security, performance, and mobility.
- *Function-oriented technology* provides the support for specific functions of e-business systems. Important functions supported by this class of technology are electronic catalog management, electronic certificate management, electronic payment support, electronic contracting support, and business intelligence support.

Integration of technology classes is a major point in realizing e-business systems. A well-designed architecture (as discussed in Chapter 6) is the starting point to obtain this.

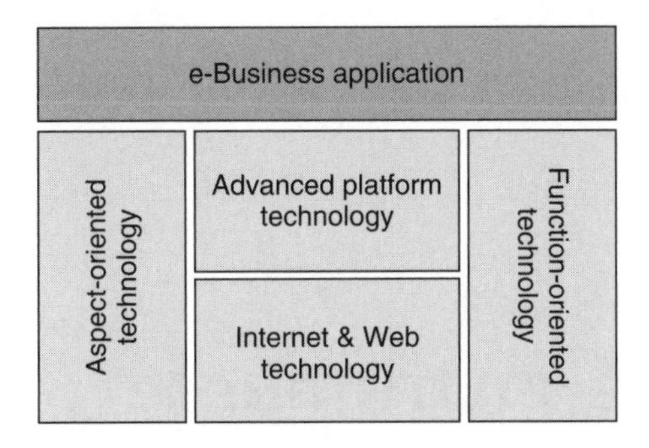

Figure 7.18 Technology classes as a basis for e-business applications

7.9.2 Questions and exercises

1 Study the electronic catalogs of a few well-known e-retailers in a specific shopping domain (such as music, books, or house accessories). Compare the catalogs with respect to the support they offer for browsing and searching. Pay attention to the number of predefined browsing sequences, the number of search criteria (search dimensions) and the possibilities to combine these.

2 The X/Open XA protocol (discussed in Section 7.4.1) uses a *two-phase commit protocol* to ensure that distributed transactions either completely succeed, or completely fail (i.e., that a transaction cannot remain partially completed). Find out how the two-phase commit protocol works.

3 In Section 7.4.3, we have mentioned a double asymmetric encryption protocol. Elaborate on this protocol and show that it indeed guarantees all four security characteristics discussed in that section.

4 Figure 7.16 shows the Ideal payment process from a customer's perspective, i.e., the process steps a customer has to perform. Specify the Ideal payment process from a retailer perspective, i.e., the process steps a retailer has to perform.

5 Try and find information about the practical usage of the RosettaNet and ebXML standards (in terms of market size, domain types, regional usage, etc.). Are there interesting differences between the usage patterns of the two standards?

8

BOAT as an analysis instrument

Learning goals

By the end of the chapter you should:

- Know and understand an approach to classify an e-business scenario;
- Know and understand an approach to analyze or design an e-business scenario;
- Be able to relate elements from the four BOAT aspects graphically;
- Understand e-business developments in a temporal setting.

8.1 INTRODUCTION

In the chapters of this book so far, we have explored the e-business space along a number of dimensions as outlined in Chapter 2 and Chapter 3. This provides a conceptual 'tool' for analyzing and designing e-business scenarios, but does not yet explain how to precisely 'handle this tool' in practice. In terms of cooking: the ingredients are there, but the overall recipe is still missing. Therefore, we provide guidelines in this chapter as to how to use the theory in this book for the following tasks:

- classifying an existing e-business scenario (Section 8.2);
- analyzing an existing e-business scenario (Section 8.3).

Designing an e-business scenario can in principle follow the same approach. After describing the basic way to perform these tasks, we next pay special attention to two additional issues to obtain a complete analysis (or design):

- getting an overview of the major dependencies between elements in the four BOAT aspects (Section 8.4);
- adding the time aspect to describe e-business developments[1] (Section 8.5).

8.2 CLASSIFYING A SCENARIO

An e-business scenario can be classified using the following steps as a starting point for analysis or design:

1 Determine the scope of the scenario. This includes the following two tasks:
  a decide which organizations are included in the scenario (and which are excluded);
  b decide for each organization which activities are included in the scenario (and which are excluded).

  Note that is not always a trivial task, certainly in complex supply chains or business networks. If this step is problematic, it may be an indication that one is actually trying to classify a combination of scenarios: an e-business network may consist of multiple, independent e-business scenarios.
2 Classify the scenario in terms of the party types involved (see Section 2.3). If this step is problematic, it may be an indication that Step 1 has not been performed correctly. If there are parties that have an unclear role or that have 'superfluous' activities, too broad a scope may have been chosen. If a party with a 'logical' role is missing or a 'logical' function is not supported, too narrow a scope may have been chosen.
3 Classify the scenario in terms of the objects manipulated (see Section 2.4). Again, if this step is problematic, it may be an indication that Step 1 has not been performed correctly. If many heterogeneous objects are identified, too broad a scope may have been chosen.
4 Classify the scenario in terms of applicable time scope or time scopes (see Section 2.5). If two very different time scopes are found, it may again be an indication that the scope of the scenario is too broad. Note that an (ultra-)dynamic time scope is typically coupled to the life-cycle (or rather 'trade cycle') of the objects identified in Step 3.

The above steps are summarized in Figure 8.1.

8.3 ANALYZING OR DESIGNING A SCENARIO

An e-business scenario can be analyzed (or designed) after it has been classified as discussed above. The following steps are used for analysis (or design):

5 Describe the scenario with respect to the four BOAT aspects in global terms (see Chapter 4 to Chapter 7). Make diagrams or graphical models where possible, as this will yield more structure and clarity than text only.

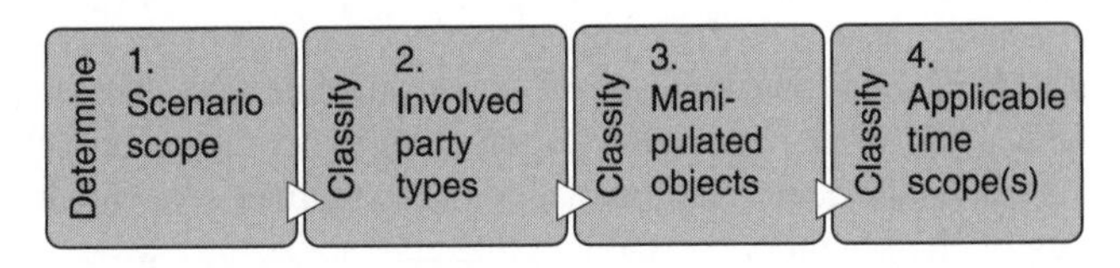

Figure 8.1 Steps to classify an e-business scenario

6 Analyze the mappings between the identified elements in the BOAT aspects in global terms. Make diagrams or graphical models where possible – we discuss a technique for this in Section 8.4.
7 Decide which BOAT aspect(s) are most relevant for the nature of the scenario, i.e., choose which aspect(s) have a 'leading character'. The most relevant aspects are usually those that distinguish the scenario best from similar scenarios. Preferably choose only one aspect, two if really necessary.
8 Analyze or design the results of Steps 5 and 6 in more detail. Start with the aspect(s) identified as 'leading' in Step 7. Usually, it is advisable to elaborate these aspect(s) most, as they most heavily determine the entire scenario.

The above analysis (design) steps are summarized in Figure 8.2. This figure complements Figure 8.1: together, they summarize the complete classification and analysis (design) approach.

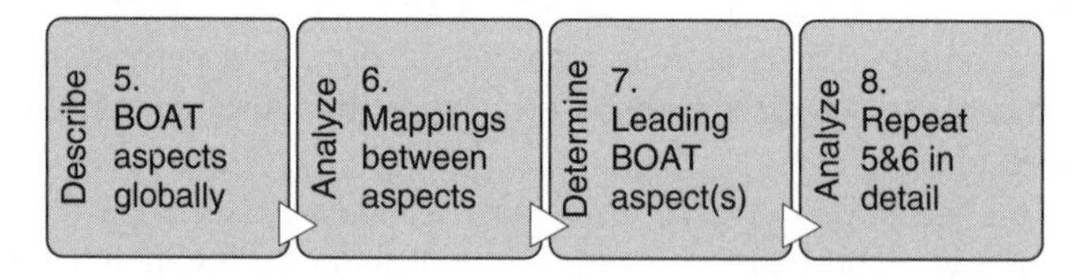

Figure 8.2 Steps to analyze an e-business scenario

8.4 BOAT ELEMENT DEPENDENCY DIAGRAM

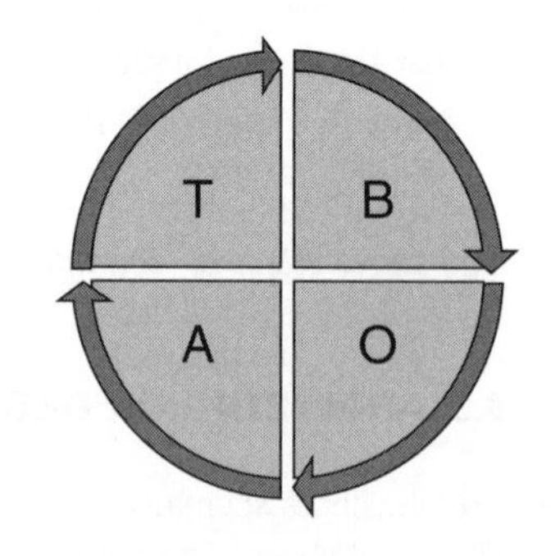

After an analysis or design of an e-business scenario has been made, the most important elements in the four BOAT aspects and their dependencies can be shown in a BOAT element dependency diagram (BEDD) to provide an overview of a scenario.

A BEDD is based on the wheel model of the BOAT framework. In a BEDD, all four mappings between BOAT aspects are summarized – as such, it represents the complete wheel model as introduced in Section 3.3. The mappings are summarized by indicating the most essential elements in each aspect and using arrows between elements in different aspects to show important dependencies between them. A dependency between elements X and Y means that the characteristics of element X have a strong influence on the characteristics of element Y.

An abstract BEDD is shown in Figure 8.3 (it is abstract as it contains only abstract elements). For each of the four BOAT aspects, the most important elements are shown in the respective quarter of the diagram. The number of elements depends on the nature of the scenario, but should preferably not be too large – otherwise, the diagram loses its overview function. The arrows indicate the dependencies

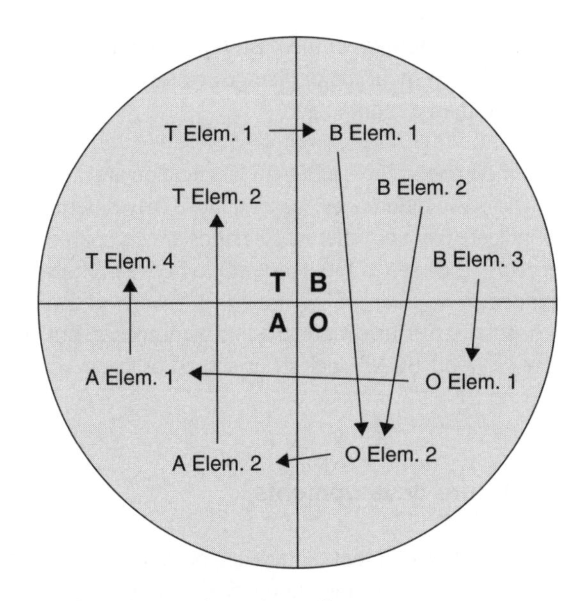

Figure 8.3 Abstract BOAT element dependency diagram

between elements of different BOAT aspects. The number of arrows crossing a boundary is an indication of the amount of the coupling between two BOAT aspects. In the example, the coupling between B and O aspects is the largest. Note that this indication needs to be used with care, as the arrows do not indicate anything about the relative importance of the dependencies. It is possible to illustrate the relative importance by means of the weights of the arrows or their colors, but this makes the BEDD harder to interpret – often it is a better idea to include only the most important dependencies, as they represent the core of the relations between the BOAT aspects.

We show a concrete BEDD (i.e., a BEDD of a concrete example e-business scenario) when revisiting the running case studies at the end of this chapter.

8.5 ANALYZING E-BUSINESS DEVELOPMENTS

As we have seen, the field of e-business is a field with rapid developments. Therefore, it is often interesting to analyze an e-business scenario over time, i.e., to analyze its development. We can do this in a retrospective way, i.e., look back at the past. We can also do this in a prospective way, i.e., try to look forward into the future.

8.5.1 Analyzing past developments

When analyzing past developments (which have been completed at the moment of analysis), typically two 'moments in time' are chosen:

1 *Past*: a carefully chosen moment in the past, typically one or more years ago.
2 *Now*: a stable moment (without major changes going on) in the very recent past, preferably not more than a month ago.

For each of the two moments in time, a BOAT classification and analysis is performed as outlined above and main differences are identified. Very different outcomes from classification may indicate that two different scenarios are compared, not two versions of the same scenario – this means that somewhere between the past and now, the scenario was replaced.

It is of course possible to use more than two moments, but given the effort required to perform a good BOAT analysis, it should be clear why this is actually necessary.

8.5.2 Analyzing future developments

When analyzing future developments (studying possibilities for scenarios to be realized), it is often a good idea to think in terms of three 'moments in time':

1 *Now*: a stable moment in the short-term future or very recent past.
2 *Near Future*: typically in the order of one year away from now.
3 *Far Future*: typically in the order of five to ten years away from now.

For each of the three moments in time, a BOAT analysis is performed as outlined above. Emphasis can (or even should) be placed on a leading BOAT aspect.

It is often worthwhile to think about the *Far Future* first to explore possibilities in an 'ideal world' in which extreme ideas are realizable. This avoids thinking in terms of too pragmatic 'current limitations' (e.g. in terms of technology or regulations). When a 'vision' has been established for the *Far Future*, the *Near Future* can be deduced as interpolated between *Now* and *Far Future*. This can be compared to the approach of *extreme thinking* as explained with change management (see Section 5.6.2).

8.6 RUNNING CASES

In this section, we conclude the discussion of the two running cases that we have seen throughout this book. For POSH, we elaborate a BOAT element dependency diagram. For TTU, we perform a short future development analysis.

8.6.1 POSH

A BOAT element dependency diagram[2] for the POSH scenario is shown in Figure 8.4. It shows the main elements of the four BOAT aspects for the scenario and the cross-aspect dependencies between these elements.

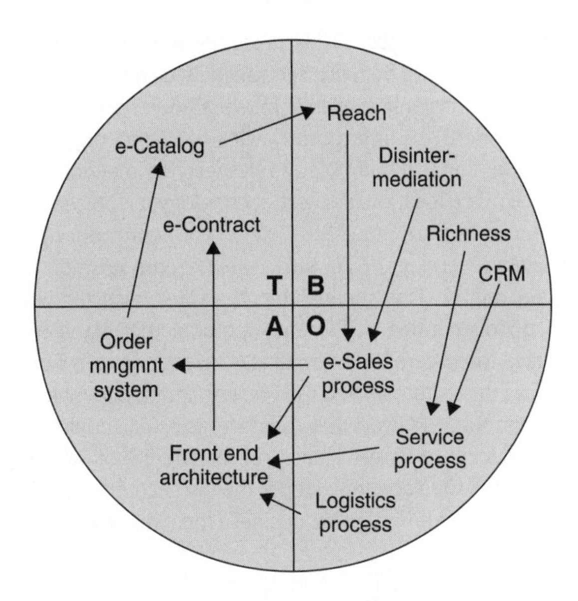

Figure 8.4 BOAT element dependency diagram for POSH scenario

In the B aspect, *extended reach, extended richness, disintermediation* and *enhanced customer relationship management* are the main elements (as discussed in Section 4.8.1). In the O aspect, the front-end processes of POSH are key elements. POSH selects the *e-sales process* (discussed in Section 5.8.1), the *service process* and the *manufacturer relationship process* as the main processes. In the A aspect, the *front-end architecture* is key to POSH (see Section 6.8.1). The structure of their order management system is considered an essential e-business element as well (again, see Section 6.8.1). In the T aspect, *e-catalog technology* is of prime interest to POSH in the current situation; *e-contract technology* is added for future developments (see Section 7.8.1).

The arrows show the main dependencies. For example, extended reach and disintermediation determine the existence and the nature of the e-sales process of POSH, so realization of reach and disintermediation depend on the implementation of these processes. In other words: the processes enable reach and disintermediation.

The diagram shows that most dependencies exist between the B and the O aspects and between the O and the A aspects. This suggests that the O aspect is the leading aspect for the POSH scenario. As there is only one dependency between the T and the B aspect, the POSH scenario is not a technology push scenario.

8.6.2 TTU

TTU projects the far future at about ten years from now. The T aspect will be the leading BOAT aspect for TTU, as communication modalities will rely heavily on technology developments. They analyze the future with respect to the two kinds of services they offer: interpretation and translation.

For their interpretation services, TTU takes the extreme position that all international business meetings will be held electronically using multi-party telepresence systems, which will be commonly available. Interpretation services will still be needed in these meetings, where the interpreter will join a meeting as a party in the telepresence meeting. For low-technology telepresence meetings, interpreters can join from their home office location. For high-technology telepresence meetings, dedicated telepresence set-ups are required. TTU can be a provider of such facilities.

For their translation services, TTU takes the extreme position that all business documents will be digital. This means that their activities for handling physical documents can be dismantled. TTU also expects that translations of official documents will have to be certified by means of electronic certificates.

TTU uses the far future situation and the present situation to make an interpolation for the medium-term future. Given that they are and will remain in a technology-push market, they decide to invest heavily in knowledge of and experience with telepresence technology. One concrete step is the installation of a TTU-owned, high-end telepresence facility at an intensive business location, such as London or New York City.

8.7 CHAPTER END

This last theory chapter of the book is again ended with a chapter summary and a set of questions and exercises.

8.7.1 Chapter summary

Analyzing or designing an e-business scenario starts with determining the exact scope of the scenario in terms of parties and activities of these parties. Next, the scenario is classified in terms of party types, objects and time scope(s). After scoping and classification, a BOAT analysis or design is performed. First, a global analysis of BOAT aspects is made, after which the dependencies are analyzed. A BOAT element dependency diagram can be used as a summarization technique here. A leading BOAT aspect is chosen (two if really necessary). Then, a detailed analysis or design is performed, where the leading BOAT aspect is elaborated in most detail.

In analyzing past and future developments, points in time should be chosen with care. For future analysis, it can be a good idea to start with a far future scenario, which is analyzed by means of extreme thinking.

8.7.2 Questions and exercises

1 Explain all dependencies in the BOAT element dependency diagram of the POSH scenario, as shown in Figure 8.4.
2 Construct a BOAT element dependency diagram for the TTU scenario. Use the description of TTU in Chapter 4 to Chapter 7 as input for the construction process.

3 Take a real-world e-business scenario. Perform a short, high-level BOAT analysis of it. Summarize the dependencies between the most important identified elements in a BOAT element dependency diagram.
4 Future developments are analyzed at various points in time, including the far future. How far away this far future actually is, depends on characteristics of the scenario at hand. Which characteristics determine this?
5 The BOAT dependency diagram of the POSH scenario (see Figure 8.4) suggests that the O aspect of BOAT is the leading aspect for this scenario. Do you agree with this observation? Explain your answer.
6 The BOAT dependency diagram of the POSH scenario (see Figure 8.4) suggests that the technology push forces of e-business are not too strong in this scenario. Should the POSH organization have more interest in these technology push forces? Motivate your answer.
7 TTU projects the extreme future of business meetings as becoming all-virtual using telepresence technology (see Section 8.6.2). Analyze the extreme other end of the future, where telepresence technology has lost all appeal and meetings are all face-to-face. Try and design a business future for TTU in this case.

9

Concluding remarks

Learning goals

By the end of the chapter you should:

- Understand the tension field between separation and integration of concerns when analyzing or designing e-business scenarios;
- Understand the importance of change in e-business settings and the importance of conceptual structures in this context.

9.1 INTRODUCTION

In this short final chapter of the book, we present a few concluding remarks – they are to be interpreted as final observations after the topics discussed in the preceding eight chapters. First, we spend a few words on the tension field of separation and integration of concerns that is so typical for a complex world like e-business. Then, we turn our attention to dealing with change, as change is omnipresent in e-business.

9.2 SEPARATION AND INTEGRATION

Given the complexity of the e-business domain, a good separation of concerns is required to understand it. In this book, we have presented a three-dimensional space for the classification of e-business scenarios. We have presented the BOAT framework as a basis for distinguishing aspects of e-business in analysis or design. These are the basic tools of this book; they are therefore repeated in Figure 9.1.

The BOAT framework is a conceptual tool aimed at separation of concerns – as such, it is an aid to arrive at clarity. But as the various aspects of e-business have an important interplay, the relations between the aspects must be given enough attention. This is explicitly treated in this book by the sections on the four mappings between

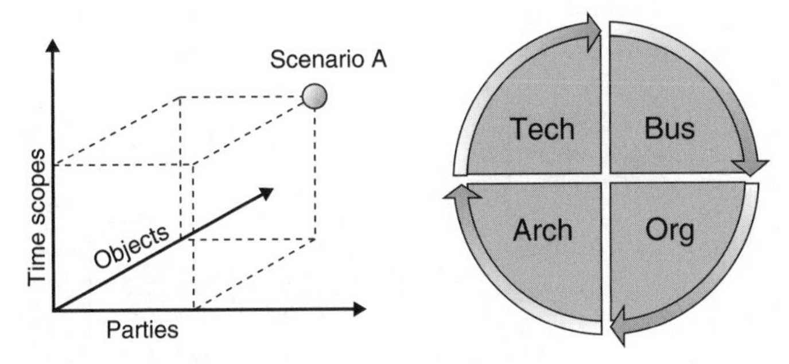

Figure 9.1 Main classification and analysis tools

the BOAT aspects (Sections 5.7, 6.7, 7.6 and 7.7). It is also reflected in the BEDD technique, which we have introduced in the previous chapter. The integration of aspects is important in e-business to arrive at consistency in analysis or design. Consequently, a good e-business analyst (or designer, for that matter) must always consciously balance between separation and integration of aspects. An iterative analysis or design approach that alternates between separation and integration can be used to deal with scenarios of high complexity.

9.3 DEALING WITH CHANGE

As indicated in the beginning of this book, e-business is a very fast-moving domain: *the only constant in e-business is change.* This implies that many details have a rather volatile character: what is modern today may be old-fashioned tomorrow – either in terminology or in technology, perhaps even in essence. Most important in this domain is therefore to understand the 'grand structures' and relationships that are not that susceptible to change. Figure 9.2 presents a 'grand overview' of the main ingredients in the BOAT framework, organized into the four BOAT aspects (in the wheel configuration as shown in Figure 9.1). This overview illustrates the 'grand structures' of e-business according to this book.

A well-structured overall view is what this book tries to convey – the focus is on important concepts, not on many details. Further details can be easily positioned within this overall view. As such, the theory presented in this book can be seen as a stable framework, the precise contents of which will vary over time. Details in the e-business field are moving targets because they change very rapidly – they can be filled into the grand structures as they evolve. As an analogy, one can view things as a well-organized wardrobe: the overall structure (in terms of classes of clothing and the relationships between them) remains relatively stable, but the individual clothing items within the wardrobe follow trends and fashions.

Of course, to be able to analyze and design current, concrete e-business scenarios in detail, thorough understanding of 'volatile details' is necessary too, as they form the practical ingredients for a scenario at a certain moment in time. In terms of our analogy: to actually get dressed, one needs concrete pieces of clothing. To make concrete e-business designs stable over time, however, it is important to base them on conceptual structures, which can be filled in differently as time proceeds.

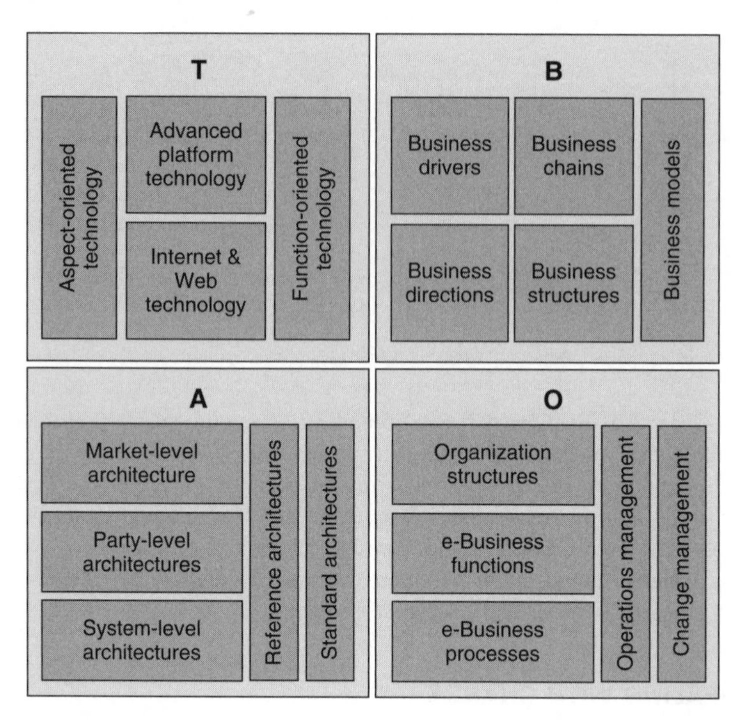

Figure 9.2 Grand overview of BOAT framework ingredients

Notes

CHAPTER 1

1 In the rest of this book, we make an exception to this rule for activities of which the efficiency is *dramatically* improved, as this enables truly new forms of business – we address this point in Chapter 4.
2 Note that this definition of e-business is not shared by all other authors. Many use a much broader definition, sometimes as broad as 'e-business is doing business with computers'. Obviously, almost all business is covered by such a broad definition, as there is hardly any contemporary business in which computers do not play a role at all.
3 The SABRE system (obviously in a much more modern version) is still in use. It now supports many more travel-related business activities than airline booking only (Wikipedia 2009a).
4 Ideas exist to even extend the Internet to the planet Mars (see e.g. http://www.itwire.com/content/view/9802/1066/), although the use of that for e-business purposes can be questioned, obviously.
5 Information and communication technologies come and sometimes go at rapid rates. Development and acceptance of new technologies are very nicely illustrated by the *hype cycle* model developed by Gartner (Fenn and Linden 2005).

CHAPTER 2

1 On the one hand, time gets more important, as business relations get more dynamic (see the extended definition of e-business that we developed in Chapter 1) and business transactions are performed faster. On the other hand, we see that e-business erases the importance of time when it comes to availability of business possibilities (we discuss this in more detail in Chapter 4).
2 By 'orthogonal' we mean that values in different dimensions are independent from each other, i.e., a specific choice in one dimension does not influence possible choices in the other dimensions. Compare Figure 2.1 to a set of axes in geometry, in which the x-, y- and z-values of a point can be chosen independently.
3 Bartering through electronic markets seemed like a way to avoid the tax system (as no money is transferred). But nowadays, tax offices have regulations for this – see e.g. the regulations about Barter Exchanges on www.irs.gov. The existence of virtual worlds with their own monetary systems (like Second Life, see www.secondlife.com) gives raise to similar issues.

4 See http://www.ebay.com.
5 Sometimes also referred to as *government-to-citizen*, which conveniently can also be abbreviated as G2C.
6 Note that digital goods are replacing physical goods that are information carriers, e.g. online music in MP3 format from commercial music sites is replacing physical CDs containing the same music.
7 This is the e-retailing business model, which we discuss in more detail in Section 4.6.1.

CHAPTER 3

1 More frameworks exist that model a complex environment. A well-known example is the Zachman framework for enterprise architecture (2002). This framework describes corporate information system development in the context of an organization, using a set of six system aspects (formulated as interrogatives) and a set of six groups of stakeholders. The Zachman framework can be related to the BOAT framework, but the mapping is not straightforward.
2 So BOAT might have been called BOIT, but that does not sound as nice . . . .
3 In practice, more elaborate waterfall models are used, possibly including several design and implementation sub-phases, a testing phase and an introduction phase.
4 Note that *aspects* in this linear approach are effectively *levels*.
5 Henderson and Venkatraman's complete model (1993) also includes diagonal relations between the four cells – we have omitted these here for reasons of clarity.

CHAPTER 4

1 The concept of *value creation* is essential in the basic notion of a *business model*. For instance, Osterwalder and Pigneur (2009) use the following definition: '*A business model describes the rationale of how an organization creates, delivers, and captures value*'.
2 Note that virtual environments have also been mentioned as communication *channels*. Modern virtual environments like Second Life do have both well-elaborated communication (channel) and presentation (media) aspects that are strongly intertwined.
3 We use the term *bricks and clicks* to refer to the integration of the principles from the old and the new economy. We also see the term *bricks and mortar* to refer to the old economy and *clicks and mortar* to refer to the integration of new and old (see e.g. Jelassi and Enders 2008).
4 This is certainly true when new communication channels are introduced. For example, in the early days of electronic retail, consumers might place orders over the Web, then start doubting whether it had worked and subsequently place the same order using a traditional channel (like a physical form via the postal service) – leading to many double deliveries.
5 See http://www.dell.com.
6 The term 'crowdcasting' is a mix of the terms 'crowdsourcing' and 'broadcasting'.
7 See http://www.innocentive.com.
8 See http://www.wikipedia.org.
9 See http://www.istockphoto.com.
10 See http://www.sellaband.com.
11 In the 2009 Sellaband business model, a band has to sell 5,000 parts at $10 each to obtain the required funding of $50,000 (as listed at www.sellaband.com). In principle, each part

can be owned by a different believer. This illustrates that crowdsourcing may indeed involve large crowds.

CHAPTER 5

1 We will revisit this issue when discussing change management in Section 5.6.2.
2 Note that we use the term 'consumer' in two very different ways: it indicates a type of party (an individual person as opposed to a business or government party) and a role of a party (consumer as opposed to provider). Although this may be confusing, the term is generally used in both these ways and circumventing this would lead to unusual terminology.
3 The notation that we use for business processes can easily be mapped to standard notations with a more formal background, such as UML Activity Diagrams (Fowler and Scott 2000) or Petri Nets (van der Aalst and van Hee 2002) or other informal notations such as Event-driven Process Chains (EPCs) (Wikipedia 2009i).
4 In our terminology, *process flow control* is executing the *control flow* of a process. In other words, *control flow* is a specification issue, *flow control* an execution issue.
5 A book discussing the issue of predicting the 'unpredictable' in a broad context and a slightly polemic style is *The Black Swan* by Nassim Taleb (2007).
6 Note that we mean characteristics here in the O aspect, i.e., characteristics that determine the way channels are used by organizations. Characteristics of a technical nature belong in the A or T aspect.
7 Note that the outgoing arcs at the split are labeled to provide more clarity to the process specification.

CHAPTER 6

1 Note that more elaborate definitions of the term 'architecture' also exist, which also pay attention to the way the structure of a software system is constructed (see e.g. Grefen 2008).
2 The term 'exploded' is also used in information systems modeling to indicate 'refined'.
3 See http://www.skype.com.

CHAPTER 7

1 Note that with discussing this mapping after the previously discussed mappings, we complete analyzing the aspect-pair-wise dependencies in the cyclical BOAT view. We revisit the topic of dependencies in the complete BOAT cycle in Section _8.3.
2 See http://www.youtube.com.
3 See http://www.flickr.com.
4 See http://www.oasis-open.org for more information.
5 See http://www.rosettanet.org for more information.
6 In the CrossWork project, both the terms BPM and WFM are used and refer respectively to the build time and execution time support for business processes. Often the terms are used as (near) synonyms (with BPM as the more modern alternative). We discuss BPM technology later in this chapter.

7 So-called *personal database systems* (like many small database management systems designed to run on personal computers) do not have the client/server organization, as they serve one single user only.
8 See http://www.wfmc.org/ for more information.
9 See http://www.skype.com.
10 Akamai Technologies, Inc.; see http://www.akamai.com.
11 See http://www.ideal.nl/?lang=eng-GB for more details.
12 See http://www.paypal.com for more details.
13 See https://twitpay.me/.
14 For example: Linden Lab, the developer of Second Life, states the following in August 2009 on their Second Life Web site: 'With nearly US$35 million traded between residents each month, the Second Life economy has grown to become one of the world's largest user-generated virtual economies.'

CHAPTER 8

1 Note that this is essentially different from the *time scopes* dimension introduced in Section 2.5. The *time scopes* dimension is used to classify the time aspect of e-business transactions, i.e., of the *operations* of an e-business scenario. The time aspect in this chapter relates to the *development* of an e-business scenario.
2 Note that we say *a* BOAT element dependency diagram, not *the* diagram. Constructing a BEDD is matter of making choices – different choices lead to a different BEDD.

References

Aalst, W. van de and K. van Hee; *Workflow Management: Models, Methods, and Systems*; MIT Press, 2002.

Acquisti, A., S. Gritzalis, C. Lambrinoudakis, and S. De Capitani di Vimercati; *Digital Privacy: Theory, Technologies and Practices*; Auerbach Publications, 2008.

Alonso, G., F. Casati, H. Kuno, and V. Machiraju; *Web Services: Concepts, Architectures and Applications*; Springer, 2004.

Alonso, G., U. Fiedler, C. Hagen, A. Lazcano, H. Schuldt, and N. Weiler; *WISE: Business to Business E-Commerce*; Proceedings of the Ninth International Workshop on Research Issues on Data Engineering; Sydney, Australia, 1999; pp. 132–139.

Angelov, S.; *Foundations of B2B Electronic Contracting*; Ph.D. Thesis; Eindhoven University of Technology, 2006.

Angelov, S. and P. Grefen; The 4W Framework for B2B e-Contracting; *Networking and Virtual Organizations*, Vol. 2, No. 1; Inderscience Publishers, 2003; pp. 78–97.

Angelov, S. and P. Grefen; *A Case Study on Electronic Contracting in On-Line Advertising – Status and Prospects*; Network-Centric Collaboration and Supporting Frameworks – Proceedings of the Seventh IFIP Working Conference on Virtual Enterprises; Helsinki, Finland; Springer, 2006; pp. 419–428.

Angelov, S. and P. Grefen; An E-contracting Reference Architecture; *Journal of Systems and Software*, Vol. 81, No. 11; Elsevier, 2008; pp. 1816–1844.

Bass, L., P. Clements, and R. Kazman; *Software Architecture in Practice*; Addison-Wesley, 2003.

Chesbrough, H.; *Open Business Models: How to Thrive in the New Innovation Landscape*; Harvard Business Press, 2006.

Chiu, D., K. Karlapalem, and Q. Li; *Views for Inter-organization Workflow in an E-commerce Environment*; Proceedings of the Ninth Working Conference on Database Semantics; IFIP, 2001; pp. 137–151.

Comer, D.; *Internetworking with TCP/IP*, Vol. 1; Prentice Hall, 2005.

Dell, M. and C. Fredman; *Direct from Dell: Strategies that Revolutionized an Industry*; Collins Business, 2006.

Dobriceanu, A., L. Biscu, A. Badica, and C. Badica; The Design and Implementation of an Agent-Based Auction Service; *International Journal of Agent-Oriented Software Engineering*, Vol. 3, No. 2/3; Inderscience, 2009; pp. 116–134.

Elliott, S. (ed.); *Electronic Commerce: B2C Strategies and Models*; Wiley, 2002.

Evans, P. and T. Wurster; *Blown to Bits: How the New Economics of Information Transforms Strategy*; Harvard Business School Press, 1999.

Fasli, M.; *Agent Technology for E-Commerce*; Wiley, 2007.

Fasli, M. and O. Shehory (eds); *Agent-Mediated Electronic Commerce: Automated Negotiation and Strategy Design for Electronic Markets*; Springer, 2007.

Fenn, J. and A. Linden; *Gartner's Hype Cycle Special Report for 2005*; Gartner, 2005.

Fowler, M. and K. Scott; *UML Distilled*; Addison-Wesley, 2000.

Grefen, P.; *Onzichtbare Architecturen – tussen Chaos en Structuur in e-Business*; Inaugural Lecture; Eindhoven University of Technology, 2003 (in Dutch).

Grefen, P.; *Introduction to (Complex) Information System Architectures*; Lecture Notes; Eindhoven University of Technology, 2008.

Grefen, P. and S. Angelov; *On tau-, mu-, pi- and epsilon-Contracting*; Proceedings of the CAiSE Workshop on Web Services, e-Business, and the Semantic Web; Toronto, Canada; Springer, 2002; pp. 68–77.

Grefen, P., H. Ludwig, and S. Angelov; A Three-Level Framework for Process and Data Management of Complex E-Services; *International Journal of Cooperative Information Systems*, Vol. 12, No. 4; World Scientific, 2003; pp. 487–531.

Grefen, P., K. Aberer, Y. Hoffner, and H. Ludwig; CrossFlow: Cross-Organizational Workflow Management in Dynamic Virtual Enterprises; *Computer Systems Science and Engineering*, Vol. 15, No. 5; CRL Publishing, 2000; pp. 277–290.

Grefen, P., N. Mehandjiev, G. Kouvas, G. Weichhart, and R. Eshuis; Dynamic Business Network Process Management in Instant Virtual Enterprises; *Computers in Industry*, Vol. 60, No. 2; Elsevier, 2009; pp. 86–103.

Henderson, J. and N. Venkatraman; Strategic Alignment: Leveraging Information Technology for Transforming Organisations; *IBM Systems Journal*, Vol. 32, No. 1; IBM, 1993; pp. 472–484.

Hoffner, Y., S. Field, P. Grefen, and H. Ludwig; Contract-Driven Creation and Operation of Virtual Enterprises; *Computer Networks*, Vol. 37, No. 2; Elsevier, 2001; pp. 111–136.

Holden, G., S. Belew, J. Elad, J. Rich; *E-Business*; Wiley Pathways, 2009.

Howe, J.; *Crowdsourcing: Why the Power of the Crowd Is Driving the Future of Business*; Crown Business, 2008.

Inmon, W., R. Terdeman, J. Norris-Montanari, and D. Meers; *Data Warehousing for E-Business*; Wiley, 2001.

Jelassi, T. and A. Enders; *Strategies for e-Business: Concepts and Cases* (2nd Edition); Prentice Hall, 2008.

Katz, J. and Y. Lindell; *Introduction to Modern Cryptography: Principles and Protocols*; Chapman & Hall/CRC, 2007.

Keen, P., C. Ballance, S. Chan, and S. Schrump; *Electronic Commerce Relationships: Trust by Design*; Prentice Hall, 2000.

Kirkman, P.; *Electronic Funds Transfer Systems: The Revolution in Cashless Banking and Payment Methods*; Blackwell, 1987.

Lazcano, A., H. Schuldt, G. Alonso, and H. Schek; WISE: Process-Based E-Commerce; *IEEE Data Engineering Bulletin*, Vol. 24, No. 1, 2001; pp. 46–51.

Leymann, F. and D. Roller; *Production Workflow: Concepts and Techniques*; Prentice Hall, 1999.

Marcus, J.; *Amazonia: Five Years at the Epicenter of the Dot.Com Juggernaut*; New Press, 2005.

McKay, J. and P. Marshall; *Strategic Management of e-Business*; Wiley, 2004.

Mehandjiev, N. and P. Grefen (eds); *Dynamic Business Process Formation for Instant Virtual Enterprises*; Springer, 2010.

Mintzberg, H.; *Structure in Fives: Designing Effective Organizations*; Prentice Hall, 1992.

Mitchell, D., C. Coles, B. Golisano, and R. Knutson; *The Ultimate Competitive Advantage: Secrets of Continually Developing a More Profitable Business Model*; Berrett-Koehler Publishers, 2003.

National Institute of Standards and Technology; *Public Key Infrastructure Technology*; ITL Bulletin July 1997; National Institute of Standards and Technology, USA, 1997.

Nelson, A. and W. Nelson; *Building Electronic Commerce with Web Database Constructions*; Addison-Wesley, 2002.

Norman, T. *et al.*; Agent-Based Formation of Virtual Organisations; *Knowledge-Based Systems*, Vol. 17, No. 2–4, 2004; pp. 103–111.

OASIS; *UDDI Executive Overview: Enabling Service-Oriented Architecture*; OASIS, 2004; www.oasis-open.org.
OASIS, OASIS ebXML Joint Committee; *The Framework for eBusiness*; OASIS, 2006.
OGF GRAAP Working Group; *Web Services Agreement Specification (WS-Agreement)*; Open Grid Forum, 2007.
O'Mahony, D., M. Peirce, and H. Tewari; *Electronic Payment Systems for E-Commerce*; Artech House, 2001.
Osterwalder, A. and Y. Pigneur; *Business Model Generation*; Self-Published, 2009.
Paavilainen, J.; *Mobile Business Strategies: Understanding the Technologies and Opportunities*; Wireless Press, 2002.
Papazoglou, M.; *Web Services: Principles and Technology*; Pearson, 2007.
Párhonyi, R.; *Micro Payment Gateways*; Ph.D. Thesis; University of Twente, 2005.
Paulson, E.; *Inside Cisco: The Real Story of Sustained M&A Growth*; Wiley, 2001.
Perkins, A. and M. Perkins; *The Internet Bubble*; Harper Business, 1999.
Phillips, P.; *E-Business Strategy: Text and Cases*; McGraw-Hill, 2003.
Pieper, R., V. Kouwenhoven, and S. Hamminga; *Beyond the Hype: e-Business Strategy in Leading European Companies*; Van Haren Publishing, 2001.
Porter, M.; *Competitive Advantage: Creating and Sustaining Superior Performance*; Free Press, 1985.
Raucci, R.; *Mosaic for Windows: A Hands-on Configuration and Set-up Guide to Popular Web Browsers*; Springer, 1995.
RosettaNet Program Office; *Overview, Clusters, Segments, and PIPS, Version 02.07.00*; RosettaNet, 2009.
Sokol, P.; *From EDI to Electronic Commerce: A Business Perspective*; McGraw-Hill, 1995.
Stevens, W.; *TCP/IP Illustrated, Volume 1: The Protocols*; Addison-Wesley Professional, 1994.
Ströbel, M.; *Dynamic Outsourcing of Services*; Research Report RZ 3236; IBM Research, 2000.
Taleb, N.; *The Black Swan: The Impact of the Highly Improbable*; Random House, 2007.
Terdiman, D.; *The Entrepreneur's Guide to Second Life: Making Money in the Metaverse*; Sybex, 2007.
Turban, E., D. King, J. Lee, M. Warkentin, and H.M. Chung; *Electronic Commerce 2002: A Managerial Perspective*; Prentice Hall, 2002.
Vacca, J.; *Public Key Infrastructure: Building Trusted Applications and Web Services*; Auerbach Publications, 2004.
VanHoose, D.; *E-Commerce Economics*; Thomson – South-Western, 2003.
Van Slyke, C. and F. Bélanger; *E-Business Technologies*; Wiley, 2003.
Vetsikas, I. and N. Jennings; *Towards Agents Participating in Realistic Multi-Unit Sealed-Bid Auctions*; Proceedings of the Seventh International Joint Conference on Autonomous Agents and Multiagent Systems, 2008; pp. 1621–1624
Wang, T., B. Kratz, J. Vonk, and P. Grefen; *A* Survey on the History of Transaction Management: From Flat to Grid Transactions; *Distributed and Parallel Databases*, Vol. 23, No. 3; Springer, 2008; pp. 235–270.
Weise, J.; *Public Key Infrastructure Overview*; Sun BluePrints OnLine, Sun Microsystems, 2001.
Whyte, W.S.; *Enabling eBusiness: Integrating Technologies, Architectures and Applications*; Wiley, 2001.
Wikipedia; SABRE; Wikipedia, 2009a; http://en.wikipedia.org/wiki/Sabre_(computer_system).
Wikipedia; Society for Worldwide Interbank Financial Telecommunication; Wikipedia, 2009b; http://en.wikipedia.org/wiki/Society_for_Worldwide_Interbank_Financial_Telecommunication.
Wikipedia; History of the Internet; Wikipedia, 2009c; http://en.wikipedia.org/wiki/History_of_the_Internet.
Wikipedia; Waterfall Model; Wikipedia, 2009d; http://en.wikipedia.org/wiki/Waterfall_model.
Wikipedia; Telepresence; Wikipedia, 2009e; http://en.wikipedia.org/wiki/Telepresence.
Wikipedia; Web Ontology Language; Wikipedia, 2009f; http://en.wikipedia.org/wiki/Web_Ontology_Language.

Wikipedia; Web 2.0; Wikipedia, 2009g; http://en.wikipedia.org/wiki/Web_2.0.
Wikipedia; X/Open XA; Wikipedia, 2009h; http://en.wikipedia.org/wiki/X/Open_XA.
Wikipedia; Event-driven Process Chain; Wikipedia, 2009i; http://en.wikipedia.org/wiki/Event-driven_process_chain.
Workflow Management Coalition; *Glossary: A Workflow Management Coalition Specification*; Workflow Management Coalition, 1994.
Lai Xu; *Monitorable Multi-party Contracts for E-Business*; Ph.D. Thesis; Tilburg University, 2004.
Zachman, J.; *The Zachman Framework for Enterprise Architecture*; Zachman International, 2002.

Index